THE CAMBRIDGE BIBLE COMMENTARY

NEW ENGLISH BIBLE

GENERAL EDITORS

P R. ACKROYD, A. R. C. LEANEY
J. W. PACKER

PSALMS 1-50

PSALMS I-50

COMMENTARY BY

J. W. ROGERSON
Senior Lecturer in Theology, University of Durham

AND

J. W. McKAY
Lecturer in Theology, University of Hull

CAMBRIDGE UNIVERSITY PRESS

CAMBRIDGE
LONDON · NEW YORK · MELBOURNE

Published by the Syndics of the Cambridge University Press
The Pitt Building, Trumpington Street, Cambridge CB2 IRP
Bentley House, 200 Euston Road, London NW1 2DB
32 East 57th Street, New York, NY 10022, USA
296 Beaconsfield Parade, Middle Park, Melbourne 3206, Australia

First published 1977

PRINTED IN GREAT BRITAIN
AT THE UNIVERSITY PRESS, CAMBRIDGE

Library of Congress cataloguing in publication data
Bible. O.T. Psalms. English. New English. 1977. Psalms.
(The Cambridge Bible commentary, New English Bible)
Includes bibliographies and indexes.
CONTENTS: [1] 1–50. – [2] 51–100. – [3] 101–150.
1. Bible. O.T. Psalms – Commentaries. I. Rogerson, John William.
II. McKay, John William. II. Title. III. Series.
BS1430.3.R63   223′.2′077   76–27911
ISBN 0 521 21463 7 hard covers (Psalms 1–50)
ISBN 0 521 29160 7 paperback (Psalms 1–50)

GENERAL EDITORS' PREFACE

The aim of this series is to provide the text of the New English Bible closely linked to a commentary in which the results of modern scholarship are made available to the general reader. Teachers and young people have been especially kept in mind. The commentators have been asked to assume no specialized theological knowledge, and no knowledge of Greek and Hebrew. Bare references to other literature and multiple references to other parts of the Bible have been avoided. Actual quotations have been given as often as possible.

The completion of the New Testament part of the series in 1967 provides a basis upon which the production of the much larger Old Testament and Apocrypha series can be undertaken. The welcome accorded to the series has been an encouragement to the editors to follow the same general pattern, and an attempt has been made to take account of criticisms which have been offered. One necessary change is the inclusion of the translators' footnotes since in the Old Testament these are more extensive, and essential for the understanding of the text.

Within the severe limits imposed by the size and scope of the series, each commentator will attempt to set out the main findings of recent biblical scholarship and to describe the historical background to the text. The main theological issues will also be critically discussed.

Much attention has been given to the form of the volumes. The aim is to produce books each of which will be read consecutively from first to last page. The introductory material leads naturally into the text, which itself leads into the alternating sections of the commentary.

The series is accompanied by three volumes of a more general character. *Understanding the Old Testament* sets out to provide the larger historical and archaeological background, to say something about the life and thought of the people of the Old Testament, and to answer the question 'Why should we study the Old Testament?'. *The Making of the Old Testament* is concerned with the formation of the books of the Old Testament and Apocrypha in the context of the ancient Near Eastern world, and with the ways in which these books have come down to us in the life of the Jewish and Christian communities. *Old Testament Illustrations* contains maps, diagrams and photographs with an explanatory text. These three volumes are designed to provide material helpful to the understanding of the individual books and their commentaries, but they are also prepared so as to be of use quite independently.

P. R. A.

A. R. C. L.

J. W. P.

CONTENTS

CONTENTS

CONTENTS

THE FOOTNOTES TO THE N.E.B. TEXT

The footnotes to the N.E.B. text are designed to help the reader either to understand particular points of detail – the meaning of a name, the presence of a play upon words – or to give information about the actual text. Where the Hebrew text appears to be erroneous, or there is doubt about its precise meaning, it may be necessary to turn to manuscripts which offer a different wording, or to ancient translations of the text which may suggest a better reading, or to offer a new explanation based upon conjecture. In such cases, the footnotes supply very briefly an indication of the evidence, and whether the solution proposed is one that is regarded as possible or as probable. Various abbreviations are used in the footnotes:

(1) Some abbreviations are simply of terms used in explaining a point: *ch(s).*, chapter(s); *cp.*, compare; *lit.*, literally; *mng.*, meaning; *MS(S).*, manuscript(s), i.e. Hebrew manuscript(s), unless otherwise stated; *om.*, omit(s); *or*, indicating an alternative interpretation; *poss.*, possible; *prob.*, probable; *rdg.*, reading; *Vs(s).*, version(s).

(2) Other abbreviations indicate sources of information from which better interpretations or readings may be obtained.

Aq.　Aquila, a Greek translator of the Old Testament (perhaps about A.D. 130) characterized by great literalness.

Aram.　Aramaic – may refer to the text in this language (used in parts of Ezra and Daniel), or to the meaning of an Aramaic word. Aramaic belongs to the same language family as Hebrew, and is known from about 1000 B.C. over a wide area of the Middle East, including Palestine.

Heb.　Hebrew – may refer to the Hebrew text or may indicate the literal meaning of the Hebrew word.

Josephus　Flavius Josephus (A.D. 37/8–about 100), author of the *Jewish Antiquities*, a survey of the whole history of his people, directed partly at least to a non-Jewish audience, and of various other works, notably one on the *Jewish War* (that of A.D. 66–73) and a defence of Judaism (*Against Apion*).

Luc. Sept.　Lucian's recension of the Septuagint, an important edition made in Antioch in Syria about the end of the third century A.D.

Pesh.　Peshitta or Peshitto, the Syriac version of the Old Testament. Syriac is the name given chiefly to a form of Eastern Aramaic used by the Christian community. The translation varies in quality, and is at many points influenced by the Septuagint cr the Targums.

Sam.   Samaritan Pentateuch – the form of the first five books of the Old Testament as used by the Samaritan community. It is written in Hebrew in a special form of the Old Hebrew script, and preserves an important form of the text, somewhat influenced by Samaritan ideas.

Scroll(s)   Scroll(s), commonly called the Dead Sea Scrolls, found at or near Qumran from 1947 onwards. These important manuscripts shed light on the state of the Hebrew text as it was developing in the last centuries B.C. and the first century A.D.

Sept.   Septuagint (meaning 'seventy'; often abbreviated as the Roman numeral LXX), the name given to the main Greek version of the Old Testament. According to tradition, the Pentateuch was translated in Egypt in the third century B.C. by 70 (or 72) translators, six from each tribe, but the precise nature of its origin and development is not fully known. It was intended to provide Greek-speaking Jews with a convenient translation. Subsequently it came to be much revered by the Christian community.

Symm.   Symmachus, another Greek translator of the Old Testament (beginning of the third century A.D.), who tried to combine literalness with good style. Both Lucian and Jerome viewed his version with favour.

Targ.   Targum, a name given to various Aramaic versions of the Old Testament, produced over a long period and eventually standardized, for the use of Aramaic-speaking Jews.

Theod.   Theodotion, the author of a revision of the Septuagint (probably second century A.D.), very dependent on the Hebrew text.

Vulg.   Vulgate, the most important Latin version of the Old Testament, produced by Jerome about A.D. 400, and the text most used throughout the Middle Ages in western Christianity.

[. . .]   In the text itself square brackets are used to indicate probably late additions to the Hebrew text.

(Fuller discussion of a number of these points may be found in *The Making of the Old Testament* in this series.)

PSALMS

NAME, CONTENT AND PLACE OF THE BOOK
IN THE OLD TESTAMENT

The name 'psalms' comes from the Greek Septuagint translation of the Bible via the Latin Vulgate (see *The Making of
the Old Testament*, pp. 147–54). The Greek word *psalmos*
denoted the twanging of a stringed instrument with the
fingers, and later came to mean a song sung to the accompani-
ment of a plucked instrument. In turn, *psalmos* is a translation
of the Hebrew *mizmōr*, which also appears to have denoted
both the playing of instruments and the singing of songs.
Strictly speaking, then, the title 'psalms' means 'songs'.
The name for the book in the Hebrew Bible is *tehillīm* or
sēpher tehillīm, meaning 'praises' or 'book of praises'.

In actual fact, neither 'songs' nor 'praises' adequately describes the content of the Psalter. In it, we find expressed by
both the individual and the congregation, prayers for help
and thanksgivings for deliverance in the face of sickness,
despair, desertion by friends, and physical danger. We find
hymns of praise to God as creator and judge of the world, as
the one who has chosen his people Israel and his dwelling in
Zion, and who has guided, supported and punished his people.
We find entreaties that God will speedily and effectively
establish his rule throughout the world, at the same time
that it is acknowledged that he is already the universal king,
controlling the forces of nature, and shaping the destinies of
the nations. We find prayers for the well-being of the king,
and traces of ceremonial used at the king's coronation and the
periodic renewal of the divine covenant with the house of
David. We find extended meditations on Israel's past history,

I

and on God's gracious revelation of his law and his will to his people. We find the whole range of human emotions in their relation to God, from extreme pessimism and doubt to simple and certain trust. Even this lengthy catalogue is not complete, thus showing the impossibility of describing the Psalter and its contents in one word or short phrase. At the end of this introduction, an attempt is made to tabulate the contents of the Psalter.

The psalms stand either in first or second place in the third section of the Hebrew Bible, the Writings (see *The Making of the Old Testament*, pp. 118–24). The English Bible has a different order for the books, with Psalms following the Pentateuch and the historical books (including Ruth, Esther and Job). This arrangement derives from the way the books of the Old Testament were grouped together in the early Christian centuries. The underlying principle was probably that the psalms (believed to be substantially by David) should precede the books attributed to Solomon (Proverbs, Ecclesiastes, Song of Songs) which in turn should precede the prophetic books bearing the names of Isaiah, Jeremiah and Ezekiel. In other words, these books appear in the order of the historical sequence of the lives of those who were believed to have been their authors.

Although there are 150 psalms, there are two major ways of numbering them, the Hebrew and the Greek. The N.E.B. follows the Hebrew numbering, while among Bibles and commentaries used by Roman Catholics, the Greek numbering has been familiar. The major differences are that Pss. 11–113 and 117–146 in the Hebrew numbering are 10–112 and 116–145 in the Greek numbering, and these differences arose from uncertainty about how to regard the verses contained in Pss. 9, 10, 114, 115, 116 and 147 (according to the Hebrew reckoning). The Greek numbering was almost certainly correct in regarding Pss. 9–10 as one psalm (and note that the N.E.B. regards them as one psalm, numbered 9–10) but it was probably incorrect in regarding Pss. 114 and 115

2

as one psalm, and in dividing 116 and 147 each into two psalms. On the other hand, modern scholarship is virtually unanimous in regarding Pss. 42 and 43 as originally one psalm, against both the Hebrew and the Greek numberings.

PSALM TITLES, AUTHORSHIP AND GROWTH OF THE PSALTER

The preface to the Library Edition of the N.E.B. Old Testament (p. xiv) notes that in the Hebrew, many psalms have titles or headings. The N.E.B. translators decided not to include them in the translation because (i) they are almost certainly not the work of the authors of the psalms, (ii) where they are historical notices they are deduced from the text of the psalm itself and rest on no reliable tradition, and (iii) where they are musical directions, they are mostly unintelligible. However, it is to be noted that the N.E.B. retained the 'doxologies' at the end of Pss. 41, 72, 89 and 106 which mark the conclusion of Books 1–4 of the Psalms respectively, as well as the notice 'Here end the prayers of David son of Jesse' at 72: 20. It can be said of all these that they are no more the work of the authors of the individual psalms than are the psalm titles. Like the titles, they were added at various times as the psalms were collected together to form the Psalter as we have it, and it is odd that in the N.E.B. they were retained where the titles were omitted.

Although the N.E.B. translators are correct in saying that the musical parts of the psalm titles are today unintelligible and that the historical notices are no more than guesses, the titles have something to contribute when we try to deduce how the psalms were collected together. The following psalms are associated with David through the phrase *le dāwīd* in the titles: 3–41 (except 33, and 10 which is a continuation of 9; see above), 51–65, 68–70, 86, 101, 103, 108–110, 122, 124, 131, 133, 138–145. Pss. 42–49, 84–85 and 87–88 are associated with the sons of Korah, while 50 and 73–83 are associated

3

with Asaph. These account for almost all of the 'named' psalms; there are thirty-four nameless or 'orphan' psalms. It will be observed that the 'Davidic' psalms fall predominantly in the first half of the Psalter (fifty-five of Pss. 1–72 are 'Davidic') while the 'orphan' psalms are found mainly in the second half. This may indicate that in the first instance, collections of 'Davidic' psalms were made, and that in the later stages of the compilation of the Psalter, anonymous psalms were added.

The meaning of the Hebrew phrase *le dāwīd* has been much discussed. Traditionally, it was taken to denote Davidic authorship. In modern scholarship, it has often been taken to mean 'belonging to the Davidic collection', while a third view is that the phrase was meant by those who added it to denote authorship, but that these editors were not guided by any reliable tradition. There is probably some truth in all three of these views.

The Old Testament contains several references to David's skill as a musician and singer (e.g. 1 Sam. 16: 17–23; 2 Sam. 1: 17–27; Amos 6: 5) and it is reasonable to assume that David was the author of some of the psalms, even if we have no means of discovering exactly which. It is also possible that from early times these psalms were headed *le dāwīd*. Later scribes are also likely to have claimed Davidic authorship for psalms by prefacing them with this title, although reliable tradition was lacking. That the phrase *le dāwīd* might also indicate a collection can be argued as follows. Beginning with Ps. 42, we have the Elohistic Psalter (Pss. 42–83), so called because an editor or editors seem to have altered the divine name in the psalms from an original 'the LORD' to 'God' (Hebrew *'elōhīm*, thus the term 'Elohistic'). This can be seen if Ps. 14 is compared with Ps. 53 in the English; and the editing is crudely apparent in the Hebrew of Ps. 80, though not in the English translation. This editorial treatment of the divine name begins immediately after the first block of 'Davidic' psalms (3–41), and it is thus reasonable to assume that

4

Pss. 3–41 once existed as a separate collection from 42–83, because they escaped this editorial work. Further, since all but one of Pss. 3–41 are entitled *le dāwīd*, it is reasonable to say that the title indicates a collection as well as authorship. If we examine the psalms ascribed to the sons of Korah, we see that most of them have an interest in Zion, the temple and worship, from which it is usually concluded that the sons of Korah were a band of temple singers. For the name Asaph, see 1 Chron. 16: 4–7; 2 Chron. 35: 15.

With the help of these points, the following suggestions can be made about the growth of the Psalter. (i) There first existed several separate collections of psalms: two Davidic collections (Pss. 3–41 and 51–72 – cp. 72: 20) probably containing genuine psalms of David and others attributed to him; a Korahite collection (Pss. 42–49, 84–85, 87–88) and an Asaphite collection (Pss. 50, 73–83). (ii) An Elohistic Psalter was compiled from three collections – the second Davidic, part of the Korahite, and the Asaphite, to form the group of psalms, 42–83. This collection was subjected to editorial revision in which the divine name 'the LORD' was changed to 'God' (*'elōhīm*). It is also possible that the Elohistic Psalter extended as far as Ps. 88, and that the editorial alteration of the divine name proceeded no further than Ps. 83. (iii) The first Davidic collection and the Elohistic Psalter were joined together. (iv) Numerous further additions were made, about which we can only guess. It is probable that Ps. 1 was composed to be the beginning of the whole Psalter, and possible that Ps. 119 at one point marked its conclusion. If this is so, then Pss. 120–134 which are each entitled 'A song of ascents' would have been attached as a block following on from Ps. 119, and Pss. 138–145 may have been a small group of Davidic psalms which were added at a late stage to the Psalter. (Pss. 135–137 lack titles, and it is impossible to say why or when they were placed after Pss. 120–134.)

The division of the Psalter into five books (Pss. 1–41, 42–72, 73–89, 90–106, 107–150) presumably dates from the time of the completion of the Psalter, probably in the third century B.C. It is usually held that the Psalter was divided into five books on analogy with the five books of the Pentateuch. However, we have already suggested that long before the Psalter was complete, Pss. 3–41 and 42–83 probably existed as separate collections, and in the commentary on Ps. 72, it is suggested that the doxology of 72: 18f. was added to that psalm before the Psalter was divided into books by means of doxologies. Ps. 72: 18f. may have served as the model for the other doxologies.

Although we know so little about how the psalms came to be arranged in their present order, the process may not have been entirely haphazard. Pss. 105 and 106 are clearly complementary, and the unrelieved pessimism of Ps. 88 is immediately followed by the affirmation 'I will sing the story of thy love, O LORD' in 89: 1.

HISTORY OF INTERPRETATION

It has long been recognized that the psalms are rich and varied in content, including praise, prayer and lament. Commentators in all ages have recognized their applicability to many situations in the religious life of the individual and the community, and it is probable that even in the Old Testament period, psalms were reinterpreted in the light of new situations. Thus, Ps. 79, which speaks of enemies defiling Jerusalem and its temple, is never quite explicit enough to enable us to identify the events for certain, and the reason may be that reinterpretation and spiritualizing of the psalm have obscured its references to the events which first called it forth. In 1 Chron. 16: 8–36, parts of Pss. 96, 105, 106 and 107 are quoted in respect of the institution of praise to God by David, after he had brought the Ark to Jerusalem.

Alongside, and not necessarily instead of, what we might call the spiritual interpretation of the psalms, there has been the historical interpretation. Traditional Jewish interpretation understood many of the psalms in the context of the life of David, and this approach was expressed already in some of the psalm titles. Thus the title of Ps. 51 reads 'To the choirmaster. A Psalm of David, when Nathan the prophet came to him after he had gone in to Bathsheba', linking the psalm with the incidents related in 2 Sam. 11–12. When, in the eighteenth and nineteenth centuries, critical scholarship began to abandon belief in the Davidic authorship of the psalms, the historical approach continued, but now, many psalms were understood in the context of the history of ancient Israel. If psalms spoke of Israel or Jerusalem surrounded by enemies, they were referred to the known crises of Israel's history, especially the siege of Jerusalem in 701 B.C. by the Assyrian king Sennacherib. An extreme form of this approach connected some, or even all, of the psalms with events of the Maccabaean revolt and the rule of the Hasmonaean dynasty (169–63 B.C.).

In the present century, psalm studies have been dominated by the form-critical and cultic interpretations. The former, associated with the German, Hermann Gunkel, sought to classify the psalms into types according to their formal structure, and then to suggest a context in the religious life of Israel for the types. The latter, associated with the Norwegian, Sigmund Mowinckel, attempted to reconstruct the worship of the Jerusalem temple, especially as it centred around the king, and it was based on material about worship among ancient Israel's neighbours, as well as upon allusions in the psalms themselves. Subsequent scholarship has criticized these pioneering efforts. Gunkel's psalm types have been considerably modified, and doubt has been cast on the validity of some of Mowinckel's reconstructions. However, the work of these scholars has left a permanent mark on the interpretation of the psalms. Classification of psalms into types on the basis of their formal pattern or structure may be subjective, and unconsciously use content as well as form; but it is useful to consider as a group the so-called individual laments (e.g. Pss. 3–7, 13–14, 17, 22, 25–26), the psalms of the kingship of

God (Pss. 47, 93, 96–99), or the psalms of Zion (Pss. 46, 48, 76, 84, 87, 122), to name only three groups. Also, attempts to reconstruct the worship of the Jerusalem temple have drawn attention to important features of ancient Israelite religion, such as the role of the king, and the covenant between God and the house of David.

No commentator, then, can fail to be indebted to the form-critical and cultic approaches to the psalms; but the usefulness of the approaches can be exaggerated. For example, to label a psalm as an individual lament is sometimes to say nothing that could not be observed by an intelligent reader, and further, if psalms are tied too closely to a particular suggested 'original setting', this may obscure the fact that the psalms were certainly reinterpreted within the Old Testament period, and seen in a fuller perspective in later Jewish and Christian interpretation. Also, concentration on the 'original setting' may sometimes make it difficult for the reader to regard a particular psalm as anything more than interesting information about obsolete ceremonies from a remote and alien culture.

In the present commentary, the writers have tried to strike a balance between the spiritual, historical, form-critical and cultic approaches, seeing value in each where appropriate. The writers have also tried to bring out the religious teaching of permanent value which they believe the psalms to contain.

THE CHARACTER OF THE N.E.B. TRANSLATION

For the translator of the Old Testament, the psalms present some major difficulties. First, it is often not clear from a given psalm what exactly it is about; it may be open to two or more interpretations depending on how a difficult Hebrew word or phrase is regarded. Sometimes, the translator will translate a psalm according to a general view of its meaning which he has arrived at not so much by looking at the psalm as a whole, but by studying the difficult Hebrew word or phrase, and comparing it with similar phrases elsewhere in the Old

Testament or in ancient Near Eastern literature. Alternatively, he may let the content of the psalm as a whole override the way in which he translates a difficult word or phrase. In such cases, translators will not claim absolute certainty for their translation; it will represent the best that they feel they can do in a difficult case.

A second reason for the difficulty in translating the psalms arises from the use and re-use of the psalms in Old Testament times, and later in the synagogue and in the church. The psalms can be understood at so many different levels that really adequate translation is impossible. One result of this is that translations of the psalms have different characters, depending on the general approach adopted by their translators. If one compares Ps. 84 in the N.E.B., the Authorized Version and the Psalter of the Book of Common Prayer, the different characters of these renderings are clearly apparent. The Prayer Book version, dating from 1540, preserves some of the early Christian Greek and Latin interpretations of the psalms, with modifications from continental Reformation sources. It presents Ps. 84 as a description of worship and pilgrimage in such a way that the earthly Jerusalem about which the psalm speaks is a veiled symbol for the heavenly Jerusalem, and the pilgrimage to Zion is a symbol for that pilgrimage which is the whole of the religious life of an individual. The Authorized Version is much more literal, and in its attempt to give a faithful rendering of the Hebrew, it sometimes produces nonsense, as in verse 5, where it has 'Blessed is the man whose strength is in thee; in whose heart are the ways of them.' On a superficial reading, the Authorized Version conveys less than the Prayer Book version. The N.E.B. adopts the view that the psalm was sung in connection with a pilgrimage to Zion in ancient Israel. It achieves a consistency of interpretation with the occasional help of a radical treatment of the Hebrew text, but unlike the Prayer Book version, allows no hints that the psalm could be seen in a wider perspective. The difference between these translations of Ps. 84 is not that

9

one is more 'correct' than the others. At one or two points, the N.E.B. is doubtless more correct from the point of view of Hebrew than the Prayer Book version, but at the same time the N.E.B. contains some conjectures that are at best only possibilities. The proper way to assess a translation is to examine it in the light of its overall approach, and in the case of the N.E.B., this approach seems to have been to render the psalms according to what the translators believed to be the setting of individual psalms in the life of ancient Israel.

Because in the present commentary the writers have sought to see the psalms in a wider perspective than their suggested original setting in ancient Israel, they have regarded the N.E.B. as a witness to the original Hebrew, but they have felt free to criticize the N.E.B. translation, and to draw attention to more traditional approaches to interpretation, where they have felt that the N.E.B. implies too narrow a view, or a misleading interpretation.

LITERARY AND POETIC CHARACTERISTICS OF THE PSALMS

The psalms are poetry, and they employ several literary devices. Some of these characteristics are apparent, even in translation. Nine psalms, 9–10, 25, 34, 37, 111, 112, 119 and 145, are acrostic psalms, in which individual lines or verses, or groups of verses, begin with successive letters of the Hebrew alphabet. Possibly, the psalmists regarded Hebrew as a special language because in it God had allowed his law and the record of his mighty deeds to be written. The alphabet perhaps symbolized the whole of the Hebrew language, and so, in composing psalms in which verses began with each successive letter of the alphabet, the psalmists were reminding themselves of the marvellous fact that the oracles of God had been recorded in Hebrew. The acrostic principle is at its most elaborate in Ps. 119, where each group of eight verses begins with a successive letter of the alphabet.

In some psalms, refrains can be noticed. In Pss. 42–43 the refrain

> 'How deep I am sunk in misery,
> groaning in my distress:
> yet I will wait for God;
> I will praise him continually,
> my deliverer, my God'

occurs at 42: 5, 11; 43: 5. In Ps. 46: 7, 11 the refrain

> 'The LORD of Hosts is with us,
> the God of Jacob our high stronghold'

is found. Refrains such as that in Ps. 46 and at 80: 3, 7, 19 suggest that they were congregational responses, while in Ps. 136, the fact that every second line is

> 'his love endures for ever'

suggests that this psalm, at least, was used antiphonally, perhaps with the congregation responding every other line with the refrain. In an ancient Hebrew manuscript discovered in caves near the Dead Sea, Ps. 145 appears with a refrain after each verse.

Hebrew poetry is not characterized by rhyme, but by stress and sense. Unfortunately, we do not know how Hebrew was pronounced in biblical times, and what is written in the commentaries about stress must inevitably rest a good deal upon conjecture. In any case, no translation can reproduce the stress in the Hebrew. The sense aspect of Hebrew poetry can, however, be recognized in translation. Often, the sense of a line is exactly reproduced in the next line:

> 'what is man that thou shouldst remember him,
> mortal man that thou shouldst care for him?' (8: 4)

> 'O LORD, who may lodge in thy tabernacle?
> Who may dwell on thy holy mountain?'   (15: 1)

Sometimes, the sense of the first line is taken up and slightly expanded in the second:

> 'The LORD is righteous in his acts;
> he brings justice to all who have been wronged' (103: 6)

or the sense of the first line may be followed by an opposite sense:

> 'The LORD watches over the way of the righteous,
>> but the way of the wicked is doomed.' (1: 6)

Another device is for the sense to be repeated, until it reaches a climax:

'O LORD, the ocean lifts up, the ocean lifts up its clamour; the ocean lifts up its pounding waves.

Mightier far than the noise of great waters, than the breakers of the sea,

Is the LORD who is on high.' (93: 3f. The N.E.B. is here adapted to follow the order of the Hebrew more closely.)

Sometimes, the poetry employs metaphor:

> 'A herd of bulls surrounds me,
>> great bulls of Bashan beset me.
>> Ravening and roaring lions
>> open their mouths wide against me' (22: 12f.)

or simile:

> 'I am like a desert-owl in the wilderness,
>> an owl that lives among ruins.
>> Thin and meagre, I wail in solitude,
>> like a bird that flutters on the roof-top.' (102: 6f.)

These are just some examples of the literary and poetic devices that are used in the Psalter, and the psalms can be much better appreciated if we bear them in mind as we read the biblical text. The psalms are religious texts, but their writers were literary craftsmen. They not only strove to find the best possible language in which to utter their prayers and praises; they also probably appreciated that poetry alone was the medium in which it was possible to come closest to the task of expressing the unspeakable mysteries of God in the language of men.

THE CONTENTS OF THE PSALTER

(Some psalms appear under more than one heading. This usually means that they are adaptable for use in different situations, but occasionally it means that the psalm's interpretation is open to debate.)

A. *Hymns*

In praise of God for what he is, good, loving, faithful, etc.: 100, 103, 111, 113, 145, 146, 150.

To God the creator: 8, 19, 24, 29, 104.

To God the bounteous provider: 65, 84, 144, 147.

To the Lord of Israel's history: 68, 78, 105, 111, 114, 117.

To God both as creator and as Lord of history: 33, 89, 95, 135, 136, 144, 148.

To God the mighty, the victorious: 68, 76, 149.

On the final victory of God and his people: 46, 47, 48, 68, 93, 96, 97, 98, 99.

'The LORD is king': 47, 93, 96, 97, 98, 99.

'Songs of Zion' (cp. 137: 3): 46, 48, 76, 84, 87, 122.

Suitable for use by pilgrims: 84, 121, 122, 125, 127.

B. *National psalms*

Prayers for deliverance or victory: 44, 60, 74, 79, 80, 83, 85, 89, 108, 126, 129, 137, 144.

Prayers for blessing and continued protection: 67, 115, 125.

General prayers for mercy or restoration: 90, 106, 123.

Psalms that call the people to obedience: 81, 95.

Royal psalms: 2, 18, 20, 21, 45, 72, 89, 101, 110, 132.

Other psalms that include prayers for the king: 61, 63, 80, 84.

Other psalms that make reference to the king: 78, 122, 144.

C. *Prayers of the individual in time of need*

For protection, deliverance or vindication in the face of persecution: 3, 5, 7, 12, 17, 25, 35, 40, 41, 54, 55, 56, 57, 59, 64, 70, 86, 120, 123, 140, 141, 142, 143.

For use in time of suffering and dereliction: 6, 13, 22, 28, 31, 38, 39, 42–43, 69, 71, 77, 88, 102, 143.

For justice or personal vindication: 7, 17, 26, 35, 69, 94, 109.

For forgiveness: 6, 25, 38, 51, 130.

Expressing a deep longing for the nearness of God: 22, 25, 27, 38, 42, 51, 61, 63, 73, 77, 84, 130, 143.

Expressing confidence or trust: 4, 11, 16, 23, 27, 52, 62, 91, 121, 131.

Suitable for use in a night vigil: 5, 17, 22, 27, 30, 46, 57, 59, 63, 108, 143.

The 'Penitential Psalms' in Christian tradition: 6, 32, 38, 51, 102, 130, 143.

D. *Thanksgiving psalms*

For national deliverance: 118 (?), 124.

For personal deliverance: 18, 30, 34, 66, 116, 118, 138.

For forgiveness: 32.

For the knowledge of God's continuing love and care: 92, 107.

See also above: A. *Hymns.*

E. *Psalms giving instruction or containing meditations on various themes*

On the Law: 1, 19, 119.

On the qualities required in the citizens of God's kingdom: 15, 24, 101, 112.

On corruption in society: 11, 12, 14, 53, 55, 58, 82, 94.

On the lot of mankind, the problem of evil and suffering, the ways of the godly and the wicked: 1, 9–10, 14, 36, 37, 39, 49, 52, 53, 58, 62, 73, 90, 92, 94, 112.

On God's judgement: 50, 75, 82.

On God's blessings: 127, 128, 133.

On God's omniscience: 139.

F. *Psalms generally accounted Messianic in Christian interpretation*

The royal Messiah: 2, 18, 20, 21, 45, 61, 72, 89, 110, 118, 132.

The suffering Messiah: 22, 35, 41, 55, 69, 109.
The second Adam, fulfiller of human destiny: 8, 16, 40.
Psalms describing God as king, creator, etc., applied to Jesus
  in the New Testament: 68, 97, 102.

G. *Special categories*

Acrostics: 9–10, 25, 34, 37, 111, 112, 119, 145.
Songs of ascent: 120–134.
Hallel: 113–118.
Hallelujah: 146–150.

✻   ✻   ✻   ✻   ✻   ✻   ✻   ✻   ✻   ✻   ✻   ✻   ✻   ✻

BOOK 1

THE TWO WAYS

1

Happy is the man   1
  who does not take the wicked for his guide
  nor walk the road that sinners tread
  nor take his seat among the scornful;
  the law of the LORD is his delight,   2
the law his meditation night and day.

  He is like a tree   3
planted beside a watercourse,
  which yields its fruit in season
    and its leaf never withers:
in all that he does he prospers.
Wicked men are not like this;   4
  they are like chaff driven by the wind.
So when judgement comes the wicked shall not stand firm,   5
nor shall sinners stand in the assembly of the righteous.
  The LORD watches over the way of the righteous,   6
    but the way of the wicked is doomed.

* This psalm may have been originally intended as a prologue to the whole Psalter because at some time Ps. 2 was
known as 'the first Psalm' (see Acts 13: 33, N.E.B. footnote).
Its central doctrines, the blessedness of the godly life (verses
1–3) and the futility of godlessness (verses 4–6), are certainly
characteristic of the psalmist's faith and are reiterated throughout the book. They are also basic to Israel's covenant faith
and reappear as promise and warning or as blessing and curse
in almost every part of the Old Testament. Their presentation
in this psalm in terms of the company a man keeps recalls the
teaching of the wisdom writers (cp. Prov. 2: 12–15, 20–2),
but the closest parallel is to be found in Jer. 17: 5–8. There
are some indications that the psalm is a fairly late composition; for example, its emphasis on the law and on reflective
meditation is reminiscent of later Jewish piety.

1–3. The way of righteousness.

1. *Happy is the man:* as much a cry of joy as a statement of
fact. This happiness is God's gift, but is available only to the
faithful (cp. Matt. 5: 3–10). They are the ones who will not
walk, stand or sit (the Hebrew uses all three verbs) with the
ungodly, that is, will spend no part of their waking life following their example. Their whole allegiance, their thinking,
behaving and belonging, implied in the terms *guide*, *road* and
seat, will be unaffected by the wicked. The *wicked*, *sinners*
and *scornful* are respectively the enemies of God in general,
those who deliberately wander from God's paths and the
proud who rebelliously scoff at God. The parallelism suggests
that the terms are used as synonyms.

2. *the law:* not simply the legal portions of the Pentateuch,
for the Hebrew word, *tōrā*, means basically 'teaching' and
may therefore be applied to the whole tradition of God's
word to man. To the psalmist it is certainly no mere collection of regulations to restrict behaviour, but rather the account
of God's revealed will which he finds a delight to study and
which imparts to him the very life of God himself (verse 3;
see more fully introduction to Ps. 119). By *meditation night*

and day, that is by continuously and quietly reciting the text to himself, the faithful learns to love and obey his God (Josh. 1: 8). This is the positive aspect of godliness; verse 1 paints the negative aspect.

3. This is not the picture of *a tree* growing naturally beside a river, but of a tree *planted* (better 'transplanted') by a gardener *beside a watercourse* or irrigation channel. The lesson of the metaphor is that spiritual happiness is God-given, not naturally attained. Furthermore, unlike the Palestinian wadis that go dry in summer, God's life-giving streams are constant, so that the tree's *leaf never withers* through drought and its *fruit* crop never fails (cp. Ezek. 47: 12). As the tree flourishes because the gardener tends it, so the godly man *prospers* because God cares for him (not because he deserves to; there is no notion of merit in this simile).

4-6. The way of the wicked.

4. *chaff:* the empty husks that were blown away when the threshed corn was tossed in *the wind*. The image is of all that is worthless and without permanence, very much in contrast to the firmly rooted, fruitful tree. Human activity without God has no lasting value.

5. *when judgement comes:* the overtones of final judgement are unmistakable, though the original author may have intended only the this-worldly sense of on-going judgement in the life of the wicked. Likewise, *the assembly of the righteous* is the present worshipping community, but can also refer to the final assize (cp. Dan. 7: 9f.). The implication is that God constantly judges the wicked in this life, but a time will come when he will conclusively remove them from among the faithful. *the righteous:* those who have a right relationship with God because of their obedience to the demands laid upon them in their covenant with him.

6. *the way of the righteous:* the road that leads to and is loved and cared for by God (cp. Ps. 119: 25-32). *the way of the wicked* leads nowhere, it has no future, it *is doomed*. The contrast in the two-ways doctrine is not between sinless perfection

and failure, but between loyalty and rebellion. There is also
no idea of merit or reward associated with the way of obedience (see on verse 3). To follow that way is to be happy (verse 1)
in the enjoyment of God's free grace and abundant love; to
reject it is to choose futility. ✳

THE LORD AND HIS ANOINTED KING

2

1   Why are the nations in turmoil?
Why do the peoples hatch their futile plots?

2   The kings of the earth stand ready,
and the rulers conspire together
against the LORD and his anointed king.

3   'Let us break their fetters,' they cry,
'let us throw off their chains!'

4   The Lord who sits enthroned in heaven
laughs them to scorn;

5   then he rebukes them in anger,
he threatens them in his wrath.

6   Of me he says, 'I have enthroned my king
on Zion my holy mountain.'

7   I will repeat[a] the LORD's decree:
'You are my son,' he said;
'this day I become your father.

8   Ask of me what you will:
I will give you nations as your inheritance,
the ends of the earth as your possession.

9   You shall break them with a rod of iron,
you shall shatter them like a clay pot.'

[a] *So Sept.; Heb.* I will repeat unto . . .

Be mindful then, you kings;   10
    learn your lesson, rulers of the earth:
worship the LORD with reverence;   11-12
    tremble, and kiss the king,*a*
lest the LORD be angry and you are struck down in mid
      course;
for his anger flares up in a moment.
    Happy are all who find refuge in him.

✻ The key to understanding this psalm is to be found in
Nathan's oracle in 2 Sam. 7: 8–16 where several promises
are given to David: that he is to rank among earth's greatest
kings, that his people are to dwell in peace undisturbed by
foreign aggression, that he is to be the founder of a dynasty
that will endure for ever, that the relationship between God
and the heir to his throne will be that which exists between a
father and his son, and that God will never withdraw his
covenanted love from him. This psalm is virtually, as one
commentator puts it, 'a poetical treatment of the prophecy
of Nathan', though the speaker is now the king himself
(verses 6f.). That does not mean, however, that it is only
appropriate on the lips of David (as quoted in Acts 4: 25f.).
Since the prophecy spoke of an everlasting dynasty, each
succeeding king was heir to the promises and had the right to
claim them for himself. It has therefore been conjectured that
the Judaean monarchs through their generations would have
recited this text on their coronation days and at other suitable
festivals during their reigns, calling for the submission of the
nations and claiming the worldwide authority promised to
their forefather.

By Christian times it was commonly accepted that the

a] tremble. . .king: *prob. rdg.; lit.* tremble and kiss the mighty one;
Heb. obscure.

19

psalm spoke prophetically of a *coming* Davidic king, the Messiah, and it is with this sense that it is so frequently cited in the New Testament. Perhaps this interpretation does not represent the psalmist's original intention, but it is entirely consonant with the general tenor of his composition, for his idealistic vision of world domination can hardly relate to anything other than religious expectation, certainly not to any known historical situation, and his presentation of the 'anointed king' is fully concordant with Isaiah's portrait of the 'Prince of peace' (Isa. 9: 6f.; 11: 4f.).

1–3. The futile conspiracy of the nations.

1. *Why:* a rhetorical question expressing not despair, as in Ps. 22: 1, but mingled astonishment and scorn at the senseless opposition to God's rule. *the nations:* not particular rebellious subject kingdoms, but all earth's pagan *peoples* who continually threaten the existence of Israel and challenge the universal rule of God. *hatch. . .plots:* the Hebrew suggests the picture of conspirators muttering together.

2. *kings of the earth. . .rulers:* the leaders of God's enemies, and so personified by Herod and Pilate in Acts 4: 25–8. In the psalms they are subject to God, usually standing in terror or reverence before him (cp. Pss. 76: 12; 102: 15). *his anointed king:* (*māshīaḥ*) the Davidic king who was anointed at his coronation (cp. 1 Kings 1: 39); in later interpretation, the coming Messiah. He does not stand alone and helpless, for conspiracy against him is also *against the LORD*.

3. The psalmist writes as if the reign of God were a present reality against which the nations are in rebellion. This is a mode of expression based on faith which gives present substance to man's hopes, making him presently certain of the ultimate realities he cannot yet see (cp. Heb. 11: 1).

4–6. God responds in derision and judgement.

4. The picture is one of majesty, as the title *The Lord* suggests (contrast 'the LORD' which represents 'Yahweh', the Hebrew personal name for God). *sits enthroned in heaven:* like a mighty king, far above the turmoil of 'the kings of the

earth'. *laughs them to scorn:* not with personal vindictiveness, but with the sovereign contempt their ridiculous plots merit (cp. Pss. 37: 13; 59: 8).

5. *then:* the Hebrew suggests something much stronger than a mid-sentence connective. It is better to begin a new sentence here, for this is the point of transition in the psalm where the laughter ends and the foolish clamour of the kings is silenced by the awful voice of God.

6. *Of me he says:* an explanatory addition by the N.E.B. translators. The speech is intended as God's response to the uproar of the kings in verse 3, thus: 'Your agitation is pointless, since it is I, the one who sits enthroned in heaven, who have set my king in Zion, a city that is under my personal protection.' The *I* is emphatic in the Hebrew. *Zion* was an ancient stronghold that became the City of David (2 Sam. 5: 7) and was sanctified by the presence of the Ark (2 Sam. 6). The name was later transferred to the temple hill which became God's *holy mountain* when the Ark was removed thither (1 Kings 8: 1); it is sometimes also used of the whole city of Jerusalem (cp. Ps. 48: 12). The name thus expresses the eternal election of David and God's abiding, protective presence with his king and people.

7–9. God's decree concerning his king.

7. *the LORD's decree:* perhaps the content of 'the warrant' presented to the king at his coronation (2 Kings 11: 12). If so, the significance of *this day* is clear, for what the king repeats is the words used on that occasion, or a poetic rephrasing of them. The theme of the decree is the pledge of adoption given to David's heir in 2 Sam. 7: 14. This declaration of sonship is variously used in the New Testament in connection with Christ's baptism (Matt. 3: 17), transfiguration (Matt. 17: 5; 2 Pet. 1: 17) and resurrection (Acts 13: 33; cp. Rom. 1: 4) and to express his unique superiority (Heb. 1: 5; 5: 5).

8. *Ask of me:* God's word always requires man's response and even the son must claim the *inheritance* that is his natural right. World domination is not promised in 2 Sam. 7, but

it is implied in the unique status of the king as God's son (cp. Ps. 89: 27).

9. If the righteous rule of God's anointed is to be established, rebellion must be quenched, and that utterly. This notion is forcefully conveyed in the image of *a clay pot* completely shattered by *a rod of iron* (either the royal sceptre or a battle-mace). The citations of this verse in Rev. 2: 27; 12: 5; 19: 15 follow the Septuagint in reading 'rule' for *break them*.

10-12. The kings of the earth are summoned to submit while there is still time.

10. *Be mindful . . . learn your lesson:* the king now adopts the role of a teacher exhorting and admonishing his troublesome 'pupils' (cp. Prov. 4: 1).

11-12. *worship the LORD with reverence:* this is the first thing a pupil must learn, for it 'is the beginning of knowledge' (Prov. 1: 7). *kiss the king:* in an act of homage, perhaps bowing before him to kiss his feet (cp. Ps. 72: 9). The N.E.B. translators, like all others, have been obliged to emend what is a very strange Hebrew sentence, 'and rejoice with trembling; kiss son', the word for 'son' even being in Aramaic. But the general sense is plain. *his anger:* not mere impatience or loss of temper, though it *flares up in a moment*, and, like his laughter (verse 4), not an outburst of personal vindictiveness, but an expression of his judgement which is necessary to ensure the promised happiness of those *who find refuge in him*. The final benediction aptly summarizes the mood and theme of confidence that pervades the whole psalm. ✳

THE LORD IS A SHIELD TO COVER ME

3

1 LORD, how my enemies have multiplied!
   Many rise up against me,
2 many there are who say of me,
   'God will not bring him victory.'

But thou, LORD, art a shield to cover me: 3
  thou art my glory, and thou dost raise my head high.
I cry aloud to the LORD,   4
  and he answers me from his holy mountain.
I lie down and sleep,   5
and I wake again, for the LORD upholds me.
I will not fear the nations in their myriads   6
who set on me from all sides.

Rise up, LORD; save me, O my God.   7
  Thou dost strike all my foes across the face
    and breakest the teeth of the wicked.
    Thine is the victory, O LORD,   8
and may[a] thy blessing rest upon thy people.

---

* The Hebrew text of this psalm has a title which runs:
'A psalm of David when he fled from Absalom, his son', the
allusion being to 2 Sam. 15: 13 – 16: 14. The worshipper
using this psalm is thus invited to see the same power of God
that supported David in so critical a time sustaining him also.
As a plea for protection it could have been used by David's
successors on the throne in times of national crisis, but it may
equally be the prayer of any worshipper describing his own
personal troubles with metaphors drawn from war or in-
surrection. Although it is the cry of a man in distress, the
psalm's dominant theme is faith in God who hears and upholds
the petitioner.

1–2. The psalmist appeals to God with a lament. The thrice
repeated statement that his foes are many emphasizes the
gravity of his plight.

1. *my enemies:* if the speaker is the king, the danger may be
from foreign invasion (see on verse 6), or from internal

[a] Thine . . . and may: *or* O LORD of salvation, may . . .

rebellion (cp. 2 Sam. 15: 12f.). The private individual using this psalm would think of personal enemies, perhaps persecutors who mock his faith (verse 2), or spiritual forces that assail him (see on verse 7).

2. '*God will not bring him victory*': it is perhaps because the psalmist's troubles are so serious that the enemies scorn his trust in God to uphold him, thinking that his condition is beyond all help, even God's. *victory:* the Hebrew word, more commonly translated 'salvation', suggests the fulfilment of all the psalmist prays for, victory over his enemies (verses 1–2), vindication of his faith (verse 4) and release from suffering and fear into the joy and peace of God's presence (verses 3, 5–6).

3–6. Despite the onslaught of the world, the knowledge of God's presence inspires confidence and peace.

3. *a shield to cover me:* for this metaphor of protection, see more fully on Ps. 18: 35. *my glory:* God's glory is his presence in radiance and holiness (see on Ps. 19: 1). When he brings victory or salvation, he gives of his glory and clothes his servants with honour and radiant joy (Ps. 21: 5f.). The experience is described in the parallel phrase, *raise my head high*, which suggests the opposite of a head bowed in dejection and misery (cp. Luke 21: 28).

4. His prayer is that God will personally intervene to rescue him from his troubles, but before uttering that prayer (verse 7), he confidently asserts that God has answered it. Cp. the prayer of Jesus at the tomb of Lazarus in John 11: 41–3. *his holy mountain:* see on Ps. 2: 6. The expectation that God's help would come from Zion (cp. Ps. 20: 2) reflects the belief that the temple was an earthly representation of God's dwelling in heaven and a symbol of his presence with his people (1 Kings 8: 27–30).

5. Such is his faith in God that the psalmist sleeps in peace (cp. Ps. 4: 8) and this for him is a proof that God's victory is already won, despite all that his enemies say. The tenses could also be translated as past: 'I lay down ... I woke again',

emphasizing the reality of his experience.

6. *the nations:* the Hebrew is perhaps more accurately rendered 'people', suggesting that the psalmist feels himself thronged or menaced by a hostile mob. The N.E.B. translation implies an attack by foreign nations, an appropriate picture if the speaker is the king. *in their myriads:* irrespective of their numerical strength.

7–8. The psalmist's prayer for help is brief, for he has complete confidence that God is victorious.

7. *Rise up, LORD:* an ancient battle cry of Israel's armies (cp. Num. 10: 35). *Thou dost strike. . .:* the psalmist's enemies are also God's enemies and are therefore powerless. God treats them with appropriate contempt, insulting them with a blow on the cheek and rendering them harmless by breaking their *teeth*. The image of wild beasts with ferocious teeth may suggest demonic oppression, as may also the picture of the menacing mob attacking from all sides in verse 6.

8. Since the enemies are at war with God, they constitute a threat to the worshipping community as well as to the psalmist. Thus the concluding expression of confidence in God's *victory* (see verse 2) passes naturally into prayer for his people. *

THE LORD HAS PUT HAPPINESS AND PEACE
IN MY HEART

4

Answer me when I call, O God, maintainer of my right, 1
I was hard pressed, and thou didst set me at large;
  be gracious to me now and hear my prayer.
Mortal men, how long will you pay me not honour but 2
  dishonour,
or set your heart on trifles and run after lies?
Know that the LORD has shown me[a] his marvellous love; 3

[a] *Prob. rdg.; Heb.* him.

the LORD hears when I call to him.

4   However angry your hearts, do not do wrong;
     though you lie abed resentful,[a] do not break silence:
5 pay your due of sacrifice, and trust in the LORD.

6 There are many who say, 'If only we might be prosperous
        again!
   But the light of thy presence has fled from us, O LORD.'
7   Yet in my heart thou hast put more happiness
     than they enjoyed when there was corn and wine in
        plenty.
8 Now I will lie down in peace, and sleep;
   for thou alone, O LORD, makest me live unafraid.

✻ The spirit of assurance and serenity that characterizes
Ps. 3 pervades this psalm as well. Though it opens with a cry
for help (verse 1), it is otherwise fully occupied with exhortation based on the psalmist's testimony to his personal experience of God's love (verses 2–5) and with a description of his
consequent inner peace and happiness (verses 6–8). It is sometimes argued that the psalm was composed for use by the
king, a priest or some other official leader as a homiletic
address to the assembled community. Yet it is also a psalm
that could be used by any worshipper whose integrity is
questioned or whose faith is criticized or ridiculed.

    1. The psalmist's plea is brief and spoken in the knowledge
that God, because he is himself righteous, will maintain his
faithful servant's *right* in the face of false accusations. His confidence is based on past experience, for he has been in narrow
straits before and God has *set* him *at large*, like some cornered
animal released to run free.

    2–5. With such trust in God's protection, he addresses his
critics.

        [a] lie abed resentful: *prob. rdg.; Heb.* say on your beds.

2. *Mortal men:* that is, in no way divine and therefore not in a position to pass judgement. Their accusations, though unspecified, seem to relate to the psalmist's standing before God. Possibly they think that his suffering is some form of punishment for insufficient faith or faulty conduct. Certainly his response is to assert that his faith is entirely sufficient, grounded as it is on a personal knowledge of God's love (verse 3) and confirmed by the experience of great joy and peace in his presence (verses 7–8). And so he begs them to show him respect (*honour*) and to disregard the *lies* and unfounded slanders (*trifles*) that have been directed against him.

3. *has shown me his marvellous love:* this translation involves emendation, but many ancient manuscripts suggest the rendering 'he has done marvellous things for the one who loves him' (or '. . . for his faithful one'). But either translation suggests a special relationship founded on the loving faithfulness that exists between God and his servant, and this is the very basis of the psalmist's confidence (see further on Ps. 5: 7).

4. He calls on his hearers to give thought to their own conduct, to beware lest the anger and resentment he has seen in them erupt into violent action or speech. Perhaps the *silence* is thought to afford an occasion for reflection on what he has said about God's love. The N.E.B. translation requires some textual changes and a slight reordering of the words; the Hebrew reads 'be angry, but do not sin, say in your heart (=think, ponder) upon your beds, but be silent'. Eph. 4: 26 may be partly based on this verse.

5. A proper faith will issue not in anger and resentment, but in obedient worship and *trust in the LORD.*

6–8. He contrasts his own peace with the agitated longings of others.

6. There are many who seek God's blessing, but they seek it in material prosperity rather than in a personal relationship with their LORD. What earthly pleasure they have known has proved transient and so they lament the passing of what they took to be God's blessing. *the light of thy presence has fled*

from us: these words contain an allusion to the priestly blessing in Num. 6: 24-6. The Hebrew can also be translated as a prayer, 'lift up the light of thy presence upon us.'

7. The psalmist tells how much the joy that God has given him exceeds the greatest *happiness* that man knows. The height of earthly pleasure is also a rare thing, whereas the joy of God is in the *heart* as a permanent possession through all troubles (cp. John 16: 22).

8. Cp. Ps. 3: 5. Sleep undelayed by anxiety or fear, whatever the present circumstances, is a blessing given by God alone and is a natural consequence of the knowledge (verse 3) and the joy (verse 7) of God s presence. ✻

IN THE MORNING GOD WILL HEAR ME

5

1 Listen to my words, O Lord,
        consider my inmost thoughts;
2 heed my cry for help, my king and my God.
3 In the morning, when I say my prayers,
        thou wilt hear me.
   I set out my morning sacrifice[a]
        and watch for thee, O Lord.
4 For thou art not a God who welcomes wickedness;
        evil can be no guest of thine.[b]
5   There is no place for arrogance before thee;
        thou hatest evildoers,
6   thou makest an end of all liars.

[a] *Or* plea.
[b] who welcomes . . . thine: *or* who protects a wicked man; an evil man cannot be thy guest.

The LORD detests traitors and men of blood.
But I, through thy great love, may come into thy house, 7
and bow low toward thy holy temple in awe of thee.

Lead me, LORD, in thy righteousness,   8
    because my enemies are on the watch;
give me a straight path to follow.

There is no trusting what they say,*a*   9
    they are nothing but wind.

Their throats are an open*b* sepulchre;
smooth talk runs off their tongues.

Bring ruin on them, O God;   10
let them fall by their own devices.

Cast them out, after all their rebellions,
for they have defied thee.

But let all who take refuge in thee rejoice,   11
let them for ever break into shouts of joy;
shelter those who love thy name,
    that they may exult in thee.

For thou, O LORD, wilt bless the righteous;   12
    thou wilt hedge him round with favour as with a shield.

✻ This is one of several psalms that may have been used in
a night vigil at the sanctuary (see p. 14, sect. C). Though a
cry for help in the face of enemies, it is permeated by an
atmosphere of trust and confidence. The opening plea is
coupled with an assertion that God will hear (verses 1–3) and
the call for protection and for just punishment of the wicked
is followed by a statement that God will bless the righteous
(verses 8–12). The basis of this assurance is the knowledge that
God has covenanted his love to his loyal servants and the

[a] *So Sept.; Heb.* he says.
[b] *Or* inscribed.

observation that the enemies are rebels and traitors who cannot stand in the presence of the king (verses 4–7). This psalm is similar to Ps. 17 in structure, theme and purpose. There is no good reason for thinking that this is a late psalm.

1–3. A plea for hearing, repeated three times to emphasize the urgency of the psalmist's need (cp. Ps. 17: 1–2).

1. *inmost thoughts:* unspoken prayers of the heart.

2. *my king and my God:* the use of the pronoun *my* is both an intimate privilege and an indication of loyalty.

3. *I set out my morning sacrifice:* the Hebrew reads 'I prepare (in the) morning'. No object is expressed, but *sacrifice* is a reasonable assumption since the Hebrew verb often refers to the ordering of sacrificial materials. It has sometimes been held that the psalm was written for use on the eve of trial by one who claims that the accusations against him are false (verse 9). If so, what he has prepared may be his case or his 'plea' (N.E.B. footnote). But the psalm is also suited for a wider use in many kinds of spiritual suffering. The image of the loyal servant thronged by the enemies of God can suggest oppression by human, demonic or psychological agencies. Typical feelings of distress symptomatic of separation from God, such as doubt, fear or guilt, can be magnified in the watches of the night and become associated with the terrors of darkness, pictured here menacing the tortured soul and obscuring his path (see on verse 9). The sufferer appeals to God for protection and quite naturally views the dawning light of day as a symbol of God's coming deliverance. Thus the offering of sacrifice at the moment of victory would be most appropriate.

4–7. His reasons for confidence. These verses are similar in form to the entrance 'torahs' (see p. 63) in Pss. 15 and 24 which describe the kind of people who find acceptance with God, though here the portrait is of God's enemies who can never remain in his presence. The psalmist, by contrasting his own loyalty with this picture of rebelliousness, claims for himself the privilege of being God's *guest* and thus of enjoying his protection, a privilege God grants only to the faithful (cp. Ps. 23: 5f.).

5–6. Their *arrogance* exalts themselves instead of God; they are conscious *evildoers* and deceitful *liars*. Indeed, they are rebels against God, *traitors* who must shrink before the wrathful presence of their king.

7. *But I:* as a faithful servant he fits none of the categories described. Yet he makes no claim to sinlessness, for his access to God depends not on his own merit, but on God's *love*. The Hebrew word is *ḥesed*, more commonly translated 'unfailing love' in the N.E.B. It describes the relationship that exists in the covenant between God and his people. God's *ḥesed* is his faithfulness to his promises of protection and blessing; the Israelite's *ḥesed* is his loyalty and his obedience to the covenant demands. The psalmist is saying, 'I am loyal, I trust in your promise. So I approach you, confident of your help.' *bow low:* as a sign of homage. The scene is the temple forecourt beside the altar of sacrifice (verse 3) with the worshipper facing the sanctuary where God was believed to be present in a special way in the Holy of Holies. In later times the Jews far from Jerusalem looked towards the holy spot to offer the spiritual sacrifice of prayer (cp. Dan. 6: 10).

8–9. Surrounded by insidious enemies he prays for safe conduct.

8. *thy righteousness:* seen in God's faithfulness to his promises to protect his servants. He prays that God will *Lead* him, making his journey *straight* and easy, as a shepherd leads his sheep (Ps. 23: 3).

9. If this psalm were used by one falsely accused (see on verse 3), his plea would be as here, that his accusers are smooth-tongued liars and not to be trusted. But any man whose trust is in God knows that whatever assails his faith must be false and *nothing but wind* beside God's love. Yet this insubstantial enemy speaks with *smooth*, seductive words that can lead the faithful astray into the yawning throat of hell. The picture of enemies with gaping jaws and active tongues suggests a

nightmarish confusion of human and demonic imagery perhaps appropriate to a night vigil setting (see verse 3). 'inscribed' (N.E.B. footnote): this alternative translation alludes to the common practice of inscribing tombs with a curse on would-be plunderers or vandals.

10–11. He calls on God to execute his justice by confounding the enemies and blessing the faithful.

10. This call is made more in a spirit of anguish than of vindictiveness, but the enemies are rebels who *have defied* God and if God's covenant is to prevail, they cannot be permitted to continue despoiling the faithful.

11. *that they may exult in thee:* the rejoicing is not simply at the enemies' downfall, though their removal releases the faithful from fear and worry, leaving them free to praise God. The joy is that of knowing God's presence, now restored after dispersal of the darkness that oppressed the soul. It is also a joy that is to be *for ever*, a supernatural joy that cannot be taken away (cp. John 16: 22). *thy name:* God's name is God himself as far as he is known or has revealed himself to men.

12. He concludes with an expression of confidence in God's power to bless and protect his servants. *shield:* see on Ps. 18: 35. ✳

COME BACK, O LORD

6

1   O LORD, do not condemn me in thy anger,
      do not punish me in thy fury.
2   Be merciful to me, O LORD, for I am weak;
      heal me, my very bones are shaken;
3   my soul quivers in dismay.
      And thou, O LORD – how long?
4   Come back, O LORD; set my soul free,
      deliver me for thy love's sake.

None talk of thee among the dead;   5
who praises thee in Sheol?

I am wearied with groaning;   6
all night long my pillow is wet with tears,
I soak my bed with weeping.
Grief dims my eyes;   7
    they are worn out with all my woes.
Away from me, all you evildoers,   8
for the LORD has heard the sound of my weeping.
The LORD has heard my entreaty;   9
the LORD will accept my prayer.
All my enemies shall be confounded and dismayed;   10
    they shall turn away in sudden confusion.

☀ It has been suggested that this is a prayer for use in time of
sickness, but the language of illness could be metaphorical
of a spiritual condition. The psalmist's main concern is that
God has withdrawn (verse 4), abandoning him to grief and
dismay, and even to death (verses 3–7). Though he feels that
this is just punishment for his sinful behaviour, he pleads for
mercy (verses 1–2), and such is the sincerity of his trust in
God's love (verse 4) that he concludes his prayer assured that
God has heard him (verses 8–10). This is the first of the seven
'Penitential Psalms' in Christian tradition (see p. 14, sect. C).
Its date of composition cannot be determined.

1–3. The psalmist pleads for mercy.

1. Cp. Ps. 38: 1. The use of the verbs *condemn* and *punish*
implies that his suffering is a disciplinary consequence of sin
and that God's *anger* or *fury* is not blind passion, but a rational
expression of his justice.

2. The suppliant's *bones*, the framework that supports and
gives solidity to his body, *are shaken* and he is *weak*. The same
poetical image depicts the languor of the soul bereft of God's
comforting and strengthening presence in Ps. 22: 14.

3. *soul:* the Hebrew *nepesh* generally denotes the life-principle in man, his essential vitality, and here, as the parallelism indicates, his 'innermost being', in contrast to his solid frame (verse 2). The Old Testament regards man as a body imbued with living breath (cp. Gen. 2: 7). The common view, found in later thought, that man consists of three parts, body, soul and spirit, belongs to the world of Greek ideas. *how long?*: a common expression in prayers for help (cp. Ps. 13: 1f.). If his suffering is corrective punishment, it must be temporary, so the psalmist, like a shaken, penitent child before his master, stammers out his plea that the chastisement end soon.

4–5. He calls on God to return and free him from this death-like existence.

4. *Come back, O LORD:* there is no greater anguish for the faithful than the sense of abandonment by God (cp. Pss. 22: 1; 27: 9), even if deserved. The sufferer knows he is receiving justice, but he has asked for mercy, and now he casts himself on the faithful *love* of God (see on Ps. 5:7), wherein lies his only hope of restoration.

5. *Sheol:* the underworld of the dead, a place of silence and gloom to which all men, good or bad, must finally descend, there to abide cut off from living men and, worst of all, from communion with God (Ps. 88: 5). But the psalmist's concern is with his present condition, not his future life. He is sick in spirit and body, he is lifeless (verse 2), the shadow of death is over him, he has lost the feeling of God's nearness and praise does not come easily to his lips. He is all but in Sheol already.

6–7. He describes his tears of penitence and anguish.

6. *tears* and *weeping* usually express spiritual and emotional rather than physical agony, and here they suggest sorrow for sin and distress at God's absence.

7. Suffering has taken the sparkle from his eyes.

8–10. In faith he declares that his prayer is heard.

8. *Away from me, all you evildoers:* cp. Matt. 7: 23. This change of mood, from anguish to triumph, has suggested to

some scholars that a priestly blessing or a prophetic oracle was uttered during a pause between verses 8 and 9. However, the statement of confidence is an integral part of the prayer itself. It demonstrates the psalmist's living trust in the faithfulness of God's promised 'love' towards his covenant people, the very basis on which he offers his plea (verse 4). Thus, having presented his request to God, he begins to act in the full assurance of faith that God has heard and will respond. *evildoers:* malevolent figures, whether human or demonic, that have helped to cause or to aggravate the psalmist's suffering (see on Ps. 3: 1, 7).

9. *The LORD has heard:* the repetition (verse 8) emphasizes his certainty. This certainty is realized now by faith or inspiration, for the experience of fulfilment lies in the future: *the LORD will accept.*

10. The 'dismay' (verse 3) he experienced in the face of God's anger will presently be the lot of his *enemies* (see verse 8) when God intervenes in judgement. *

GOD IS A JUST JUDGE

7

O LORD my God, in thee I find refuge;   1
    save me, rescue me from my pursuers,
    before they tear at my throat like a lion   2
    and carry me off beyond hope of rescue.
O LORD my God, if I have done any of these things –   3
    if I have stained my hands with guilt,
    if I have repaid a friend evil for good   4
    or set free an enemy who attacked me without cause,
may my adversary come after me and overtake me,   5
    trample my life to the ground
    and lay my honour in the dust!

6   Arise, O LORD, in thy anger,
        rouse thyself in wrath against my foes.
  Awake, my God who hast ordered that justice be done;
7   let the peoples assemble around thee,
        and take thou thy seat on high above them.
8   O LORD, thou who dost pass sentence on the nations,
        O LORD, judge me as my righteousness deserves,
        for I am clearly innocent.
9   Let wicked men do no more harm,
      establish the reign of righteousness,[a]
      thou who examinest both heart and mind,
        thou righteous God.

10   God, the High God, is my shield
        who saves men of honest heart.
11   God is a just judge,
      every day he requites the raging enemy.

12   He sharpens his sword,
      strings his bow and makes it ready.
13   He has prepared his deadly shafts
      and tipped his arrows with fire.
14   But the enemy is in labour with iniquity;
  he conceives mischief, and his brood is lies.
15   He has made a pit and dug it deep,
      and he himself shall fall into the hole that he has made.
16   His mischief shall recoil upon himself,
      and his violence fall on his own head.

17   I will praise the LORD for his righteousness
      and sing a psalm to the name of the LORD Most High.

[a] the reign of righteousness: *or* the cause of the righteous.

✳ It has sometimes been thought that this psalm was composed for the accused man who wished to call on God to vindicate his innocence (see on Ps. 5: 3), but it is likely that it had a less limited use in ancient Israel, as is partly suggested by the Hebrew title which designates it a psalm that David 'sang to the LORD concerning Cush a Benjamite'. We know nothing of this Cush, but at the time of Absalom's rebellion David was bitterly pursued by some of Saul's people, the Benjamites (2 Sam. 16: 5; 20: 1), and the psalm itself depicts a sufferer who is relentlessly hounded by enemies. In his plight he appeals for help (verses 1–2), pleads his devotion to the cause of justice (verses 3–5) and prays God to establish his righteousness (verses 6–9). He then concludes with a psalm of praise expressing his confidence that God as a just judge will end the present reign of evil (verses 10–17).

1–2. His cry for help.

1. *in thee I find refuge:* a common theme in the prayers of the individual (e.g. Ps. 57: 1); here it sounds a note of trust and confidence at the very beginning of the psalm. It may be interpreted spiritually, but could also suggest that the sufferer has sought sanctuary in the temple. *my pursuers:* the Hebrew reads 'all my pursuers', suggesting that no specific enemies are in mind.

2. Comparison with wild animals in the psalms suggests ferocity, cruelty and terror (see on Ps. 17: 12).

3–5. He solemnly protests his devotion to justice. The whole sentence is in the form of an oath: 'if I am guilty of these crimes . . . then *may my adversary* punish me in his fury.' The repeated invocation of the LORD *my God* (verse 1) adds solemnity and authority to the oath.

4. It is not moral perfection that the psalmist claims. The specific charges here relate to just dealings with his fellows, the principles of law and order in society. He has not himself acted unjustly, nor has he apathetically turned a blind eye on wanton violation of the common laws of justice. In other words, he has been a socially responsible citizen, behaving uprightly himself and ensuring that others did the same in

37

their dealings with him. The theme is appropriate in a psalm addressed to God as 'a just judge' (verse 11).

5. The three-fold formulation adds strength and effectiveness to the curse. The metaphor (cp. Ps. 143: 3) likens his 'pursuers' (verse 1) to a hunter or a fighting man who may *overtake* him, *trample* him underfoot and *lay* him *in the dust* of death. *my honour:* literally 'my glory', that is simply 'me' (see also Pss. 30: 12; 57: 8).

6–9. He appeals to God to act as judge and bring justice to men.

6. *Arise, O LORD:* with this ancient war-cry (see Ps. 3: 7) he summons God to battle against the *foes*, who must now be likened to a hostile army. But the scene is as much the courtroom as the battle-field, for God's *anger* and *wrath* are rational expressions of his *justice*. On the call to *Awake*, see on Pss. 17: 15; 44: 23.

7. The scene is now the heavenly court where God sits enthroned as judge and *the peoples* of the earth are summoned for the last assize (cp. Dan. 7: 9f.). *take thou thy seat:* the Hebrew actually reads 'return', suggesting the sense of God's absence while wickedness appears to triumph.

8. It is to this universal judge, who will *pass sentence* of acquittal or condemnation *on the nations*, that he presents his plea of *righteousness*, his claim to be *innocent* of socially irresponsible behaviour (see verse 4).

9. By using the image of last judgement, which is probably as much poetic as the other word-pictures in the psalm, he has set his own appeal for present vindication within the wider context of prayer for the inauguration of God's rule on earth. This is indeed the whole intention of the curses and pleas for judgement in the psalms, that *wicked men* may *do no more harm* and that *the reign of righteousness*, God's eternal purpose, may be established on earth. God's judgement is not dependent on the accounts of often biassed witnesses, for he can examine man's *heart and mind*, or literally 'heart and kidneys', the seats of intellect and emotion respectively.

10–17. He sings the praise of God as judge and envisages the final passing of judgement. Verses 1–9 address God in the second person, verses 10–17 praise him in the third person.

10. *my shield:* see on Ps. 18: 35. The Hebrew of this verse is awkward, but the N.E.B.'s translation *the High God* corresponds well with the title in verse 17. *men of honest heart* are those who uphold social justice (verse 4) and long for its final establishment (verse 9), that is, those whose minds are attuned and loyal to the purposes of God expressed in his covenant.

11. *every day he requites the raging enemy:* this translation requires two alterations to the Hebrew which reads 'and God is angry every day'. Both renderings imply that God's judicial wrath against evil never rests.

12. No subject change has been indicated, so presumably *He* is God, depicted as a warrior preparing his weapons for battle against the enemy. But in translation the N.E.B. has removed an opening phrase which could suggest that the subject of the sentence is the enemy, not God: 'If he does not repent, but *sharpens* . . .'

13. God's *shafts* are his lightnings (Ps. 18: 14), but the poet is still developing his military metaphor. *arrows tipped* with inflammable materials were used as incendiary devices in ancient warfare.

14. *the enemy* is now a pregnant woman giving birth to a *brood* of *lies*. Though the various stages of conception, labour and birth are mentioned, they are simply introduced as synonyms for the sake of the parallelism. Likewise *iniquity*, *mischief* and *lies* are poetic synonyms and are not intended to represent different degrees in the growth of evil.

15. Now the enemy has become a hunter digging a *pit* to trap some wild animal, but his wickedness has proved self-destructive (cp. Ps. 9: 15). In this psalm the enemies have been likened to a lion, a warrior, accusers, wicked men, a pregnant woman and a hunter. Such is the fluidity of psalm imagery that it is impossible to identify the foe with any one class of persons. The psalms remain adaptable for use in different

situations; the pictures used here may even be interpreted with reference to oppression by supernatural forces (cp. on Ps. 5: 3, 9).

16. The boomerang effect on sin (cp. Prov. 26: 27; Matt. 26: 52).

17. *I will praise:* his vindication, whilst anticipated by faith, is not yet realized in experience (see on Ps. 6: 8; 13: 5). *the name of the LORD:* that is God himself as he is known to men. *Most High:* Hebrew *'elyōn*, a title which must have been applied to the God of Israel only after David's conquest of Jerusalem, because it is first used of the god of the pre-Israelite inhabitants of the city in Abraham's time. It is well suited to the present context where the psalmist looks to his God as universal sovereign, for the old Jerusalemite god is called 'creator of heaven and earth' in Gen. 14: 19, 22. ✳

CROWNED WITH GLORY AND HONOUR

8

1   O LORD our sovereign,
      how glorious is thy name in all the earth!
      Thy majesty is praised high as the heavens.

2   Out of the mouths of babes, of infants at the breast,
          thou hast rebuked[a] the mighty,
    silencing enmity and vengeance to teach thy foes a lesson.

3 When I look up at thy heavens, the work of thy fingers,
      the moon and the stars set in their place by thee,

4   what is man that thou shouldst remember him,
      mortal man that thou shouldst care for him?

5   Yet thou hast made him little less than a god,
      crowning him with glory and honour.

6   Thou makest him master over all thy creatures;

[a] *Prob. rdg.; Heb.* founded.

40

thou hast put everything under his feet:
all sheep and oxen, all the wild beasts,   7
    the birds in the air and the fish in the sea,   8
    and all that moves along the paths of ocean.
    O LORD our sovereign,   9
how glorious is thy name in all the earth!

✻ This hymn of praise shows much in common with the story of creation in Gen. 1, though it does not necessarily post-date that account. Its theme is God's purpose for man who, as he contemplates the majesty of God reflected in the vastness of the universe, becomes aware of his own insignificance, and yet knows that God has graciously blessed him and appointed him master of the earth. However, as the writer of Heb. 2: 6–9, where verses 4–6 are quoted, correctly notes, 'in fact we do not yet see all things in subjection to man'. But he argues that though the kingly likeness of God in man, of which Gen. 1 and Ps. 8 speak, is obscured by sin, it is restored in Jesus who bears 'the stamp of God's very being' (Heb. 1: 3) and has been 'crowned now with glory and honour' (Heb. 2: 9).

1. *our sovereign:* these are the words of an individual worshipper (verse 3) acknowledging that his personal communion with God depends on his membership of God's covenant community. They also express fitting reverence and praise before the creator whose glory and *majesty* encompass and are reflected in *the heavens* and *in all the earth. thy name:* God's revealed presence.

2. Yet the paradox that calls forth his song of wonder is that 'to shame what is strong, (this universal) God has chosen what the world counts weakness' (1 Cor. 1: 27). The faithful may feel like mere *babes* before the *enmity* of the world, but it is through them that God works his purpose. Moses and Jesus were hardly *the mighty* of their day, but through them

God performed his greatest acts of salvation, *silencing* the hateful powers in mankind that had held his people in bondage. God's *foes* may be historical persons and nations (Ps. 2: 1–3) or mythological beings and disruptive cosmic forces (Ps. 74: 13; 89: 10; 93: 3). The N.E.B.'s rendering is but one of many different attempts to interpret a very obscure verse, but alternative translations usually preserve the same general sense. Matt. 21: 16 is based on the Septuagint (cp. Revised Standard Version).

3. The worshipper becomes acutely aware of his own involvement in this paradox when he looks at the night sky and considers that its infinite immensity is the personal handiwork of God, *the work of* his *fingers*.

4. Cp. Ps. 144: 3; Job 7: 17f. *mortal man:* literally 'son of man', that is a being of the human kind, not in any sense divine. The thought of this verse is in keeping with the notion of human frailty found in verse 2. *remember:* as the parallel *care for* suggests, this verb implies action on behalf of mankind, not simply a calling to mind.

5. *little less than a god:* or 'than God (himself)'. The translation 'than the angels' (Heb. 2: 7) takes the Hebrew *'elōhīm* in its plural sense of 'divine beings' (cp. Ps. 58: 1; 82: 1). It is part of the great paradox that man, who is so puny and insignificant beside the rest of creation, is unique in God's purpose, being alone of all creatures made in God's 'image and likeness' (Gen. 1: 26) yet prevented from attaining full divine status (Gen. 3: 22f.). *crowning him:* man's commission is to 'rule over . . . every living thing' (Gen. 1: 28). For this task God gives him the attributes of royalty, *glory and honour* (cp. Ps. 21: 5).

6. Cp. Gen. 1: 26, 28. *everything under his feet:* man is granted complete victory and authority over his world; God's command in Gen. 1: 28 is that he 'subdue' the earth. Christ assumes this authority in the New Testament (1 Cor. 15: 27; Eph. 1: 22).

7–8. Man's rule is comprehensive; his subjects are not only

domestic animals, but also *the wild beasts, the birds . . . the fish* (Gen. 1: 26, 28) and *all* the strange creatures that inhabit the great deep (cp. Gen. 1: 21).

9. It is no part of Old Testament belief that man has gained his own mastery over his environment. This is God's gift to him (verse 5) and his only fitting response is the reverent wonder and praise that opens and permeates the whole psalm. *

THE LORD IS KING, PROTECTOR OF THE POOR
9-10

* The decision to treat Pss. 9 and 10 as one continuous poem goes back as far as the Septuagint and Vulgate. Taken together they form an acrostic (see p. 10), though the alphabetic sequence is broken, especially at the beginning of Ps. 10. It is also notable that Ps. 10 has no title in the Hebrew, contrary to the general rule in Book 1. Although opinions differ about the unity of the two psalms, a possible solution is that someone has re-edited and broken up an original acrostic. The alphabetic structure disappears in the description of the wicked man in 10: 2–11, suggesting that this section has displaced some older component. The mood of these verses is certainly different from that of the rest of the two psalms. 9: 1 – 10: 1 and 10: 12–18 are both a victorious hymn of praise and a call for the activation of God's promise to rule as king and execute justice. Indeed 10: 12–18 re-echoes the themes and prayers of 9: 1 – 10: 1 (see commentary) and in both parts there is an undergirding of confidence and hope. However, the effect of the introduction of 10: 2–11 is to turn Ps. 10 into a prayer for help in the face of oppression, to change its victory cry (10: 16) into a 'lament' (10: 17). None the less, a thematic unity remains. The psalmist contemplates the conflict between God and evil, contrasting the assured triumph of God with the present oppression of the wicked. But herein lies the very problem that calls forth his prayers for intervention: faith says that God is sovereign and is just, and

yet the wicked lord it and prosper in human affairs. This gap between faith and experience, which is too wide to bridge with reasoned arguments, evokes the anguished 'Why?' and the pleas for action. And yet it is on the side of faith that the psalmist takes his firm stance: God, who will judge victoriously among the nations (Ps. 9), will surely bring justice to them that are downtrodden by the ungodly (Ps. 10). Perhaps the best comment on this problem in the Psalter is to be found in Ps. 73. The acrostic form is sometimes regarded as a sign of post-exilic writing, though there is no good reason why this psalm could not have been composed earlier. ✳

1   I will praise thee, O Lord,[a] with all my heart,
     I will tell the story of thy marvellous acts.
2   I will rejoice and exult in thee,
     I will praise thy name in psalms, O thou Most High,
3   when my enemies turn back,
     when they fall headlong and perish at thy appearing;
4   for thou hast upheld my right and my cause,
     seated on thy throne, thou righteous judge.
5   Thou hast rebuked the nations and overwhelmed the
     ungodly,
   thou hast blotted out their name for all time.
6   The strongholds of the enemy are thrown down for
     evermore;
   thou hast laid their cities in ruins, all memory of them is
     lost.
7   The Lord thunders,[b] he sits enthroned for ever:
   he has set up his throne, his judgement-seat.
8   He it is who will judge the world with justice
   and try the cause of the peoples fairly.

[a] thee, O Lord: *so Sept.; Heb.* the Lord.
[b] thunders: *prob. rdg.; Heb. unintelligible.*

So may the LORD be a tower of strength for the oppressed, 9
    a tower of strength in time of need,
that those who acknowledge thy name may trust in thee; 10
    for thou, LORD, dost not forsake those who seek thee.
Sing psalms to the LORD who dwells in Zion, 11
    proclaim his deeds among the nations.
For the Avenger of blood has remembered men's desire, 12
    and has not forgotten the cry of the poor.

Have pity on me, O LORD; look upon my affliction, 13
    thou who hast lifted me up[a] and caught me back from
        the gates of death,
    that I may repeat all thy praise 14
and exult at this deliverance in the gates of Zion's city.

The nations have plunged into a pit of their own 15
        making;
their own feet are entangled in the net which they hid.
Now the LORD makes himself known. Justice is done: 16
    the wicked man is trapped in his own devices.
    They rush blindly down to Sheol, the wicked, 17
        all the nations who are heedless of God.
    But the poor shall not always be unheeded 18
    nor the hope of the destitute be always vain.
Arise, LORD, give man no chance to boast his strength; 19
    summon the nations before thee for judgement.
Strike them with fear, O LORD, 20
let the nations know that they are but men.
Why stand so far off, LORD, **10**
    hiding thyself in time of need?

[a] thou . . . me up: *prob. rdg.*; *Heb.* from those who hate me.

✻ 9: 1–4. The psalmist offers praise to God whose victories he himself has witnessed.

1. Each of the four lines of verses 1–2 begins with '*ālep*, the first letter of the Hebrew alphabet, but in the rest of the psalm the subsequent letters indicated below are only used to open each stanza. Thankful *praise*, like all true religious expression, comes from the *heart* (Deut. 6: 5), not simply from the lips (Isa. 29: 13). *marvellous acts:* the Hebrew word *niplā'ōt*, used frequently in the Psalter, usually refers to the great redemptive miracles of Israel's history (cp. Ps. 106: 7), but may also suggest deeds of deliverance in the psalmist's own life and experience.

2. True praise *will rejoice* in God for what he is, or has revealed himself to be (his *name*), as well as recount his gracious acts (verse 1). The title *Most High* is very appropriate in this psalm which celebrates God's universal sovereignty (see on Ps. 7: 17).

3. Stanza *bēt*. The reason for praise is God's victory, portrayed here firstly as the triumphant *appearing* of God and the panic-stricken rout of the psalmist's *enemies*.

4. Secondly, God is depicted as *judge* upholding the *cause* of the psalmist in a lawsuit, for his victory is the outworking of his righteousness. His *throne* is a symbol of his judicial power (verse 7).

5–8. The eschatological aspect of God's victory: personal experience of God's saving intervention (verses 3–4) causes the psalmist to think of what it prefigures, namely the greater, final triumph (verses 5–6) and judgement (verses 7–8) that are yet to come.

5. Stanza *gīmel*. As creation was by the spoken word of God (Ps. 33: 6; cp. Gen. 1: 3, 6, 9, etc.) and involved the giving of names (Gen. 2: 18–23), so when God has *rebuked the nations* and *blotted out their name*, he has terminated their existence. *the nations:* the traditional enemies of Israel defeated in the great saving events of history, especially in the exodus and the settlement, are a symbol of all powers that war

against God's people. They are *the ungodly* and must be totally vanquished in the end.

6. The pictures in this verse are probably based on memories of the conquest of Canaan and the curse on Amalek in Exod. 17: 14, but the poet's mind is still on the future finality (*for evermore*). The past tenses in verses 5–6 are instances of the Hebrew 'prophetic perfect' which describes the predicted event as though it had already happened, as it has, of course, in the mind and declared purpose of God. *strongholds:* a conjectural translation (?). The Hebrew reads 'the enemy has gone – desolations for ever'.

7. Stanza *hē* (there is no stanza beginning with the fourth letter, *dālet*). *thunders: hōmeh,* an emended form of the last word of verse 6 transposed to the beginning of this verse to maintain the metrical structure and the alphabetic sequence. *his throne, his judgement-seat:* cp. verse 4 and Ps. 7: 7f.

8. Cp. Pss. 96: 13; 98: 9; Acts 17: 31. It is not the enemies or the nations that will give ultimate judgement, but God (cp. Ps. 82).

9–12. God's judgement must result in deliverance for the oppressed and encouragement for the faithful.

9. Stanza *wāw*. Unlike the enemy strongholds that fail to give protection (verse 6), God is a sure refuge, *a tower of strength in time of need* (cp. Ps. 46: 7, 11).

10. Cp. Ecclus. 2: 10. *those who acknowledge thy name:* those who love and worship God as he has revealed himself and who obey his demnads (cp. Ps. 8:1). *seek thee:* possibly by visiting the sanctuary, but certainly by an inward turning to God.

11. Stanza *zayin*. Knowledge of God's victory gives courage to the faithful to sing God's praise and to bear witness to *his* great *deeds* of salvation. *the LORD who dwells in Zion:* the temple, as an earthly counterpart of God's heavenly abode, is a symbol of his presence with his people (see on Ps. 2: 6 and 11: 4).

12. *the Avenger of blood:* the LORD himself. Man's life is a

sacred gift from God (Gen. 2: 7) and ultimately belongs to him alone. Hence blood shed by a murderer cries out to God for vengeance (Gen. 4: 10; 9: 5f.). *men's desire:* the Hebrew actually reads 'them', that is the oppressed who acknowledge God's name (verses 9f.). *the poor:* it is uncertain whether the Hebrew word denotes the lowly and humble, that is the godly, or the poor and afflicted, that is the victims of social injustice. Certainly these two classes are not always distinguishable, and perhaps both are intended. In 10: 2 the poor is indeed one who is hounded by the wealthy, but in 10: 12–14 he is also a man who commits himself to God (see also on Ps. 40: 17).

13–14. Though God is the conquering king and judge, the final realization of his victory has not yet arrived and there is still need to pray for its fulfilment in the midst of present suffering and oppression.

13. Stanza *ḥēt*. Since the psalmist clearly identifies himself with the afflicted poor, it may be best to retain the traditional reading and translate 'my affliction at the hands of those who hate me'. Any kind of suffering, whether from illness or from oppression, if it sap the vitality in man, brings him close to *the gates of death* and dims his vision of the nearness of God (cp. Ps. 6: 5). But the worshipper has already experienced the healing presence of God and prays for full restoration.

14. He seeks total release to rejoice and sing God's *praise*. Rescued from 'the gates of death' (verse 13), he seeks *the gates of Zion's city*, for Zion is the place of God's dwelling (verse 11) and so symbolizes divine vitality, the very antithesis of death.

9:15–10:1. Continuing his prayer for present realization of God's victory, the psalmist contemplates the fate of the wicked and calls for the activation of the judgement that he celebrates.

15. Stanza *ṭēt*. As in verses 5–6, the setting is the final overthrow of *The nations*, but the theme of the last assize is no longer prominent. The metaphors here come from hunting

and illustrate the belief that wickedness is self-destructive
(see Ps. 7: 15f.).

16. *Now:* the N.E.B.'s use of the present tenses grasps the
mood of the Hebrew perfects (see on verse 6). God's judgement is yet to come, but it may be anticipated in the present
by faith, since it is a self-revelation of his eternal nature.

17. Stanza *yōd. They rush blindly:* the Hebrew reads 'they
return', as to the place where by nature they belong, namely
the land of death.

18. Stanza *kap.* God is faithful and 'will not cast off his
servants for ever' (Lam. 3: 31). *the poor:* see on verse 12.

19–20. As in verses 5–7, God acts against the enemy both
in battle and in judgement. *Arise, LORD:* reminiscent of
Israel's ancient war-cry in Num. 10: 35. *they are but men:*
that is, frail and in no sense divine (see on Ps. 8: 4). Men and
nations are apt *to boast* in their apparent superiority, but real
strength lies with God alone.

10: 1. Stanza *lāmed. Why:* as in Ps. 22: 1, this is a plea for
intervention, not a request for explanations. The psalmist's
sense of dereliction is very real and is perhaps a greater cause
of anguish than any physical sufferings. ✳

The wicked man in his pride hunts down the poor: 2
may his crafty schemes be his own undoing!
The wicked man is obsessed with his own desires,   3
and in his greed gives wickedness*a* his blessing;
arrogant as he is, he scorns the LORD   4
and leaves no place for God in all his schemes.
His ways are always devious;   5
thy judgements are beyond his grasp,*b*
and he scoffs at all restraint.

[a] wickedness: *transposed from first line of verse 4.*
[b] beyond his grasp: *prob. rdg.; Heb.* on high before him.

49

6 He says to himself, 'I shall never be shaken;
    no misfortune can check my course.'[a]
7 His mouth is full of lies and violence;
    mischief and trouble lurk under his tongue.
8   He lies in ambush in the villages
    and murders innocent men by stealth.
    He is watching[b] intently for some poor wretch;
9 he seizes him and drags him away in his net;
  he crouches stealthily, like a lion in its lair
    crouching to seize its victim;
10   the good man[c] is struck down and sinks to the ground,
    and poor wretches fall into his toils.
11 He says to himself, 'God has forgotten;
    he has hidden his face and has seen nothing.'

☼ 10: 2-11. Turning his thoughts from future judgement to
the present conditions of mankind, the psalmist vividly depicts the ways of the wicked and their oppression of the poor.
The alphabetic structure is absent from this section.

2. *The wicked man:* man in rebellion against God. *in his
pride* he boasts in his own strength and self-sufficiency (verses
4, 6).

3. *is obsessed with:* literally 'praises'. He sets his mind on
his own desires and makes them his praise instead of God.

4. And so he *leaves no place for God.* He denies, not that
God exists, but that God cares or has the power to intervene
(cp. Ps. 14: 1).

5. *are . . . devious:* the more common translation is 'prosper'. The crux of the problem is precisely that the wicked
appear to succeed though their ways are opposed to God's

[a] my course: *prob. rdg.; Heb.* which.
[b] *Prob. rdg.; Heb.* storing up.
[c] the good man: *prob. rdg.; Heb. om.*

(Ps. 73: 2–12). *he scoffs:* literally 'he puffs', that is openly showing his contempt with some physical gesture.

6. '*I shall never be shaken*': the righteous man makes this claim in faithful dependence on God (Ps. 16: 8), but the wicked man makes it in arrogant self-sufficiency.

7. Paul uses this verse in his description of human corruption in Rom. 3: 14.

8. It is uncertain whether this accusation of highway robbery and murder is to be interpreted literally. The language, as in the next verse, is probably metaphorical, but it is also closely reminiscent of Hos. 6: 9 where the priests of Shechem are accused of precisely these crimes. In the absence of a strong police system, bandits were a constant threat to travellers in ancient Israel and in the Near East in general (cp. Luke 10: 30).

9. *like a lion:* see on Ps. 17: 12.

10. *the good man:* this addition by the N.E.B represents an attempt to restore a semblance of alphabetic sequence, but it is purely conjectural. *toils:* an uncommon English word meaning 'net', 'snare'. The Hebrew reads 'by his mighty ones', but it is not very clear what that signifies.

11. *He:* either the wicked man who 'scorns the LORD' (verse 4), or the poor wretch who feels that God has forsaken him by hiding himself in time of need (verse 1). *hidden his face:* in disinterest, or possibly in displeasure, if the speaker is the poor man and he feels that his suffering is some kind of punishment for sin, though there is no other evidence to support such an interpretation in this psalm. *

Arise, LORD, set^a thy hand to the task;   12
   do not forget the poor, O God.
Why, O God, has the wicked man rejected thee   13
   and said to himself that thou dost not care?

[a] *Or* who settest.

14 Thou seest that mischief and trouble are his companions,
   thou takest the matter into thy own hands.
   The poor victim commits himself to thee;
   fatherless, he finds in thee his helper.

15   Break the power of wickedness and wrong;
   hunt out all wickedness until thou canst find no more.

16 The LORD is king for ever and ever;
   the nations have vanished from his land.

17   Thou hast heard the lament of the humble, O LORD,
   and art attentive to their heart's desire,

18   bringing justice to the orphan and the downtrodden
   that fear may never drive men from their homes again.

⁕ 12–15. The psalmist resumes his prayer for the protection
of the poor (9: 9 – 10: 1), confident that God is in control.
The triumphant mood of Ps. 9 has returned.

12–13. Stanza *qōp. Arise . . . Why:* these words echo his
earlier prayer (9: 19 – 10: 1) and again call for a response in
action. God must terminate injustice and show that he cares.

14. Stanza *rēsh.* In the spirit of Ps. 9 the psalmist reasserts
his faith in God's sovereignty. *fatherless:* that is, lacking protection. In Israel, as in the ancient Near East generally, the king
was in theory responsible for the care of orphans, and all
helpless people. But ultimately it was God who was their
guardian.

15. Stanza *shīn. Break the power:* literally, 'break the arm',
that is, take away the power to do harm.

16–18. The psalm ends with the confident note on which
Ps. 9 opened. God is king and will not fail his people.

16. *The LORD is king:* is a statement of faith for the present
and of hope for the future. It expresses the conviction that
God's authority is absolute now and that it will be seen to be

so by all in the end. It is this belief in the sovereignty of God
that is so strongly asserted in 9: 1–8 and forms the basis of the
psalmist's confidence throughout. The absolute rule of God
must mean the end of all opposition, and so the disappearance
of *the nations*.

17. Stanza *tāw. art attentive to their heart's desire:* literally,
'you will establish their heart, you will incline your ear',
that is, you will listen to their prayer and strengthen their
faith.

18. *justice to the orphan and the downtrodden:* see on verse 14.
that fear . . . again: this is an interpretation rather than a translation, but it captures the mood of the Hebrew well. The closing note is one of security and trust. *

THE LORD'S EYE IS UPON MANKIND

11

In the LORD I have found my refuge; why do you say to 1
    me,
   'Flee to the mountains like a bird;
see how the wicked string their bows 2
    and fit the arrow to the string,
    to shoot down honest men out of the darkness'?
When foundations are undermined, what can the good 3
    man do?
   The LORD is in his holy temple, 4
  the LORD's throne is in heaven.
His eye is upon mankind, he takes their measure at a
    glance.
The LORD weighs just and unjust 5
    and hates with all his soul the lover of violence.
   He shall rain down red-hot coals upon the wicked; 6

brimstone and scorching winds shall be the cup they
    drink.
7 For the LORD is just and loves just dealing;
    his face is turned towards the upright man.

* There is no indication of personal suffering in this psalm,
only a passing mood of despondency at the condition of
society. Like Lot in ancient times, the psalmist is advised to
make good his escape from the decadent community in which
he lives, but in God he finds reassurance and hope. God
is in control and is watching over his people. This is not a
prayer for help, but a psalm of confidence, like Ps. 23. It
contains nothing that would indicate its date of composition.

1–3. When he looks at society he feels despair.

1. *'Flee to the mountains like a bird'*: run and hide like a
defenceless creature. The Hebrew reads 'Flee to your mountain, O bird.' Since the reference to 'red-hot coals' and
'brimstone' in verse 6 recalls the judgement on Sodom and
Gomorrah (Gen. 19: 24), the poet probably had in mind the
similar counsel given to Lot to 'Flee to the hills' (Gen. 19:
17). But the psalmist finds *refuge* with God, perhaps in the
temple (verse 4, see also on Ps. 7: 1). It is not necessary to
imagine that any particular counsellors followed him thither;
the *you* most likely refers to voices of despair speaking within
him.

2. These are general observations on the Sodom-like
quality of life in society rather than comments on the psalmist's own suffering. The *wicked* (see on Ps. 1: 1) act with stealth
under cover of darkness (cp. Ps. 64: 3f.).

3. Though presented by the N.E.B. as the psalmist's comment on the advice in verses 1–2, this reads like a continuation
of the counsel of despair. The *foundations* are the fundamental
principles of law and order in society.

4–7. When he looks to the LORD his confidence is renewed.

4. The voices of despair fade when he thinks of *the LORD*

54

enthroned as judge (cp. Ps. 9: 7), scrutinizing *mankind* with
his judicial gaze that penetrates all hearts and minds (Ps. 7:
9). *The LORD is in his holy temple* (cp. Hab. 2: 20): the parallelism shows that this must be given a spiritual interpretation.
The king of the universe cannot be contained in any building,
for 'Heaven itself, the highest heaven, cannot contain' him
(1 Kings 8: 27). The *temple* is an earthly representation of
God's heavenly abode, just as God's *throne . . . in heaven* is
symbolized by the Ark in the Holy of Holies (cp. Isa. 6: 1).
It could therefore be either the Solomonic temple itself (cp.
on verse 1) or contemplation of the spiritual counterpart that
inspires the psalmist's confidence.

5. As 'the LORD . . . loves just dealing' (verse 7), he is
totally at enmity with *the lover of violence*. But he is the omniscient and omnipotent judge who *weighs* all men in his scales
of justice.

6. And *the wicked* will be visited with the judgement of
Sodom and Gomorrah (see on verse 1). It is from *the cup* of
God's wrath, not his cup of salvation (Ps. 116: 13), that they
will drink.

7. But the LORD's *face is turned towards the upright man* to
bless him (cp. Num. 6: 24-6). ✳

THE LORD'S WORDS ARE PURE

12

Help, LORD, for loyalty is no more;   1
  good faith between man and man is over.
One man lies to another: 2
they talk with smooth lip and double heart.
  May the LORD make an end of such smooth lips   3
  and the tongue that talks so boastfully!
  They said, 'Our tongue can win the day.   4
Words are our ally; who can master us?'

5 'For the ruin of the poor, for the groans of the needy,
   now I will arise,' says the LORD,
      'I will place him in the safety for which he longs.'

6 The words of the LORD are pure words:
   silver refined in a crucible,
   gold[a] seven times purified.

7 Do thou, LORD, protect us[b]
   and guard us from a profligate and evil generation.[c]

8 The wicked flaunt themselves on every side,
      while profligacy stands high among mankind.

* This may be a communal prayer or the plea of an individual. Surrounded by deceit, the psalmist would cry out with
Elijah 'I alone am left, and they seek to take my life' (1 Kings
19: 10, 14). The situation is similar to that in Ps. 11, but here
the worshipper finds comfort in God's promises which, unlike man's words, can be trusted.

1-4. The psalmist cries for help and prays for an end to
the deceit and corruption in society.

1. *loyalty . . . good faith*: this rendering in abstract terms
depends partly on emendation and the Hebrew is better
represented by the translation 'the loyal man (*ḥāsīd*, see on
Ps. 30: 4) . . . faithful men'. His complaint is virtually identical to Elijah's in 1 Kings 19: 10 (cp. Micah 7: 2), that the people
amongst whom he lives have forsaken the ways of God and
are hostile to the faithful.

2. Social intercourse is totally lacking in sincerity. Men
make a pretence of friendship to cover up their treachery.
The *smooth* flattery on their *lips* is utterly hypocritical and
issues from a *heart* that thinks one thing, but speaks to deceive.

[a] gold; *prob. rdg.; Heb.* to the earth.
[b] *So some MSS.; others* them.
[c] a profligate and evil generation: *prob. rdg.; Heb.* the generation which
is for ever.

Whilst this is presented as a comment on society as a whole, the individual psalmist or the worshipping community would doubtless have particular persons or groups in mind.

3-4. The prayer for help passes into a call for judgement. The *tongue* 'is a small member but it can make huge claims' (Jas. 3: 5), and when it does so, it speaks *boastfully*, uttering proud words of self-sufficiency (cp. Ps. 10: 6), claiming a personal strength they think can be matched by no-one not even God: *They said, '. . . who can master us?'* Thus does man usurp the place of God.

5. God answers with an oracle promising protection. Some scholars have thought that this verse was spoken by a prophet or priest. This may have happened when the psalm was used liturgically by the whole congregation, but the individual alone at prayer should equally hear God speak of comfort and hope as he meditates on these words of divine assurance (see also on Ps. 27: 8, 14). He should also be encouraged by the memory that God arose to deliver his people once before when their *groans* were heard in Egypt, thus vindicating his faithfulness (Exod. 2: 24).

6-8. The psalmist acknowledges the trustworthiness of God's word and renews his plea.

6. *The words of the LORD:* all God's promises, of which that in verse 5 is a typical and representative example. Unlike the deceitful speech of men (verse 2), God's words are *pure*, true and reliable. Like *refined silver* or *purified gold*, they contain no hidden dross or deceit. The Hebrew could be translated 'in a crucible on the ground', indicating the method of refining.

7-8. Encouraged by God's word, the psalmist now ends his prayer by repeating his plea for help. However, a statement of trust and confidence, such as is commonly found in other psalms of this type (see on Ps. 6: 8), would follow most naturally as a conclusion after the oracle and its acceptance. It may therefore be better to translate (as the Authorized Version): 'Thou, LORD, wilt protect . . . generation, though the wicked flaunt themselves . . .' The psalm would then end with a triumphant and confident assertion that God will keep his own and that nothing the wicked may do or say can separate them from his love (cp. Rom. 8: 37–9). The Hebrew of verse 7 is awkward and many commentators resort to emendation. *flaunt themselves:* better 'prowl around'. *

HOW LONG, O LORD?

13

1 How long, O LORD, wilt thou quite forget me?
  How long wilt thou hide thy face from me?
2 How long must I suffer anguish in my soul,
      grief in my heart, day and night[a]?
  How long shall my enemy lord it over me?
3 Look now and answer me, O LORD my God.
  Give light to my eyes lest I sleep the sleep of death,
4   lest my adversary say, 'I have overthrown him',
      and my enemies rejoice at my downfall.
5   But for my part I trust in thy true love.
      My heart shall rejoice, for thou hast set me free.
6 I will sing to the LORD, who has granted all my desire.

* This is a prayer for help by one who in his distress feels forsaken by God (verse 1) and yet rejoices, trusting in his love (verses 5–6). Such is the constant dilemma of faith, fully exemplified in Christ's cry of dereliction on the cross (Matt. 27: 46) and reflected in the joyous praise of his saints amidst unspeakable suffering (cp. Acts 16: 22–6; Rom. 5: 3). Like its sentiment this psalm attaches itself to no particular age or situation.

[a] and night: *so Sept.; Heb. om.*

1–2. The psalmist's cry of desolation.

1. *hide thy face:* withdraw your blessing as a deliberate expression of displeasure (contrast Num. 6: 24–6); God does not *forget* accidentally. This language reflects the depth of the psalmist's feelings, as does the four-fold repetition of the cry *How long* (cp. Ps. 6: 3), but his reason and his faith encourage him to offer his prayer and expect a response, trusting that God has not completely withdrawn.

2. *my enemy:* the term is used collectively; cp. the plural in verse 4. The figure may suggest persecution and scorn, adding to the inner *grief* and *anguish* that already torments him *day and night.*

3–4. He prays for help.

3. *Look* upon me and bless me, instead of hiding your face in anger, and *answer me*, instead of forgetting me (see verse 1). *death* is everything that God is not, a purposeless, joyless, paralyzing *sleep.* It encroaches on man in this life, pulling him down into its shadow of sickness, lifelessness and futility, and destroying his communion with God (see also on Ps. 6: 5). So when the psalmist prays *Give light to my eyes*, he is asking God to restore his vitality, health and joy. 'Grief dims my eyes' (Ps. 6: 7), but God's presence brings light and life.

4. See on verse 2. If his *adversary* be allowed to *rejoice at* his *downfall* while he puts his trust in God (verse 5), then God's honour and faithfulness suffer.

5–6. He anticipates the joy of deliverance.

5. The change of mood, seen particularly in the confident assertion of his belief that God has somehow already *set* him *free*, illustrates the vitality of the psalmist's *trust in* God's *true love*, his faithfulness to his loyal followers (see on Ps. 5: 7). There is no need to suppose, as some do, that a priestly oracle or blessing must have been uttered between verses 4 and 5 (cp. on Ps. 6: 8); it is his faith that permits him to *rejoice* in suffering.

6. *has granted all my desire:* the Hebrew speaks of God's granting rather than of man's desiring and is perhaps better

translated as in the Authorized Version: 'hath dealt bounti-
fully with me.' *

THERE IS NO GOD?

14

1[a]   The impious fool says in his heart,
        'There is no God.'
    How vile men are, how depraved and loathsome;
        not one does anything good!
2   The LORD looks down from heaven
        on all mankind
    to see if any act wisely,
        if any seek out God.
3 But all are disloyal, all are rotten to the core;
        not one does anything good,
        no, not even one.

4   Shall they not rue it,
    all evildoers who devour my people
        as men devour bread,
        and never call upon the LORD?
5   There they were in dire alarm;
    for God was in the brotherhood of the godly.
6   The resistance of their victim was too much for them,
        because the LORD was his refuge.
7 If only Israel's deliverance might come out of Zion!
    When the LORD restores his people's fortunes,
    let Jacob rejoice, let Israel be glad.

* Just as Ps. 11 reviews the lack of law and order in society
[a] *Verses 1–7: cp. Ps. 53: 1–6.*

and Ps. 12 the prevalence of corruption and deceit, so Ps. 14 deals with the universality of godlessness. Also, as Ps. 11 compared the situation with that in the days of Sodom and Gomorrah, so this psalm likens it to conditions before the Flood (verses 1–3). But all three psalms show how confidence is restored when the faithful turns to God and contemplates his power or goodness. In its present form this psalm may date from the exile (verse 7), but its thought is timeless. It recurs in Book 2 as Ps. 53 with some variations, the most significant being the substitution of the title 'God' for 'the LORD' (see further, p. 5).

1–3. The psalmist laments the godlessness of mankind.

1. *The impious fool* is not a simple-minded person; he could be a very clever man, but he is one who has closed his mind to God (cp. Rom. 1: 22). He is not a militant atheist. He may not even be interested in the question of God's existence and probably never states openly, '*There is no God*'. These are words he *says in his heart*, they represent his inner disposition. He lives and behaves as though there were no need to reckon with any God. For him God is simply irrelevant (cp. Ps. 10: 4). The consequence of this kind of attitude is always depravity in some form (cp. Rom. 1: 28–32). *How vile men are:* as in Ps. 12: 1–2, the psalmist may have specific categories of person in mind, but this and his following statements are framed as generalizations about human degradation, suggesting a comparison with the corruption that existed, according to Gen. 6: 5–13, before the Flood.

2. *looks down:* cp. Ps. 102: 19. Similarly God 'saw' the wickedness of mankind in Noah's day (Gen. 6: 5, 11) and 'came down to see' the corruption of Babel and Sodom (Gen. 11: 5; 18: 21). *if any act wisely:* unlike the fool of verse 1, the wise man will *seek out God*, for 'the fear of the LORD is the beginning of knowledge, but fools scorn wisdom and discipline' (Prov. 1: 7; cp. Ps. 111: 10). The contrast between folly and wisdom is a common feature of the wisdom literature. *The LORD . . . God:* it is doubtful whether the psalmist

had any distinction in mind. The former title predominates in Book 1, but sometimes it alternates freely with the latter, e.g. in Pss. 16: 1–2; 17: 1, 6.

3. On the generalization, see on verse 1; but verse 4 clearly indicates that *all* does not include the faithful, 'my people'. Paul cites parts of verses 1–3 in Rom. 3: 10–12 to illustrate his argument about universal human corruption.

4–7. The psalmist's thoughts now turn to judgement and with renewed confidence he offers prayer for the deliverance of his people.

4. *Shall they not rue it:* the more common rendering is 'Have they no knowledge', that is, presumably, of the punishment that awaits them. But the N.E.B.'s translation is equally possible and seems to fit the context better. Since the *evildoers*, whose oppressive acts are as natural to them as eating bread, are clearly the godless fools of verses 1–3 (cp. Ps. 10: 2–11), *my people* must be the community of the faithful.

5. The psalmist envisages a reversal of present conditions at the appearing of God. His picture is undoubtedly one that holds hope for the future, though it may be based on some past historical event, such as the deliverance from oppression in Egypt.

6. *The resistance of their victim:* the more usual translation is 'the plans of the poor', the poor being the oppressed faithful (see on Ps. 9: 12). On the strength that comes from finding *refuge* in *the LORD*, see also Pss. 46 and 62. Verses 5–6 correspond to Ps. 53: 5, but there are many differences (see on Ps. 53: 5).

7. It has been thought that this final prayer, expressed in the form of a wish, is an addition from exilic times, but it could equally be the worshipper's prayer for his people at any time of persecution. The synonymous terms *Jacob* and *Israel* would then denote, not the national unit, but the faithful community that is afflicted by 'evildoers' within the territorial borders of Israel (see on verse 4). *Zion* was the place of God's abiding

presence and hence a symbol of the source from which *Israel's deliverance might come* (cp. Pss. 3: 4; 20: 2). ✷

WHO MAY DWELL IN GOD'S PRESENCE?

15

O LORD, who may lodge in thy tabernacle?   1
Who may dwell on thy holy mountain?
The man of blameless life, who does what is right   2
and speaks the truth from his heart;
   who has no malice on his tongue,   3
who never wrongs a friend
and tells no tales against his neighbour;
the man who shows his scorn for the worthless   4
and honours all who fear the LORD;
who swears to his own hurt and does not retract;
who does not put his money out to usury   5
and takes no bribe against an innocent man.
He who does these things shall never be brought low.

✷ Archaeology has uncovered a number of inscriptions, in some respects reminiscent of Ps. 15, showing that worshippers in the ancient world were frequently given instruction (torah) about conditions for admission to the sanctuary, but generally these texts take the form of a list of ritual requirements. Here the teaching is ethical, suggesting that the psalmist's question is at least as much about entry to personal communion with God as about admittance to a building. But liturgical use cannot be excluded, for Ps. 24 contains a similar entrance torah (Ps. 24: 3–6) which may have been sung at the temple gates, the people asking the question and the priest responding. The requirements of Ps. 15 are not unlike those Jesus laid on his disciples, especially in Matt. 5. It is impossible to date this psalm.

1. Since the temple on Mount Zion was a symbol of God's presence with his people (see on Pss. 2: 6 and 11: 4), the question admits of both a ritual and a spiritual interpretation. *thy tabernacle:* an archaic designation of the sanctuary dating from the wilderness period (cp. Ps. 27: 5). The tent may also betoken hospitality, a privilege God extends to the faithful. They alone may *lodge* or *dwell* with him as his 'guest' (Ps. 5: 4).

2–5. The list of conditions is not exhaustive and can be supplemented from Pss. 5: 4–6; 24: 4f.; Isa. 33: 14–16. The psalmist is not so much giving rules as painting a portrait of the kind of man who can remain in God's presence.

2. The first requirement is integrity, but not only of action. His deeds and words must express the disposition of *his heart* (cp. Ps. 24: 4; Matt. 5: 8). *blameless:* rather 'sincere'; the Hebrew word suggests a whole-hearted devotion to God that will issue in doing his will (*what is right*).

3. The second requirement is consideration for others in conversation. *has no malice:* the more literal 'wanders about on his tongue' graphically characterizes the gossip's thoughtless and unbridled use of speech.

4a–b. The third requirement is a right perspective. *the worthless:* the ungodly. The psalmists knew how their way of life could seem attractive to the faithful (Ps. 73: 3, 10), but in God's eyes it is indeed 'worthless' (Ps. 49: 5–20) and so merits his and his people's *scorn* (Pss. 37: 13; 52: 6).

4c. The fourth requirement is constancy; the word of the godly man must be thoroughly reliable. *swears to his own hurt:* he takes no oath that might cause someone else to suffer (contrast Matt. 14: 6–10).

5a–b. The final requirement is unselfish and honest use of money. It is not lending that is prohibited, but *usury* (cp. Exod. 22: 25). Exorbitant interest rates and bribery were the curse of the poor in ancient Israel (cp. Isa. 33: 15), but no man who truly fears God can exploit people for profit (Ezek. 22: 12).

5c. It is frequently held that this is a promise of material security, but what the psalmist seeks is entry to God's presence (verse 1), and there he will find a far superior kind of stability and blessing (cp. Pss. 1: 3; 16: 11). *

IN GOD'S PRESENCE IS THE FULLNESS OF JOY

16

Keep me, O God, for in thee have I found refuge.	1
I have said to the LORD,	2
'Thou, Lord, art my felicity.'	
The gods whom earth holds sacred are all worthless,	3
and cursed are all who make them their delight;[a]	
those who run after them[b] find trouble without end.	4
I will not offer them libations of blood	
nor take their names upon my lips.	
Thou, LORD, my allotted portion, thou my cup,	5
thou dost enlarge my boundaries:	
the lines fall for me in pleasant places,	6
indeed I am well content with my inheritance.	
I will bless the LORD who has given me counsel:	7
in the night-time wisdom comes to me in my inward parts.	
I have set the LORD continually before me:	8
with him[c] at my right hand I cannot be shaken.	
Therefore my heart exults	9
and my spirit rejoices,	

[a] are all worthless . . . delight: *prob. rdg.; Heb. obscure.*
[b] after them: *prob. rdg.; Heb. obscure.*
[c] with him: *prob. rdg.; Heb. om.*

my body too rests unafraid;
10   for thou wilt not abandon me to Sheol
nor suffer thy faithful servant to see the pit.
11   Thou wilt show me the path of life;
in thy presence is the fullness of joy,
in thy right hand pleasures for evermore.

* Like Pss. 4, 11, 23, this is a psalm of confidence. Thus the opening prayer for protection is immediately followed by a statement of faith (verses 1–2). Other gods have nothing to offer (verses 3–4) compared with the assurance that comes from the LORD (verses 5–8) with whom there is security and joy (verses 9–11). The psalm is suited for use by any worshipper who knows the reality of God's presence, but for Christians through the ages it has gained a fuller meaning when applied to Christ who is pre-eminently the 'faithful servant' (verse 10; cp. Acts 2: 25–8, 31; 13: 35). The date of writing cannot be determined.

1–2. The psalmist's prayer and profession of faith.

1. *Keep me:* a prayer for continual protection and assurance, and, if used in time of trouble, a plea for intervention. *in thee have I found refuge:* these words summarize the mood of dedication and confidence that pervades this psalm (cp. Ps. 7: 1).

2. In the rest of the poem the psalmist expands upon this confession. His *felicity* (literally 'good') is the security and joy that is found in the presence of the LORD (verses 5–11) and him alone (verses 3–4; cp. Ps. 73: 25).

3–4. The psalmist spurns all other gods.

3. The Hebrew may be literally rendered: 'as for the holy ones who are in the land, they and the noble, in whom is all my delight'. The N.E.B. understands 'holy ones' as *gods* and by a series of conjectural changes makes the whole verse into a denunciation of idolatry. The alternative possibility, adopted

66

in most earlier English translations, is to understand 'holy ones' as 'the loyal, the saints', and by the simple omission of the troublesome 'and' to read 'they are the noble . . .', thus making the verse into a declaration of allegiance to (delight in) the community of the faithful. Amongst them the psalmist finds those that are truly to be admired, the real nobility of this earth, and, in contrast, he rejects the ways of apostates that lead to endless trouble (verse 4).

4. Again the Hebrew is obscure, but the allusion is now more clearly to pagan cults. *libations of blood:* probably the pouring of animal blood in some idolatrous ritual, but the nature of this offering is uncertain. *take their names upon my lips:* probably in cultic usage, invoking their power or offering them homage.

5–8. Having expressed his exclusive allegiance to the LORD, he offers praise for the security that is now his portion.

5. A man's *allotted portion* is his share of land, property or food. *my cup* would suggest the idea of food, but *my boundaries* suggests land and property. The pictures are probably complementary, indicating that God is his everything: 'having thee, I desire nothing else on earth . . . God is my possession (portion) for ever' (Ps. 73: 25f.).

6. *the lines . . .:* the portions measured by line and distributed by lot. The metaphor is reminiscent of the traditions of the allotment of land in Josh. 13–19, but it speaks of a richer, spiritual *inheritance*, in some ways comparable to that of the priestly tribe of Levi who received no land in the distribution; the LORD was their 'allotted portion' too (Josh. 13: 14).

7. *counsel . . . wisdom:* God shows man 'the path of life' (verse 11) and guides him in the way (Ps. 32: 8). It is in his *inward parts*, his innermost self (conscience?; literally 'kidneys', cp. Ps. 7: 9), that he receives this guidance, particularly in the quiet moments, as in the *night-time*, when he may be still and hear the counselling voice of God (cp. Pss. 4: 4; 17: 3).

8. With his attention *continually* turned to *the LORD* he

finds a strength and confidence that enable him to meet adversity without being *shaken* (cp. Pss. 11, 12, 14).

9–11. He exults in the confident hope and great joy that communion with God inspires.

9. *heart . . . spirit . . . body:* the parallelism shows that these are used as synonyms meaning simply 'I'. *my spirit:* the N.E.B. has introduced a slight emendation to read literally 'my liver', another term denoting the innermost self (cp. verse 7), but the Hebrew reads 'my glory', suggesting a faculty of praise that is God-given (see on Ps. 30: 12).

10. The confidence expressed here is akin to the hope glimpsed in Ps. 49: 15 and Ps. 73: 24. If used in time of suffering, this verse could also be a prayer for present deliverance, but the psalmist does not expect to escape ultimate physical death. He merely finds it unbelievable that the joy of God's presence that he now knows will end beyond death in the gloom of *Sheol* where none praise him (Ps. 6: 5). Although there is yet no reasoned doctrine of after-life in these words, their hope was not misrepresented when later interpreted in this sense in the New Testament.

11. This verse probably continues the double thought of present felicity and future expectation. Thus *the path of life* is the way of present fellowship with the God who gives life, but it is also a road that must lead somewhere other than to Sheol where there is neither life nor God (see Ps. 30: 3, 5, 9). Likewise, the *presence* of God brings *joy* now in a *fullness* beyond comparison with earth's greatest joys (Ps. 4: 7), and yet not to be compared with the 'glory' that awaits (Ps. 73: 24). To enter into this experience of God's presence is to embark on a life-long journey that leads to eternal (*for evermore*) joy. Later biblical teaching about life after death continues to lay stress on closeness to God or the sense of divine presence, rather than on a supposition that man in some way possesses an everlasting element within himself (cp. John 17: 3). *

MY PLEA IS JUST: I SHALL SEE GOD'S FACE

17

Hear, LORD, my^a plea for justice,   1
    give my cry a hearing,
    listen to my prayer,
    for it is innocent of all deceit.
Let judgement in my cause issue from thy lips,   2
let thine eyes be fixed on justice.
Thou hast tested my heart and watched me all night long;   3
    thou hast assayed me and found in me no mind to evil.
I will not speak of the deeds of men;   4
    I have taken good note of all thy sayings.
I have not strayed from the course of duty;   5
    I have followed thy path and never stumbled.
I call upon thee, O God, for thou wilt answer me.   6
Bend down thy ear to me, listen to my words.

    Show me how marvellous thy true love can be,   7
    who with thy hand dost save
    all who seek sanctuary from their enemies.
Keep me like the apple of thine eye;   8
    hide me in the shadow of thy wings
from the wicked who obstruct me,   9
from deadly foes who throng round me.
They have stifled all compassion;   10
    their mouths are full of pride;
they press me hard,^b now they hem me in,   11
on the watch to bring me^c to the ground.

---

[a] my: *so Sept.; Heb. om.*
[b] they press me hard: *prob. rdg.; Heb.* our footsteps.
[c] me: *so Pesh.; Heb. om.*

12 The enemy is like a lion eager for prey,
    like a young lion crouching in ambush.
13 Arise, LORD, meet him face to face and bring him down.
    Save my life from the wicked;
14   make an end of them[a] with thy sword.
    With thy hand, O LORD, make an end of them;[a]
    thrust them out of this world in the prime of their life,
    gorged as they are with thy good things,
        blest with many sons
    and leaving their children wealth in plenty.
15 But my plea is just: I shall see thy face,
    and be blest with a vision of thee when I awake.

* The psalmist pleads for protection and, because he has
been faithful (verses 1–5), feels assured that God in his love
will answer (verses 6–7), even though he is hunted and
hemmed in by deadly foes (verses 8–12). He therefore calls
for judgement on his enemies and confidently awaits God's
blessing (verses 13–15). Since he expects God's help to come
in the morning, this psalm, like Ps. 5 and several others, is
well suited for use in a night vigil (see p. 14, sect. C). It also
compares with Ps. 5 in its structure, its atmosphere of confidence and its expression of loyalty to the covenant with God.
There is nothing in the psalm itself that could tell us when it
was written.

1–2. A plea for hearing and for justice.

1. The triple appeal suggests urgency (cp. Ps. 5: 1). It has
been suggested that this psalm, like Pss. 5 and 7, is the prayer
of an accused man on the eve of trial, but it is also suited to
more general use (see on Ps. 5: 3). *justice* is not merely acquittal
in a court of law; it is the expression of God's covenanted
love (verse 7) towards his faithful servants. Besides, the psalm-

[a] make an end of them: *prob. rdg.; Heb. unintelligible.*

70

ist expects more than a legal decision, for he seeks the protection of God's covering wings (verse 8) and ultimately a vision of his presence (verse 15). This is the language of spiritual need and experience. *innocent of all deceit:* his confidence of hearing lies partly in the sincerity of his prayer.

2. *judgement:* he requires more than a verbal decision. He is asking for the execution of justice, for active intervention to deliver him from his oppressors (verses 13–14).

3–7. Protesting his loyalty he confidently calls upon God to demonstrate his love and save him.

3. By keeping vigil before God, perhaps in the sanctuary, in the quiet of the *night* he has laid himself open to undisturbed scrutiny and God has *tested* and *assayed* him as thoroughly as a silversmith would analyse his metal to determine its quality (cp. Ps. 66: 10).

4. His delight is in God's law, not in the way of the world (cp. Ps. 1: 2); his mind is on the things of the Spirit, not on the things of the flesh (Rom. 8: 5, Revised Standard Version). The Hebrew of verses 4–5 is awkward and the N.E.B. translation is partly a paraphrase.

5. His claim is complete loyalty, not moral perfection.

6. *for thou wilt answer me:* his certainty depends partly on his claim of loyalty (verse 5), partly on the sincerity of his prayer (verse 1), but mainly on his trust in God's love (next verse).

7. He calls for the miraculous (*marvellous*, see on Ps. 9: 1) intervention of God. He has been loyal to the covenant and now God must show the faithfulness of his *love* (see on Ps. 5: 7). *seek sanctuary:* the setting may be the temple (as in Ps. 5: 7), but the phrase can be spiritually interpreted. God's *hand* is a symbol of his might, as often in the Exodus story (cp. Exod. 3: 20; 13: 9).

8–12. He prays for protection from the enemies that beset him.

8. *the apple of thine eye:* the pupil, here a symbol of that which is most precious and to be guarded with the greatest

care. The same notion of intimacy and tenderness is contained in the phrase *the shadow of thy wings* which likens God to a mother bird sheltering her young. The metaphor is enlarged upon in Deut. 32: 11.

9. The psalmist's life with God is like a path which he walks (verse 5), but he finds his way obstructed by foes who *throng round* him like huntsmen encircling their prey.

10. *They have stifled all compassion:* the Hebrew reads literally 'they have closed their fat'. 'Fat' may stand for a fat heart and that is a symptom of rebellion against God in Ps. 119: 70. The parallelism supports this interpretation, for *pride* is boasting in self instead of in God. The description of the enemies' rebelliousness sharply contrasts with the psalmist's avowal of loyalty (verses 3–5) and is presented as a motive for God to act (cp. Ps. 5: 4–7).

11. Resuming the metaphor of verse 9, he tells how like huntsmen the enemies have him cornered and close in on him watching intently for the moment to strike. The N.E.B. translation of this verse requires a small adjustment to some very clumsy Hebrew which is given a literal rendering in the footnote.

12. Comparison with the *lion* suggests ferocity and cruelty, perhaps appropriately in a psalm suited for vigil use (see on Ps. 5: 3, 9). In the psalms enemies are frequently likened to wild beasts, usually, as here, of a terrifying species (e.g. bulls in Ps. 22: 12 or wild dogs in Ps. 59: 6). However, the imagery is fluid (cp. on Ps. 7: 15). In the present passage they have also been declared rebels and compared to huntsmen. Hence they should not be identified exclusively with one particular group, for example accusers in a lawsuit. They are a figure of all, physical or spiritual, that assails the psalmist's soul and will convey different images to individual users of the psalms.

13–14. He calls on God to implement his justice and put an end to the rebellious foe.

13. Like a warrior-hero, God must intercept this enemy who is 'crouching' ready to spring (verse 12) and must

bring him down. The change to the singular, *him,* results from the comparison with a lion, but points again to the fluidity of the imagery. The *wicked* are the rebellious who do not walk in the way of God's covenant with Israel (Ps. 1).

14. The Hebrew of this verse is in some disarray. The N.E.B. interprets it as a call for the extermination of the enemy, characterized as gross personalities who have more than plenty of this world's goods and who have made wealth and pleasure their gods. However, *many sons* and *wealth in plenty* are generally regarded as signs of God's favour in the Old Testament (cp. Deut. 13: 17; 15: 4). Furthermore, a double prayer to curse the wicked and bless the faithful at this point would make the structural correspondence between Pss. 17 and 5 even closer. Some commentators have indeed translated the last part of verse 14 as a plea for blessing: 'but as for your treasured ones, fill them full, let their sons be satisfied, and may they let their abundant blessing fall on their children.'

15. The psalm ends with an expression of confidence that God will act in the morning. *when I awake:* the pronoun *I* is not expressed in the Hebrew. The Vulgate and Septuagint offer the equally correct rendering 'when you awake'. If the psalmist has been keeping vigil, then he has not been asleep (cp. verse 3). The God of Israel, it may be claimed, 'never slumbers, never sleeps' (Ps. 121: 4), but equally the sufferer, whose distress is partly occasioned by God's apparent inactivity, may, with poetic licence, exclaim, 'Bestir thyself. Lord; why dost thou sleep?' (Ps. 44: 23; cp. 78: 65), and in the ritual of his vigil regard the dawning day as a token of hope that his saviour will 'arise' (verse 13) and come to his aid. *a vision of thee:* to *see* his *face* is the ultimate blessing God grants to the faithful (cp. Job 42: 5; Matt. 5: 8). ✳

GOD KEEPS FAITH WITH HIS ANOINTED KING

18

✻ A second version of this psalm with only minor variations is found in 2 Sam. 22 where it is said to be a 'song David sang to the LORD' near the end of his reign, 'on the day when the LORD delivered him from the power of all his enemies and from the power of Saul' (2 Sam. 22: 1). The same historical note appears in the Hebrew text of the Psalter and it does accord well with the content of the psalm itself. For here we see the thanksgiving of a warrior-king who, looking back over his life, recognizes the strength that has come from God (verses 1–3). In time of danger he had called to the LORD (verses 4–6) who came in power (verses 7–15) and rescued him (verses 16–19). He for his part had followed God's way (verses 20–4) and was therefore able to rejoice in the knowledge of God's loyalty to the loyal (verses 25–9). Acknowledging God as the one who gives him strength for war and makes him victorious over his foes (verses 30–45), he ends his song with an ascription of praise in the context of which he anticipates similar blessings for his descendants (verses 46–50). But whilst the psalm is appropriate to David, it would, like Ps. 2, have been used by his heirs and successors to whom God's promises of blessing and protection also extended (2 Sam. 7: 12–16). It may have been sung as a hymn of thanksgiving on special occasions of deliverance or victory, or perhaps at the festivals as a general offering of praise for God's continuing and unfailing care. To the Christian it speaks prophetically, like Isa. 53, of Christ's faithfulness in suffering and his victory over death. ✻

1   I love thee, O LORD my strength.
2[a] The LORD is my stronghold, my fortress and my champion,

[a] *Verses 2–50: cp. 2 Sam. 22: 2–51.*

my God, my rock where I find safety,
my shield, my mountain refuge, my strong tower.
I will call on the LORD to whom all praise is due,   3
and I shall be delivered from my enemies.
When the bonds of death held me fast,   4
destructive torrents overtook me,
the bonds of Sheol tightened round me,   5
the snares of death were set to catch me;
then in anguish of heart I cried to the LORD,   6
I called for help to my God;
he heard me from his temple,
and my cry reached his ears.
The earth heaved and quaked,   7
the foundations of the mountains shook;
they heaved, because he was angry.
Smoke rose from his nostrils,   8
devouring fire came out of his mouth,
glowing coals and searing heat.
He swept the skies aside as he descended,   9
thick darkness lay under his feet.
He rode on a cherub, he flew through the air;   10
he swooped on the wings of the wind.
He made darkness around him his hiding-place   11
and dense*a* vapour his canopy.*b*
Thick clouds came out of the radiance before him,   12
hailstones and glowing coals.
The LORD thundered from the heavens   13
and the voice of the Most High spoke out.*c*

[a] *Prob. rdg., cp. 2 Sam. 22: 12; Heb.* dark.
[b] *Prob. rdg.; Heb. adds* thick clouds.
[c] *Prob. rdg.; Heb. adds* hailstones and glowing coals.

14 He loosed his arrows, he sped them far and wide,
    he shot forth lightning shafts and sent them echoing.
15 The channels of the sea-bed were revealed,
    the foundations of earth laid bare
    at the LORD's rebuke,
    at the blast of the breath of his[a] nostrils.
16 He reached down from the height and took me,
    he drew me out of mighty waters,
17 he rescued me from my enemies, strong as they were,
    from my foes when they grew too powerful for me.
18 They confronted me in the hour of my peril,
    but the LORD was my buttress.
19 He brought me out into an open place,
    he rescued me because he delighted in me.

✳ 1-3. The LORD is my stronghold.

1. *I love thee:* not in 2 Sam. 22; the Hebrew verb, an unusual one, denotes a strong, intimate affection.

2. The various titles metaphorically suggest refuge and security. They derive from a picture of military strength in the impregnability of a Judaean mountain fortress. The psalmist may have had the stronghold at Engedi in mind, the place where David himself spent much of his time as an outlaw (1 Sam. 22-4), but equally the language may be completely traditional and stereotyped, for the same figures are also used frequently in other psalms (e.g. Ps. 31: 2).

3. Such conviction of God's faithfulness, like all religious certainty, is obtained, not by reason, nor by self-persuasion, but by experience, as the following verses show.

4-6. In time of peril the psalmist had called on God for help.

4. *the bonds of death:* in 2 Sam. 22: 5 'the waves of death',

[a] *Prob. rdg.; Heb.* thy.

which suits the parallelism better. The imagery is, of course, metaphorical, signifying great danger and the proximity of death (cp. Jonah 2: 2–6). Waves, floods, *torrents*, etc., are common symbols of destruction, for in ancient mythology the deep was the mysterious sphere of all earth's harmful forces (cp. Ps. 42: 7).

5. The metaphor changes: *Sheol*, the unseen world of the dead, and *death* itself are now likened to huntsmen laying *snares* for their prey.

6. *from his temple:* the allusion here is more probably to God's dwelling in heaven than to the Solomonic temple, though the two were inseparably interrelated (see on Ps. 11: 4).

7–15. God comes amid earthquake (verse 7), fire (verse 8), the darkness of gathering storm-clouds (verses 9–11) and the final outburst of tempest (verses 12–15). Similar pictures recur frequently in the Old Testament. They speak of God's majesty and power (Ps. 29: 4) that bring terror on earth but inspire confidence among the faithful (cp. Ps. 97: 1–9).

7. God's anger is the expression of his judgement against the *earth* and all in it that causes his servant to suffer. Such is the majesty of his coming in judgement that earth must either rejoice, if faithful (Ps. 96: 11–13), or quake to the very *foundations of the mountains*, the most stable feature on its surface.

8. This picture of God as a *smoke-* and *fire*-breathing monster is little more than a dramatic characterization of his wrath, though it does also draw on traditional imagery. Smoke and fire attended God's appearance on Mount Sinai (Exod. 19: 18) and *glowing coals* feature in the visions of Isaiah (Isa. 6: 6) and Ezekiel (Ezek. 10: 2).

9. *thick darkness:* that is, of a dense, lowering storm-cloud (see verse 11; cp. Exod. 19: 16).

10. *a cherub:* here a personification of *the wind*, conceived as a winged creature conveying God's cloud-chariot (cp. Ps. 104: 3). Sculptured figures with wings known as cherubim

77

stood in the inner sanctuary of the temple (1 Kings 6: 23-8)
and in his visions Ezekiel saw winged, centaur-like creatures
that he called cherubim accompanying God's chariot-throne
(Ezek. 10; cp. Ezek. 1). Like the psalmist, he also describes
God's coming amid wind and clouds (Ps. 18: 9-12; Ezek.
1: 4) with fire, radiance, glowing coals and lightning shafts
(Ps. 18: 8, 12, 14; Ezek. 1: 4, 13). The picture is one of majestic
splendour, of the heavenly king coming down on his cherub-
drawn storm-chariot to visit his kingdom, the earth (cp. Ps.
68: 4, 33 and see on Ps. 99: 1).

11. Though God shows himself in many ways to men, yet
he remains the unseen God, invisible to human sight (cp.
1 Kings 8: 12).

13. *thundered . . . the voice:* cp. Ps. 29: 3-9. *the Most High:*
this title designates God 'creator of heaven and earth' in Gen.
14: 19, 22 and thus appropriately here betokens his sovereignty
over the world (see on Ps. 7: 17).

14. *his arrows:* the *lightning shafts* that accompany the thunder, the weapons that make the earth tremble (verse 7; cp.
Ps. 77: 17f.).

15. Even the sea with its hostile, death-bearing waters (see
on verse 4) retreats before the stormy wrath of God so that
the sea-bed is *laid bare* revealing the hidden *channels* of the deep
and the mysterious *foundations of earth. the blast of the breath of
his nostrils:* see on verse 8.

16-19. The climax of this graphic display of power is
striking, not a terror-laden devastation of earth, but the
gentle, compassionate rescue of God's servant. As the drama
returns to a human level, we are reminded that it began with
the prayer of one man lost amid *enemies . . . too powerful for*
him, a small voice in a vast hostile world. The storm language
was never intended as a prelude to a cataclysm; its purpose was
to highlight God's majesty and declare his infinite power to
protect against even impossible odds.

16. *mighty waters:* the waters of death into which he was
sinking like a drowning man (see verse 4).

18. *my buttress:* my support on which I could lean.

19. *into an open place:* where there was complete freedom after the restriction of being hemmed in by enemies (cp. Ps. 4: 1). *he delighted in me:* the fact of his rescue confirms this and the verses that follow explain why (cp. Ps. 41: 11). *

The LORD rewarded me as my righteousness deserved; 20
my hands were clean, and he requited me.
For I have followed the ways of the LORD   21
and have not turned wickedly from my God;
all his laws are before my eyes,   22
I have not failed to follow his decrees.
In his sight I was blameless   23
and kept myself from wilful sin;
the LORD requited me as my righteousness deserved   24
and the purity of my life in his eyes.

With the loyal thou showest thyself loyal   25
and with the blameless man blameless.
With the savage man thou showest thyself savage,   26
and*a* tortuous with the perverse.
Thou deliverest humble folk,   27
and bringest proud looks down to earth.
Thou, LORD, dost make my lamp burn bright,   28
and my God will lighten my darkness.
With thy help I leap over a bank,   29
by God's aid I spring over a wall.

* 20–4. The LORD delights in his servant because he is faithful. This is not an arrogant statement of self-righteousness, nor

[a] With the savage . . . savage, and: *or* With the pure thou showest thyself pure, but . . .

a claim to sinlessness, for the psalmist knows that both his strength and his blamelessness come from God himself (verse 32). His theme is God's unfailing loyalty to those who are loyal to him (verse 25) and in this section he pleads his own fidelity. Nor is this a matter of boasting, for he is completely aware of his own weakness and of the need for humility (verse 27). His only boast is in God who saved him when he was utterly helpless.

20. *righteousness:* the right response to God's love in loyalty and obedience (cp. on Ps. 1: 5). *my hands were clean:* I showed integrity of conduct (cp. Ps. 24: 4).

21-2. *the ways of the LORD:* as revealed in *his laws* (Ps. 1: 2, 6).

23. *blameless:* in loyalty (see verse 25).

25-9. In praise of God's loving faithfulness.

25. *the loyal:* the ḥāsīd, the one who responds in trust and obedience to God's own loyalty or ḥesed, his loving and faithful promise to protect and bless his people (see on Ps. 5: 7). *blameless:* the parallelism shows that integrity of single-hearted devotion is meant, not sinlessness.

26. *With the savage . . . savage:* this rendering provides a good parallel to the next line and makes the whole verse the contrasting counterpart of verse 25, though the older translation (N.E.B. footnote) is perfectly straightforward and acceptable.

27. This is a common theme of psalmody, expressed more fully in the Song of Hannah (1 Sam. 2: 1-10) and the Magnificat (Luke 1: 46-55). *humble folk:* virtually a synonym for 'the loyal' (see on Ps. 9: 12). *proud looks:* proud men, the opposite category, those who boast in their own prowess rather than God's (cp. Ps. 10: 2-6).

28. *make my lamp burn bright:* a natural metaphor for life, health or prosperity (cp. Prov. 13: 9), but since the speaker is the king, there may be additional significance in this acknowledgement that his light comes from God, for his own function was to be 'the lamp of Israel' (2 Sam. 21: 17).

29. *I leap over a bank . . .:* a metaphor suggesting renewed
vitality and strength based on the picture of a warrior-hero
assaulting enemy defences. ✳

The way of God is perfect,   30
the LORD's word has stood the test;
he is the shield of all who take refuge in him.
What god is there but the LORD?   31
What rock but our God? –
the God who girds me with strength   32
and makes my way blameless,
who makes me swift as a hind   33
and sets me secure on the*a* mountains;
who trains my hands for battle,   34
and my arms aim an arrow tipped with bronze.

Thou hast given me the shield of thy salvation,   35
thy hand sustains me, thy providence makes me great.
Thou givest me room for my steps,   36
my feet have not faltered.
I pursue my enemies and overtake them,   37
I do not return until I have made an end of them.
I strike them down and they will never rise again;   38
they fall beneath my feet.
Thou dost arm me with strength for the battle   39
and dost subdue my foes before me.
Thou settest my foot on my enemies' necks,   40
and I bring to nothing those that hate me.
They cry out and there is no one to help them,   41
they cry to the LORD and he does not answer.
I will pound them fine as dust before the wind,   42

[a] So Sept.; Heb. my.

like mud in the streets will I trample them.[a]

43 Thou dost deliver me from the clamour of the people,
and makest me master of the nations.

A people I never knew shall be my subjects;

44 as soon as they hear tell of me, they shall obey me,
and foreigners shall come cringing to me.

45 Foreigners shall be brought captive to me,
and emerge from their strongholds.

* 30–45. His help, strength and victory come from God
alone.

30. *The way of God is perfect:* here God's dealings with his
people are in mind, as the parallelism shows (cp. Deut. 32: 4,
but contrast verse 21 above). *the LORD's word:* his promises
(see on verse 25). *stood the test:* proved reliable, like silver
tested in a refiner's furnace (cp. Ps. 12: 6).

31. *rock:* a figure of strength and security (see on verse 1;
cp. Ps. 19: 14).

32. See on verses 20–4. *makes my way blameless:* like God's
own way, which is perfect (verse 30). For a similar concept,
see Lev. 19: 2.

33. *a hind:* noted for its speed and sure-footedness in difficult mountainous terrain, both indispensable qualities in a good
warrior.

34. *who trains . . . :* cp. Ps. 144: 1.

35. *the shield of thy salvation:* or 'your saving shield' (cp.
Ps. 3: 3). *thy providence:* literally 'thy humility' (the Authorized Version translates 'thy gentleness'). This Hebrew word is
not normally applied to God, but something of its meaning
here may be seen in Ps. 113: 5f. God is likened to some heroic
warrior who leads the king through the battle-field to victory,
protecting him with his magnificent shield, supporting him

[a] *Prob. rdg., cp. 2 Sam. 22: 43; Heb.* will I empty them out.

with his powerful hand and humbly affording him all the greatness and acclaim.

37–45. The language of these verses may seem harsh and even offensive to the modern reader, but the pictures it paints are all drawn from ancient battle-scenes and mean little more than that God, who has delivered the king from his foes, now grants him victory and dominion over them. This vision is based not on sheer political ambition, but on God's covenant with David which promises its fulfilment (see on Ps. 2). But the establishment of God's righteous rule on earth must be preceded by the complete eradication of all enmity and rebellion (see on Ps. 2: 9; cp. Rev. 20: 11 – 21: 8) and it is important that the king's success in effecting this should depend solely on strength that comes from God himself.

40. *my foot on my enemies' necks:* a symbolic expression of victory preceding execution in Josh. 10: 24–6.

41. *they cry to the LORD:* the psalmist seems to be thinking mainly of pagans turning to the God of Israel as a last resort when all else has failed. But *he does not answer* because their plea has no foundation in faith (contrast verse 25).

43. *master of the nations:* cp. Ps. 2: 8–12.

44. The king's fame becomes so great that *foreigners* submit to him without a battle, in much the same way as Toi, king of Hamath, sought to win David's approval by sending him presents (2 Sam. 8: 9f.).

45. *emerge from their strongholds:* a picture of exhausted defenders surrendering themselves. *

The LORD lives, blessed is my rock, 46
high above all is God who saves me.

O God, who grantest me vengeance, 47
who layest nations prostrate at my feet,
who dost rescue me from my foes and set me over my 48
enemies,

thou dost deliver me from violent men.

49   Therefore, LORD, I will praise thee among the nations
      and sing psalms to thy name,

50   to one who gives his king great victories
      and in all his acts keeps faith with his anointed king,
      with David and his descendants for ever.

✳ 46–50. Concluding praise.

46. *The LORD lives:* life and the power to give life are of the
very essence of godhead (cp. Ps. 16: 11; John 10: 10). *my rock:*
the psalmist's closing praise resumes the theme of his opening
ascription (verse 2; cp. verse 31).

47. *vengeance:* if executed on human initiative, can amount
to little more than vindictiveness, but if it is granted by or
comes directly from God, it will be an expression of his justice
(cp. Rom. 12: 17–19).

49. As they become subject to the LORD's anointed, *the
nations* will hear God's *praise* proclaimed amongst them and
so will be brought to the knowledge of his glory (cp. Ps. 96:
3, 10). Paul cites this verse in Rom. 15: 9 in support of his
claim that God intended the gospel to be preached to the
Gentiles.

50. *keeps faith:* according to the promises he made to David
(2 Sam. 7: 8–16). *his anointed king (māshīaḥ):* that is both *David*
and *his descendants* (see on Ps. 2: 2). At this point, with the
reminder that God's promises are *for ever*, the psalm looks
beyond history into the eternity of God's kingdom and the
unending rule of his Messiah. ✳

THE GLORY OF GOD AND THE PERFECTION
OF HIS LAW

19

The heavens tell out the glory of God,   1
the vault of heaven reveals his handiwork.
One day speaks to another,   2
night with night shares its knowledge,
    and this without speech or language   3
    or sound of any voice.
Their music goes out through all the earth,   4
    their words reach to the end of the world.
In them a tent is fixed for the sun,
who comes out like a bridegroom from his wedding 5
    canopy,
rejoicing like a strong man to run his race.
    His rising is at one end of the heavens,   6
    his circuit touches their farthest ends;
    and nothing is hidden from his heat.

The law of the LORD is perfect and revives the soul. 7
    The LORD's instruction never fails,
    and makes the simple wise.
The precepts of the LORD are right and rejoice the heart. 8
    The commandment of the LORD shines clear
    and gives light to the eyes.
The fear of the LORD is pure and abides for ever.   9
The LORD's decrees are true and righteous every one,
more to be desired than gold, pure gold in plenty,   10
    sweeter than syrup or honey from the comb.
    It is these that give thy servant warning,   11
    and he who keeps them wins a great reward.

12   Who is aware of his unwitting sins?
      Cleanse me of any secret fault.

13   Hold back thy servant also from sins of self-will,
         lest they get the better of me.
      Then I shall be blameless
      and innocent of any great transgression.

14 May all that I say and think be acceptable to thee,
      O LORD, my rock and my redeemer!

* This psalm falls into three distinct sections: a hymn celebrating God's majesty written in the skies (verses 1–6), a hymn
in praise of the law, its beauty and power for good (verses
7–11), and a prayer for strength to live a life acceptable to God
(verses 12–14). The differences in style, vocabulary and metre
are particularly striking in the Hebrew, but even in English
the transitions are unmistakable. It may be that the psalmist,
like the author of Ps. 108, has reused parts of older independent
psalms, but if so, he has created a new psalm that is internally
coherent. Creation and the law, or the universe and the scriptures, are pre-eminently the media of divine revelation. As the
worshipper considers the former, he becomes aware of his own
lowliness (verse 12, cp. Ps. 8), and as he contemplates the
latter, he is moved to seek grace to obey (verses 13f., cp. Ps.
119). The emphasis on the law is reminiscent of late Jewish
piety and suggests a post-exilic date for the final composition.
   1–6. The glory of God in the heavens.
   1. God's *glory* in the Psalter is usually his presence revealed
in all its splendour, such that it evokes the response in obeisance
and adoration men afford to a king (cp. Ps. 3:3). Though seen
in all creation, there is no more impressive reflection of his
majesty than in the vast *vault of heaven* (Gen. 1:6f.), whose
stars are neither gods nor mere accidents of time, but *his*
personal *handiwork* (cp. Ps. 8:3). Like the attendants round

86

God's throne (Isa. 6: 3; Rev. 4: 8), they *tell out* (literally 'keep on telling') his glory in an unending song.

2–3. *speaks:* literally 'bubbles forth speech' in a continuous stream, like a fountain. *day* and *night* have each their separate knowledge to impart: the former tells of splendour, warmth and life, the latter of mystery, immensity and repose. They are like the seraph choir singing alternately one to the other the praises of God (Isa. 6: 3), but it is far from easy for man fully to comprehend their message, for they communicate *without speech or language or sound of any voice.*

4a–b. And yet this inarticulate silence is more eloquent than speech, for it *goes out* to the limits of the inhabited world, crossing all language barriers, reaching even those who themselves are 'without speech or language'. For those who have ears to hear this strange silence is the *music* of heaven and its *words* are the praises of the creator. By citing this verse in Rom. 10: 18 Paul likens the universal proclamation of the gospel to the cosmic revelation of God.

4c. *In them:* the heavens. *is fixed:* literally 'he has fixed'; the sun can have no home other than the *tent* (probably the dome of the sky itself) that God has made for it, because it is also his 'handiwork' (verse 1). To most ancients it was a very important deity, but to the psalmist the chief witness to God's glory.

5. *like a bridegroom:* radiant in splendid attire, fresh, youthful and happy. *his wedding canopy:* either the place where the groom prepared himself for the wedding, or the place of the marriage ceremony, or the nuptial chamber; the allusion is uncertain. *like a strong man:* heroic in appearance, full of life and eager *to run his race* (cp. Judg. 5: 31). Some commentators see an allusion to the myth of a sun-god who rises daily from the ocean bed where he spends each night with his bride. Even so, this is no more than a simile to the author who may equally have been thinking of a human bridegroom or athlete.

6. *nothing is hidden from his heat:* if the silence of the skies can speak even to the deaf, then the brilliance of the sun must reach the blind also. *his circuit:* it was the universal belief of the

ancients that the sun journeyed around the earth daily (cp. Eccles. 1: 5).

7–11. The perfection of God's law. *law, instruction, precepts, commandment, decrees* are five of the eight terms used regularly in Ps. 119 (see introduction to Ps. 119).

7. *The law:* not the moral law written in the heart, but the expression of God's will embodied in scripture, particularly in the Pentateuch. Unlike the universe, it speaks directly to men and through it 'God' (verse 1) comes to be known more personally as *the LORD*. It is *perfect*, without flaw, but its perfection lies in its life-giving spirit rather than in the literal correctness of its *instruction*, for like the good shepherd, the LORD himself, it *revives the soul* (Ps. 23: 3), or like God's wisdom, it *makes* even *the simple wise*, thus bringing them new life (Prov. 9: 4–6).

8. This verse repeats the theme of the last. The law is *right*, without crookedness, but its rightness lies again in its life-giving quality, for like the presence of God himself, it will *rejoice the heart* (Ps. 4: 6f.), or like the *commandment* of the wisdom teacher, it *shines clear and gives light* as a lamp illuminating the path (Prov. 6: 23).

9. *The fear of the LORD:* here a synonym for the law, though more correctly man's proper response to it (see verse 11). Like the law which 'makes wise' (verse 7), it is frequently said to be 'the beginning of wisdom' (Ps. 111: 10; Prov. 1: 7). *pure and abides for ever:* without blemish, it contains the finality of divine revelation. *true:* dependable (see on Ps. 25: 5).

11. Both the law and the skies are witness to God's glory, but where the message of the heavens may be heard and not understood, the law gives explicit direction and *warning*. Yet its *reward* is available only to him who responds, *who keeps* its precepts. When the 'decrees' are approached with reverential 'fear' (verse 9), the faithful *servant* finds the promised reward of life and joy, wisdom and enlightenment (verses 7–8). By converse with the law he drinks of its life-giving spirit and is led into the very presence of God where alone such joys may

be found, more desirable than anything else on earth (verse 10; cp. Ps. 4: 6–8).

12–14. The psalmist prays for forgiveness and for strength to be faithful.

12–13. Through contemplating the universe and the law the worshipper is brought face to face with God himself in all his glory and perfection, and through this experience discovers his own unworthiness. Like Job or Isaiah (Job 42: 6; Isa. 6: 5), he becomes aware of a deep sinfulness that encompasses all his conscious and *unwitting* actions and feels a need to be cleansed. His desire to *be blameless and innocent* is therefore not a puritanical determination to attain moral perfection, but a prayer that God will make him fit to continue in the enjoyment of his presence.

14. The final and only basis for hope of continued acceptance is the faith that God is *my rock and my redeemer. my rock:* a place of refuge 'where I find safety' (Ps. 18: 2). *my redeemer:* cp. Job 19: 25. Technically the term applies to the next of kin who is bound by the obligations of kinship to restore the honour or the property of a relative who, for example, has fallen into slavery or debt. In the present context it is used figuratively of redemption from slavery to sin. ✳

THE LORD GIVES VICTORY TO HIS ANOINTED

20

May the LORD answer you in the hour of trouble!   1
The name of Jacob's God be your tower of strength,
give you help from the sanctuary   2
    and send you support from Zion!
    May he remember all your offerings   3
    and look with favour on your rich sacrifices,
give you your heart's desire   4
    and grant success to all your plans!

5   Let us sing aloud in praise of your victory,
        let us do homage to the name of our God!
      The LORD grant all you ask!

6   Now I know
      that the LORD has given victory to his anointed king:
        he will answer him from his holy heaven
        with the victorious might of his right hand.

7 Some boast of chariots and some of horses,
      but our boast is the name of the LORD our God.

8   They totter and fall,
      but we rise up and are full of courage.

9   O LORD, save the king,
        and answer us[a] in the hour of our calling.

* The peculiar structure of this psalm can be explained by assuming that it was composed for liturgical use. Two possible settings suggest themselves. In 2 Chron. 20 the people are seen assembled in the temple in time of war to seek God's help. The king stands to offer prayer and a Levite is moved to speak prophetic words of encouragement, exhorting the community to faith in God's protecting power. At some such assembly the king's own prayer for help (cp. Pss. 44, 60) could well have been followed by a congregational recitation of Ps. 20: 1–5. Verses 6–8, telling of the certainty of God's aid, would then have been spoken by some cultic official, or perhaps by the king himself, and the people would have responded with the closing prayer in verse 9. On the other hand, since the psalm itself betrays no sense of immediate urgency, it could also have been sung in the same sort of way at festivals, but as part of the people's continuing intercession for the king (cp. Ps. 72), expressing their faith in and their longing for the fulfilment of

[a] O LORD ... answer us: *so Sept.; Heb.* Save, O LORD: let the king answer us.

God's promise of ultimate triumph to the house of David (see on Ps. 2). Consequently, it may also be interpreted in the same way as those other psalms that speak of God's 'anointed king' (verse 6; cp. Pss. 2: 2; 18: 50), that is with reference to his coming king, the Messiah.

1–5. The people intercede on behalf of their king.

1–2. *the hour of trouble:* may be present or anticipated, depending on the setting in which the psalm is used. *The name . . . :* the confidence expressed in verses 6–8 underlies the language used in this prayer. God's *name* is no magical formula (cp. Acts 19: 13), but a symbol of his revealed self, his presence active among men. It was believed somehow to dwell in the *sanctuary* on Mount *Zion* (Deut. 12: 5; 1 Kings 8: 29), which itself stood as a token of God's abiding and protecting presence (see on Ps. 2: 6). The title *Jacob's God* also inspires assurance, for it declares *the LORD* to be the God who has chosen Israel (= Jacob, see Gen. 32: 28) for his own people and pledged them his protection (cp. Ps. 46: 7, 11).

3. The allusion may be to *offerings* and *sacrifices* accompanying the singing of the psalm.

4–5. . . . *success to all your plans!:* that is, in so far as they accord with God's will. But the king's *desire* is to see *victory* and that is fully in accordance with God's purpose as declared in his covenant with David (Ps. 2: 8). The Hebrew word for *victory* is more commonly translated 'salvation'. It actually expresses both ideas and also implies the vindication of faith, in this instance faith in the promise to David (see further on Ps. 3: 2).

6–8. The certainty of God's help is declared.

6. *Now I know:* the apparently sudden change to confidence could suggest that an oracle might have been uttered during a ritual pause after verse 5 – compare the sequence in 2 Chron. 20: prayer for help (verse 6–12), pause (verse 13), oracle (verses 14–17), concluding praise (verses 18–19). But this is only a conjecture and the psalm can be read without difficulty as an uninterrupted, coherent whole, for the mood of

confidence is already strongly present in verses 1–5. *his holy heaven:* God's heavenly dwelling, the spiritual reality of which the sanctuary in Zion, whence help was initially sought (verse 2), is the earthly representation and counterpart (see on Ps. 11: 4). *his right hand:* symbolic of strength.

7. Cp. Ps. 33: 16f.; Isa. 31: 1. *chariots* and *horses* were the most formidable war machine known to ancient man, but all man's material strength, no matter how powerful and terrifying, is completely ineffectual to overthrow God's purposes for 'his anointed' (cp. Ps. 2: 1–6).

9. A concluding prayer offered by the people, re-echoing the opening theme of the psalm. *save:* or 'grant victory' (see on verse 5). *the hour of our calling:* 'the hour of trouble' (verse 1) has been an occasion, not for despair, but for turning to God in prayer, for a renewal of faith and the strengthening of confidence in God (cp. Ps. 50: 15). ✻

THE KING REJOICES IN GOD'S MIGHT

21

1 The king rejoices in thy might, O LORD:
   well may he exult in thy victory,
2   for thou hast given him his heart's desire
     and hast not refused him what he asked.
3   Thou dost welcome him with blessings and prosperity
     and set a crown of fine gold upon his head.
4 He asked of thee life, and thou didst give it him,
   length of days for ever and ever.
5   Thy salvation has brought him great glory;
   thou dost invest him with majesty and honour,
6   for thou bestowest blessings on him for evermore
     and dost make him glad with joy in thy presence.
7   The king puts his trust in the LORD;

the loving care of the Most High holds him
unshaken.

Your hand shall reach all your enemies: 8
your right hand shall reach those who hate you;
   at your coming you shall plunge them into a fiery 9
    furnace;
   the LORD in his anger will strike them down,
    and fire shall consume them.
It will exterminate their offspring from the earth   10
   and rid mankind of their posterity.
For they have aimed wicked blows at you,   11
they have plotted mischief but could not prevail;
but you will catch them round the shoulders[a]   12
and will aim with your bow-strings at their faces.

Be exalted, O LORD, in thy might;   13
   we will sing a psalm of praise to thy power.

---

* A comparison between verse 2 and Ps. 20: 4f. has suggested
to some commentators that this psalm was composed as a
thanksgiving for victory to correspond with Ps. 20's prayer
in anticipation of battle. Others have held, largely on the basis
of verse 3, that it is a coronation hymn. Both these suggestions,
though speculative, are within the bounds of possibility, but
the language is not sufficiently specific to limit the psalm to
either setting. The opening thanksgiving (verses 1–7) appears
to have reference to the whole circle of divine gifts bestowed
on the LORD's anointed, while the second part (verses 8–12)
looks forward in confidence to the final cosmic victory of God
and the king. It is therefore best to give the psalm a more
general application and to see it along with Ps. 20 as part of
Israel's continuing celebration of God's covenant with David.
As such it may also be regarded as prophetic of the coming

[a] but you ... shoulders: *mng. of Heb. words uncertain.*

Messiah (see p. 20). It is regularly used in this sense in the
Christian Church at the feast of the Ascension to celebrate
Christ's kingship and anticipate his ultimate triumph.

1–7. With thanksgiving the congregation enumerates the
king's blessings.

1. What the *king* celebrates is more than the success of some
military expedition; it is God's *victory* (or 'salvation'; see on
Ps. 20: 5), something that has not yet been fully realized
(verses 8–12). The king's rejoicing is thus largely an expression
of faith in God's promise, though every earthly triumph
would be seen as an example of its outworking.

3. This verse looks beyond the historical coronation ceremonies to the ultimate divine favour bestowed on the Davidic
monarch. God is portrayed as a bounteous host coming to
welcome the king as his guest. The *crown of fine gold* that he
gives is thus less a symbol of earthly authority here than a
token of the rich *blessings and prosperity* (literally 'good') that
God has in store for the king. The picture is not dissimilar to
that in Ps. 23: 5.

4–6. *life . . . for ever and ever:* the hope of eternal continuity
in the Davidic tradition is attached to the dynasty, not to individual monarchs (2 Sam. 7: 16). At the personal level, which
is clearly intended here, these words, rather than signifying an
unending prolongation of life, must relate to its quality. Hence
this 'life' is a present reality in the king's experience, something God has already given him, and its character is clearly
seen in verse 6 where the *for evermore* is attached to God's
blessings and to *joy in* his *presence.* As in Ps. 16: 11, it is the
vitalizing awareness of God's personal presence uniting man
to eternity and engendering in him the hope, or even the
assurance, of unending bliss (see further on Ps. 73: 24).

5. *Thy salvation:* see on verse 1. *glory . . . majesty and honour:*
all divine attributes (cp. Ps. 8: 1, 5). The king's splendour is
given by God and is a reflection of the divine splendour.

7. The sure ground on which the king's *trust* is founded is
God's *loving care* (*ḥesed;* see on Ps. 5: 7), or his unfailing

94

promise of blessing and protection, in this instance as expressed in his covenant with David (2 Sam. 7: 8–16). *the Most High:* a title that denotes God's universal sovereignty, and hence his power to fulfil his promise (see on Ps. 7: 17).

8–12. The people anticipate God's or the king's final victory. It is uncertain who the 'you' in these verses refers to, but since the king's victory is also God's (see on Ps. 20: 4–5), precise definition is unimportant.

8. *hand . . . right hand:* symbols of power.

9. *at your coming:* literally 'in the time of your presence'. God's presence brings blessing to the faithful (verse 6), but it cannot be so with his enemies. To them it must express *anger*. *plunge them into a fiery furnace:* the Hebrew reads 'make them as a fiery furnace', suggesting the picture of a besieged city set on fire with the enemy still inside.

10. Here is no historical victory, but God's final overthrow of all evil. The worldwide scale of this vision is in keeping with the messianic hope implicit in the promise to David as reflected in verses 1–7. On the theme of the extermination of God's enemies, see on Ps. 18: 37–45.

11. The identity of God and king in the *you* of this verse is suggested by a comparison with Ps. 2: 2 where it is against both that *mischief* is *plotted*.

13. A final cry of praise. As in Ps. 20, this concluding verse resumes the thought of the first by exulting in God's *might*, but it is no longer simply the king who rejoices. His people too may now *sing*, for his victory has secured God's blessing for them as well. *

MY GOD, MY GOD, WHY HAST THOU FORSAKEN ME?

22

* This psalm is in two parts, a cry for help (verses 1–21) and a hymn of praise (verses 22–31), and both parts relate to the psalmist's present condition. He is neither praising God for

past deliverance, nor promising praise for future deliverance, but is asking for help now and simultaneously praising God for giving it. Some commentators have therefore argued that there were originally two separate psalms. Others have held that the psalm was composed to accompany the different stages in a festival drama portraying the ritual humiliation and restoration of the king. A further possibility is that a priestly oracle or blessing followed verse 21, thus providing a basis in hope for the utterance of anticipatory praise in verses 22–31. Each of these suggestions contains an element of plausibility, but the passage from supplication to praise is a common feature in other prayers for help where it is based on the confidence that arises from trust in God's faithfulness, encouraging the sufferer to anticipate the joy of deliverance and 'rejoice in the LORD', even in the midst of his distress (see also on Pss. 6: 8; 13: 5). A priestly utterance would indeed have helped to stimulate the faith needed to take this step, but the psalmist's meditation on God's faithfulness and the trust of his forefathers in verses 3–5 could have had the same effect. The heading attached to this psalm in the Septuagint contains the phrase 'concerning the help that comes at daybreak', perhaps implying that it would be suitable for use in a night vigil (see p. 14, sect. C). The soul's longing for God's nearness amid nightmarish sufferings and the confident hope of satisfaction are certainly the themes of other vigil psalms.

The early church believed that this psalm spoke prophetically of the suffering of Christ who himself uttered its opening words on the cross (Matt. 27: 46; Mark 15: 34). In the Gospels the description of the by-passers' jeers (Matt. 27: 39f.; Mark 15: 29; Luke 23: 35) and the taunts of the chief priests, lawyers and elders on Calvary (Matt. 27: 43) are drawn directly from verses 7–8, while the division of Jesus' clothes is expressly presented as a fulfilment of verse 18 (John 19: 23f.; cp. Matt. 27: 35). Verses 14–16 vividly anticipate the agonies of Christ and to some extent variant readings make the correspondence even closer (see verse 16). It is not surprising that this psalm is

traditionally used on Good Friday, but it is equally suited to
other occasions, for a sense of dereliction in suffering (verses
1–2, 11, 19) is also the experience of many faithful individuals
who can trace in it their own tale of distress and hope. ✳

My God, my God, why hast thou forsaken me   1
   and art so far from saving me,[a] from heeding my
      groans?
O my God, I cry in the day-time but thou dost not   2
     answer,
   in the night I cry but get no respite.
And yet thou art enthroned in holiness,   3
   thou art he whose praises Israel sings.
In thee our fathers put their trust;   4
   they trusted, and thou didst rescue them.
Unto thee they cried and were delivered;   5
  in thee they trusted and were not put to shame.
But I am a worm, not a man,   6
   abused by all men, scorned by the people.
All who see me jeer at me,   7
make mouths at me and wag their heads:
   'He threw himself on the LORD for rescue;   8
  let the LORD deliver him, for he holds him dear!'
But thou art he who drew me from the womb,   9
   who laid me at my mother's breast.
Upon thee was I cast at birth;   10
  from my mother's womb thou hast been my God.
  Be not far from me,   11
for trouble is near, and I have no helper.
  A herd of bulls surrounds me,   12

[a] Or, *with slight change,* from my cry.

97

great bulls*a* of Bashan beset me.

13   Ravening and roaring lions
      open their mouths wide against me.

14   My strength drains away like water
          and all my bones are loose.
      My heart has turned to wax and melts within me.

15   My mouth*b* is dry as a potsherd,
          and my tongue sticks to my jaw;
          I am laid*c* low in the dust of death.*d*

16   The huntsmen are all about me;
          a band of ruffians rings me round,
      and they have hacked off*e* my hands and my feet.

17   I tell my tale of misery,
      while they look on and gloat.

18   They share out my garments among them
      and cast lots for my clothes.

19   But do not remain so far away, O LORD;
      O my help, hasten to my aid.

20   Deliver my very self from the sword,
          my precious life from the axe.

21   Save me from the lion's mouth,
          my poor body*f* from the horns of the wild ox.

✻   1–5. A cry of dereliction and a basis for hope.
    1. *My God:* the repetition implies anguish of soul, yet the
pronoun *my* indicates continued longing and faith. The ques-

[a] great bulls: *lit.* bisons.
[b] *Prob. rdg.; Heb.* My strength.
[c] I am laid: *prob. rdg.; Heb.* thou wilt lay me.
[d] I am . . . death: *should possibly follow verse 17.*
[e] and they have hacked off: *prob. rdg.; Heb.* like a lion.
[f] my poor body: *prob. rdg.; Heb.* thou hast answered me.

tion *why* is not a request for reasons, but a cry of despair. The
sense of forsakenness is real and it is something the psalmist
cannot understand, but what he seeks is *saving* help, not an
explanation. *groans:* literally 'roaring' like a lion.

2. God's absence is unceasing *in the day-time* and at *night.*
This is the very cause of anguish, not simply something that
adds to it, and is more unbearable than physical illness or the
mockery of foes.

3. Despite his feelings of perplexity and despair, the knowledge that God is king, the Holy One and the praise of Israel,
is a sure foundation for faith and hope. *holiness* characterizes
God as the one apart from and above the limitations and im-
perfections of mankind, 'the wholly other', and also as the
pure, righteous and exalted one who cannot therefore be
untrue to his promises. The N.E.B. rendering of this verse is a
paraphrase. The Hebrew reads 'Thou art holy, enthroned on
the praises of Israel', a compressed expression recalling the
eternal 'Holy, Holy, Holy', the praise that rises before the
heavenly throne, the song in which God's people at worship
share (Isa. 6: 3; Rev. 4: 8).

4-5. *trust . . . trusted . . . trusted:* repeatedly the trust of his
forefathers was vindicated and this thought now gives him
courage and comfort since he too commits himself in faith to
God. Probably he thinks primarily of the great salvation
events of the nation's history, such as the exodus, but perhaps
also of the faith of his more immediate forebears.

6-11. He contrasts his own lot with that of his forefathers,
but recognizing God's lifelong protection, feels encouraged to
renew his appeal for help.

6. *abused, scorned,* trampled underfoot like *a worm,* not even
viewed with the common respect generally accorded to *a man,*
his is the condition of the servant in Isa. 52: 14; 53: 3 who is
despised because disfigured by suffering. But though men may
shrink in horror from one in bodily, mental or spiritual torment, God does not (verse 24).

7. The various gestures clearly express scorn and abhorrence (cp. Lam. 2: 15).

8. *He threw himself:* following the Septuagint; the verb is imperative in the Hebrew. *for rescue:* better 'let him rescue him'. *for he holds him dear* is a sarcastic comment pouring scorn on the psalmist's faith: 'God clearly holds him dear; that is why he suffers!' This abusive attitude may rest on a religious dogmatism that declares suffering to be a sign of divine disfavour or it may be simply a manifestation of natural human abhorrence of pain and disfigurement, but it is to be sharply contrasted with the compassion of divine love (verse 24). These contrasting attitudes are well illustrated in Jesus' parable of the Good Samaritan (Luke 10: 29–37).

9–10. Though there is no implication that he has always been faithful, he does believe that God has cared for him from birth. Jeremiah and Isaiah's 'servant' both suffered like the psalmist and in a comparable way they were aware that God had chosen them *from the womb* (Jer. 1: 5; Isa. 49: 1, 5).

11. Contemplation of God's care for his forefathers and for himself gives him courage to throw himself on God for help again and renew his cry (verse 2).

12–21. Detailing the unimaginable terrors that beset him, he repeats his cry for help.

12–13. Four word-pictures are used to describe his suffering. Firstly, he likens it to being surrounded by *great bulls* and *Ravening and roaring lions*, metaphors that suggest nightmarish terror. This imagery may characterize his scornful persecutors (verses 6–8), but wild beasts in the psalms frequently symbolize a cruelty and ferocity that is probably demonic (see on Pss. 5: 9; 17: 12; 57: 4), and the psalmist's problem is at least as much spiritual as physical. *Bashan:* an area of rich pastureland in northern Transjordan, and so producing fat cows (Amos 4: 1) and strong bulls.

14. The second picture is of illness and death, a metaphor that may symbolize recession of joy and purpose and encroachment of lifelessness and futility, a sickness in spirit that

comes with the sense of dereliction (cp. on Pss. 6: 5; 13: 3).
The image of the dissolving body recalls the picture of death
in Ezek. 37 where the corpses have become desiccated and the
bones have fallen apart.

15. These symptoms manifest themselves as the vital sap
and moisture of the body begins to evaporate. Death is the
negation of life, the very antithesis of everything that is God,
and so the feeling of being *laid low in the dust of death* is a
symptom of the absence of God. The reading *My mouth* is
obtained by emendation, but it suits the parallelism. *I am laid
low* also depends on an emendation, but it obliterates the
notion of divine punishment contained in the Hebrew (see
N.E.B. footnote) which could suggest that God has forsaken
the psalmist because of sin.

16. The third metaphor, like the first, shows the night-
marishness of the psalmist's sufferings: rough hunters close in
for the kill, take their prey and lop off his dangerous *hands* and
feet. The picture is even more terror-filled in the Hebrew
which reads 'dogs', not *huntsmen*, suggesting the attack of a
half-savage pack of thugs. *hacked off:* the text is difficult,
though it is obvious that a verb is needed rather than the
Hebrew 'like a lion' (N.E.B. footnote). The Septuagint has
'pierced', linking this verse unmistakably with the crucifixion
accounts in the Gospels.

17. The fourth picture is of lost solitude in a hostile world
impatient for his death so that his clothes, his last remaining
possession, can be shared out. *I tell my tale of misery:* the
Hebrew reads 'I may count all my bones', that is, I am reduced
to a skeleton.

19. Alone in his friendless world, he renews his plea that
God abandon him no longer (cp. verses 1, 11), a plea made
more urgent after consideration of his plight.

20. *my very self:* unnecessarily emphatic; better simply
'me'. *my precious life:* literally 'my only one', suggesting that
life is the only thing left to hope for. *the axe:* Hebrew reads

'the power of the dog', probably referring back to verse 16, but the N.E.B. has removed the dog from that verse too.

21. *lion . . . ox:* a reference to verses 12–13. *my poor body:* so the Septuagint. But this verse could be translated: 'Save me from the lion's mouth, and from the horns of the wild ox. Thou hast answered me!' The final exclamation would then be an expression of the faith that makes the transition to rejoicing and praise in verses 22–31 possible. *

22   I will declare thy fame to my brethren;
        I will praise thee in the midst of the assembly.
23   Praise him, you who fear the LORD;
        all you sons of Jacob, do him honour;
     stand in awe of him, all sons of Israel.
24   For he has not scorned the downtrodden,
        nor shrunk in loathing from his plight,
     nor hidden his face from him,
        but gave heed to him when he cried out.
25 Thou dost inspire my praise in the full assembly;
        and I will pay my vows before all who fear thee.
26   Let the humble eat and be satisfied.
     Let those who seek the LORD praise him
        and be*a* in good heart for ever.
27 Let all the ends of the earth remember and turn again to
            the LORD;
     let all the families of the nations bow down before him.*b*
28   For kingly power belongs to the LORD,
           and dominion over the nations is his.
29   How can those buried in the earth do him homage,

[a] and be: *so Sept.; Heb.* may you be.
[b] *So Sept.; Heb.* thee.

how can those who go down to the grave bow before
    him?
But I shall live for his sake,
    my posterity*a* shall serve him.   30
This shall be told of the Lord to future generations;
    and they shall justify him,   31
    declaring to a people yet unborn
    that this was his doing.

✻ 22–6. Convinced that his prayer is heard, he declares his
intention to praise the LORD and calls on the faithful to join in
his song.

22. Cp. Heb. 2: 12. *fame:* literally 'name', that is all that
God has revealed himself to be. *brethren:* fellow-worshippers
gathered in *assembly*. This new story of God's saving activity
will give inspiration to the faithful, while their sharing in his
song of praise will add strength to the sufferer's faith and help
to increase his joy.

23. *fear:* that is, *stand in awe of,* or offer reverence and worship to. *sons of Jacob . . . sons of Israel:* not the whole nation, but
the faithful gathered for worship who hear his song.

24. Though men may have *shrunk in loathing* from the sight
of suffering, God has reached out in compassion to heal (see
verses 6–8). God's *face* is *hidden* when he withdraws his blessing
or his presence (cp. Ps. 13: 1): the psalmist accepts in faith that
God has not forsaken him forever.

25. *Thou dost inspire my praise:* God is not only the object,
but also the source of true praise. In suffering praise does not
come easily and must be inspired by God himself (cp. Ps. 51:
15). *pay my vows:* by fulfilling a vow made while suffering to
bring a sacrifice in thanksgiving for restoration (Ps. 50: 14;
66: 13), or perhaps by offering the praises he has just promised
to give. *all who fear thee:* the faithful worshippers (see verse 23).

[a] But I . . . posterity: *prob. rdg.; Heb. obscure.*

26. *the humble:* the faithful who *seek the LORD* (cp. Zeph. 2: 3). He invites them to *eat and be satisfied*, to approach God as he has done and have their spiritual hunger satisfied (cp. Matt. 5: 6; John 6: 35). It has sometimes been held that the psalmist is inviting the poor in an act of charity to partake of his sacrifice, but the parallelism and a comparison with 23: 5 suggest that the language is probably metaphorical of spiritual blessing. *be in good heart for ever:* literally 'may your heart live for ever'; the gift of God to those who seek him is eternal life, experienced as his ever present vitalizing power in the inner being.

27-31. With overflowing confidence and joy he calls on all men to worship God and looking down the ages hears God's praises sung in generations yet unborn.

27. *all the ends of the earth:* the whole world and its inhabitants. To *remember . . . the LORD* is to call him to mind and so to acknowledge and worship him, to *bow down before him*; cp. Exod. 20: 24, where the N.E.B. has translated the same Hebrew verb with the English verb 'to invoke'.

28. It is not because he has been delivered from suffering that the psalmist wants the nations to praise God; it is because God is king.

29-30. The encroachment of death could have destroyed the psalmist's will to *bow before* God in worship and praise (see verses 14-15), but he rejoices in the confidence that he will *live for* God's *sake*, that is, that he will be restored and will sing God's praises and bear witness to his wonderful deeds. Although he himself cannot live for ever, his *posterity* will take up his hymn and worship God in his kingly power. But the N.E.B. translation depends on emendations. The Hebrew reads 'All the fat ones of the earth shall eat and worship, all who go down into the dust shall bow down before him. He cannot keep his own soul alive; posterity will serve him.' 'The fat ones' are presumably the proud and wealthy who will put aside their arrogance and worship God along with all other mortal men. Even so, the Hebrew does not entirely make good sense, and the versions give different readings, some of which are followed by the N.E.B.

30–1. *justify him:* regard him as righteous. The praises of God will be sung by *generations* to come who will continue to bear witness to God's wonderful works. *that this was his doing:* literally 'that he acted'. ✷

THE LORD IS MY SHEPHERD

23

The LORD is my shepherd; I shall want nothing.   1
   He makes me lie down in green pastures,   2
and leads me beside the waters of peace;
   he renews life within me,   3
and for his name's sake guides me in the right path.
Even though I walk through a valley dark as death   4
I fear no evil, for thou art with me,
thy staff and thy crook are my comfort.

Thou spreadest a table for me in the sight of my enemies;   5
   thou hast richly bathed my head with oil,
     and my cup runs over.
   Goodness and love unfailing, these will follow me   6
     all the days of my life,
     and I shall dwell in the house of the LORD
     my whole life long.

✷ The psalmist's presentation of God as the caring shepherd (verses 1–4) and the bountiful host (verses 5–6) radiates a warmth of confidence in God's goodness and love and an assurance of life and peace in his presence that have made this the best loved of all the psalms in the Psalter. It cannot be dated; its sentiment is timeless.

1–4. The shepherd guides, protects and provides for his sheep.

1. *The LORD* is frequently described as *shepherd* of his whole people (cp. Pss. 95: 7; 100: 3), and it is because the individual worshipper belongs to the LORD's flock that he can say *my shepherd*, confident of his personal care (cp. Luke 15: 3–6). The title 'shepherd' is also given to kings (2 Sam. 5: 2) and to Jesus as both God and King (John 10: 11).

2. Cp. Rev. 7: 17. *leads:* the eastern shepherd goes before the flock. *waters of peace:* literally 'waters of rest', that is, streams beside which the sheep may rest and be refreshed. The picture of refreshing streams and luxuriant verdure reminds the worshipper of these features in God's primaeval paradise (Gen. 2: 9f.) and in his future kingdom (Ezek. 47: 1–12; Rev. 22: 1f.) betokening the gracious gift of his life-giving Spirit both here and hereafter (see on Ps. 36: 8). These are symbols of human experience and hope that are perhaps more vividly appreciated against the background of hot and arid desert fringes where pasturage and water are not always plentiful (cp. Isa. 49: 9f.). The phrase 'waters of rest' also recalls the description, in a similar vein, of God's land as his promised rest for his people (Ps. 95: 11; cp. Heb. 4: 1–11).

3. *he renews life:* spiritual and physical reinvigoration are both in mind, for they cannot be isolated from each other (see on Pss. 6: 5; 30: 2f.). *for his name's sake:* true to himself, or to prove himself exactly what he has revealed himself to be. *the right path:* literally 'the paths of righteousness', the way that is cared for and protected by God (cp. Ps. 1: 6).

4. *a valley dark as death:* dark ravines are the traditional lurking-places of wild beasts, robbers and evil spirits, hence a symbol of any circumstances that give rise to *fear*. But as the sheep know their shepherd will defend them with his *staff* or club and herd them to safety with his *crook*, so man finds *comfort* and strength in the knowledge of God's guarding and guiding presence (cp. Ps. 16: 8). The more familiar and literal translation, 'valley of the shadow of death', contains the same

metaphor, for *death* is also a symbol of *evil* or whatever causes fear. It deprives man of the life, health and joy that God gives and is even pictured as a rival shepherd herding the wicked into Sheol (Ps. 49: 14).

5–6. The faithful is the guest of a gracious and bountiful God.

5. *in the sight of my enemies:* oriental hospitality includes protection. The knowledge of God's presence no more removes adversity than it does dark valleys, but there is rich blessing even in the face of suffering in the assurance of his protection and the knowledge that 'nothing in all creation... can separate us from the love of God' (Rom. 8: 39). The rich *oil* and the brimming *cup* are signs of festive rejoicing and sumptuous entertainment (contrast Luke 7: 46).

6. The banquet God provides for his faithful servant lasts more than a day. To him God's *love unfailing* (see on Ps. 5: 7) is a promise of lifelong welfare or *Goodness*. Since *these* always *follow* (literally 'pursue') him, what need he fear the 'evil' (verse 4) or the 'enemies' (verse 5) that may also pursue him occasionally? The mention of *the house of the LORD* may suggest a sacrificial setting in the temple, the worshippers being received as guests at God's table (cp. Ps. 36: 8), but a figurative interpretation is also suggested by the rest of the psalm which speaks of the assurance of his presence at all times, even in life's vicissitudes (see also Ps. 27: 4). ✳

THE LORD IS THE KING OF GLORY

24

The earth is the LORD's and all that is in it,   1
     the world and those who dwell therein.
For it was he who founded it upon the seas   2
     and planted it firm upon the waters beneath.

3   Who may go up the mountain of the LORD?
       And who may stand in his holy place?
4   He who has clean hands and a pure heart,
       who has not set his mind on falsehood,
           and has not committed perjury.
5   He shall receive a blessing from the LORD,
           and justice from God his saviour.
6   Such is the fortune of those who seek him,
       who seek the face of the God of Jacob.[a]

7   Lift up your heads, you gates,
           lift yourselves up, you everlasting doors,
       that the king of glory may come in.
8   Who is the king of glory?
       The LORD strong and mighty,
           the LORD mighty in battle.
9   Lift up your heads, you gates,
           lift them up, you everlasting doors,
           that the king of glory may come in.
10   Who then is the king of glory?
       The king of glory is the LORD of Hosts.

✻ It is usually thought that this psalm accompanied an annual
procession with the Ark into the temple, the questions and
answers representing the words sung respectively by a priest
at the gate and the people seeking entry. This is a possible
interpretation, though there is no direct evidence in the Old
Testament that the Ark was taken out of the temple to be
carried in processions. Other interpretations are also possible.
The opening verses sing of a majesty so great that the poet
rightly asks who may stand before such a God (verses 1–3),
but he rejoices in the knowledge that God will both receive
and bless the man who is faithful and true (verses 4–6). Hence,

[a] the face . . . Jacob: *so Sept.; Heb.* your face, O Jacob.

with eager jubilation he looks for the appearing of this glorious king and summons the portals to let him enter (verses 7–10). This may therefore be the joyous prayer of any who come to the sanctuary to 'seek the face of the God of Jacob' (verse 6). It is indeed possible to think of it being sung in a variety of ways, for it is equally suited to private devotional use and to dramatized congregational worship, but the poetic forms must not be so circumscribed by hypothetical ritual interpretations that the cry of the heart is smothered. Most scholars would agree that this is a pre-exilic psalm. Traditionally Christians use it on Ascension Day.

1–2. The psalmist rejoices that the God whose presence he has come to seek is sovereign lord and creator of the whole earth.

2. It is because he is creator that God is sovereign. *the seas . . . the waters beneath:* the ancients believed the earth to rest on a mighty cosmic ocean. Before time began its waters were in a perpetual state of turbulence, but God brought them under control, *founded* the earth and *planted it firm* on this ocean. Thus creation is sometimes portrayed as a victory over the unruly powers of the sea and the continuance of order in the universe is ascribed to the power and kingship of God (cp. Ps. 93).

3–6. These verses are in the form of an entrance torah giving instructions about conditions for admission to God's presence (see on Ps. 15), but the exultant mood continues as the psalmist expresses his conviction that blessings await the faithful in God's presence.

3. 'Heaven itself, the highest heaven, cannot contain' the universal God of verses 1–2, 'how much less' the temple on Mount Zion (1 Kings 8: 27), but this *holy place* on *the mountain of the LORD* stands as a symbol of his presence with his people (see on Ps. 2: 6) and so it is thither the pilgrims *go up* (cp. Ps. 122: 4) to seek his face (verse 6).

4. *He who has clean hands and a pure heart* is the man who shows integrity in deed and intention (Ps. 15: 2; cp. 73: 1; Matt. 5: 8). He has *his mind* fixed firmly on God, not on the

things opposed to God's will (*falsehood*), and his word is thoroughly reliable (cp. Ps. 15: 4). *committed perjury:* too legalistic, better 'sworn deceitfully'.

5. *justice:* rather 'vindication'. It is the constant longing of the faithful to see God fulfil his promises of *blessing* (see on Ps. 5: 7) and vindicate their trust in him as their *saviour*.

6. *fortune:* the more familiar translation 'the generation of those who', that is, 'the type of men who', is equally acceptable. *seek* translates two different words, but both may denote the act of visiting the sanctuary or the inner purpose of the heart. To enter into God's presence, to feel 'his face shine' in blessing (Num. 6: 25), is the 'one thing' that the faithful *seek* (Ps. 27: 4, 8). *God of Jacob:* Israel's God; the title reminds of God's promise and the people's obligation in the covenant (see on Ps. 20: 1).

7–10. With a jubilant shout the psalmist bids the gates open high to admit the glorious king of the universe.

7. In the language of poetry he endues his physical environment with supernatural qualities. The *gates* are personified and become, as it were, the *everlasting doors* of heaven. He bids them not simply open (contrast Ps. 118: 19), but *Lift up* their *heads*, for they must extend beyond the skies to admit the one whom 'heaven itself cannot contain' (see on verse 3). It is on the entry of God himself, not just of the Ark or a procession, that the worshipper's expectation is focused. *king of glory:* or 'glorious king'; God's glory is his presence in radiance and holiness (see on Ps. 19: 1).

8. Pursuing his poetic imagery, the psalmist likens the coming of God to the triumphal entry of a conquering king. The personified gates issue a challenge to the worshipper in the role of king's herald, and he first announces his master as *the LORD*, Israel's God, proclaiming that he has shown himself *mighty in battle*. The allusion is to the subjugation of the chaotic primaeval waters in creation (see on verse 2).

10. In response to a further challenge, God is identified as *the LORD of Hosts*, that is, as king over all the hosts of heaven

and earth. The appearance of this title in connection with the
Ark in 1 Sam. 4: 4 and of the similar title 'LORD of the count-
less thousands of Israel' when the Ark was carried in procession
from Sinai (Num. 10: 36) would lend support to the liturgical
interpretation of this psalm, but it also appears in other con-
texts where the Ark is not mentioned and here it suitably
denotes God's kingship over the whole of creation (cp. Ps.
46: 7). *

REMEMBER ME IN THY UNFAILING LOVE

25

Unto thee, O LORD my God, I lift up my heart.   1
In thee I trust: do not put me to shame,   2
   let not my enemies exult over me.
   No man who hopes in thee is put to shame;   3
   but shame comes to all who break faith without cause.
      Make thy paths known to me, O LORD;   4
      teach me thy ways.
   Lead me in thy truth and teach me;   5
      thou art God my saviour.
   For thee I have waited all the day long,
      for the coming of thy goodness, LORD.[a]
Remember, LORD, thy tender care and thy love unfailing,   6
      shown from ages past.
   Do not remember the sins and offences of my youth,   7
      but remember me in thy unfailing love.
   The LORD is good and upright;   8
therefore he teaches sinners the way they should go.
   He guides the humble man in doing right,   9
   he teaches the humble his ways.

    [a] for the coming . . . LORD: *transposed from end of verse 7.*

10   All the ways of the LORD are loving and sure
       to men who keep his covenant and his charge.

11   For the honour of thy name, O LORD,
       forgive my wickedness, great as it is.

12   If there is any man who fears the LORD,
       he shall be shown the path that he should choose;

13   he shall enjoy lasting prosperity,
       and his children after him shall inherit the land.

14   The LORD confides his purposes to those who fear
       him,
       and his covenant is theirs to know.

15   My eyes are ever on the LORD,
   who alone can free my feet from the net.

16   Turn to me and show me thy favour,
       for I am lonely and oppressed.

17   Relieve the sorrows of my heart
       and bring me out of my distress.

18   Look at my misery and my trouble
       and forgive me every sin.

19   Look at my enemies, see how many they are
       and how violent their hatred for me.

20   Defend me and deliver me,
       do not put me to shame when I take refuge in thee.

21   Let integrity and uprightness protect me,
       for I have waited for thee, O LORD.[a]

22 O God, redeem Israel from all his sorrows.

✻ This is an acrostic psalm (see p. 10), though the alphabetic
sequence shows a few slight irregularities, some of which are
seen again in Ps. 34, perhaps suggesting that the two psalms

[a] O LORD: *so Sept.; Heb. om.*

were the work of the same poet. Both lack a verse beginning with the sixth letter and both have an extra verse at the end. Here, apart from the last verse which is a prayer for Israel, the psalmist personally seeks God's protection, guidance and pardon, particularly in verses 1–7, 16–21, but offers his prayer with confident trust in God, whose goodness, justice and loving care form the main themes of verses 8–15. The acrostic form is sometimes seen as an indication of post-exilic writing.

1–7. Prayers for protection, guidance and pardon.

1. Verse *'ālep. my heart:* or 'my whole being'; God is the object of all his longings.

2. Verse *bēt.* His *trust* rests on the promises of God, the 'love unfailing' shown by him in the covenant he made with his people in ages past (verse 6). *my enemies:* probably the ungodly who jeer at the sufferer, taking a perverted pleasure in the thought that God has let him down (cp. Ps. 22: 7–8).

3. Verse *gīmel. hopes in:* or 'waits for'; it is not fleeting aspiration, but patient and expectant waiting for God that will not be disappointed (cp. Rom. 5: 3–5). *who break faith:* the parallelism suggests a meaning opposite to 'who hopes', hence not apostates to paganism, but all who fail to endure in faith. *without cause:* or 'to no purpose'.

4. Verse *dālet. thy paths . . . thy ways:* the roads that lead to and are loved and cared for by God (cp. Ps. 1: 6), a metaphor for the life lived in accordance with his will. Hence *Make . . . known to me . . . teach me* is a prayer that his eyes may be opened to the deeper meaning of God's law and that he may be given the grace to follow it. This insight and power, he later affirms, is given to all who are faithful and 'fear the LORD' (verse 12).

5. Verse *hē.* God's *truth* (*'emet*) is his dependability, the quality of being true to promise, and therefore is often coupled, as in verse 10 below, with his *ḥesed* or loving faithfulness to his covenanted word (see on Ps. 5: 7). Hence *Lead me in thy truth* is a prayer, not for intellectual enlightenment,

but for grace to live in and be led by the awareness of God's faithfulness.

There is no couplet between verses 5 and 6 representing the letter *wāw* and verses 5 and 7 are both longer than any other in the psalm. The N.E.B.'s rearrangement of the text contributes to the solution of both these problems, but it should be noted that the similar Ps. 34 also lacks a verse beginning with *wāw*.

6. Verse *zayin. Remember:* and so bring to life. *tender care:* the Hebrew word suggests the warmth of a mother's feeling for her child. *love unfailing: ḥesed,* see on verse 5. *shown from ages past:* the appeal is not to the antiquity, but to the enduring quality of God's love and faithfulness.

7. Verse *ḥēt. remember the sins . . . remember me:* the contrast is poignant. His prayer is that God will not judge on the basis of a wayward past, but will receive him as one who now seeks the fellowship of his *unfailing love. sins and offences:* inadvertent and deliberate errors respectively.

8–15. He sings of God's goodness, justice and faithfulness, the ground of his confidence and his prayer.

8. Verse *ṭēt. good and upright:* the two words qualify each other; God's beneficence is not sentimental, because he is upright, and his justice is not harsh, because he is good. Thus gently, but firmly, he *teaches . . . the way* (see verse 4) to *sinners,* not the openly rebellious, but those who, perhaps through ignorance, go astray.

9. Verse *yōd. the humble:* the godly, but the word may also suggest poverty, whether physical or spiritual (see on Pss. 9: 12 and 40: 17).

10. Verse *kap.* The relationship between God and worshipper is reciprocal faithfulness. God for his part is *loving* (*ḥesed*) *and sure* (*'emet,* see verse 5), true to his gracious promises of protection and blessing, while the worshipper pledges loyalty and obedience to *his covenant and his charge,* the obligations laid on Israel in the law.

11. Verse *lāmed.* This prayer for forgiveness interrupts the

hymn of praise in verses 8–15, but it aptly follows a statement
of God's love and man's duty in verse 10 that may well prompt
feelings of guilt and shortcoming. *For the honour of thy name:*
to be true to your nature as you have revealed it in your
promises (cp. Ps. 23: 3).

12. Verse *mēm. fears:* stands in awe and reverence before.
'The fear of the LORD' is virtually a synonym for true religion.
shown the path: see verse 4.

13. Verse *nūn.* The consequence of walking God's 'path'
(verse 12) is a life of blessing and this embraces a man's
children because they are brought up in a godly home. *the land:*
not vast estates, but the inheritance promised to Abraham
(Gen. 15: 7) and to Israel (Deut. 4: 1). This is God's land, the
place of *lasting prosperity*, and therefore a symbol of both
physical and spiritual blessing (cp. Matt. 5: 5).

14. Verse *sāmek. his purposes:* not secret confidences or
extraordinary disclosures, but the meaning of *his covenant*
revealed to those who would walk in fellowship with God.
This verse makes the same point as verses 10 and 12 and
further answers the prayer of verse 4.

15. Verse *'ayin. My eyes are ever on the LORD:* that is,
watching expectantly for his promised blessing (cp. Ps. 123:
2). *the net:* the hunter's trap (Ps. 9: 15), here a metaphor for the
entangling perplexities of life.

16–21. Prayers for deliverance and protection.

16. Verse *pē. Turn to me:* or 'look on me', that is, the opposite of 'hide thy face from me' (cp. Ps. 22: 24). *I am lonely:*
probably because shunned by former friends (cp. Ps. 31: 11f.).

17. Verse *ṣādē. Relieve:* this is an emended reading, but it is
almost universally accepted and it suits the parallelism better
than the Hebrew 'are enlarged'.

18. Verse *rēsh.* This verse should begin with *qōp* and
scholars have suggested various emendations to make it do so,
but the N.E.B. preserves the Hebrew. *my misery and my
trouble:* the parallelism suggests that his suffering is punishment

for *sin. forgive:* literally 'take away', implying that his sin weighs on him like a burden.

19. Verse *rēsh. my enemies:* see verse 2.

20. Verse *shīn. do not put me to shame:* resuming his opening prayer (verses 2–3).

21. Verse *tāw. integrity and uprightness:* these are clearly qualities the psalmist wishes to see in his own life, but he has portrayed them as guardian angels, perhaps in recognition that they are essentially virtues that a man derives from his walk with God, attributes of God himself. *I have waited:* see on verse 3; cp. verse 5.

22. A concluding prayer for the nation. This may be a later liturgical addition to adapt the psalm for congregational use, but it could equally be that the psalmist himself added these words to his hymn, knowing that he enjoys the blessings of the covenant only by virtue of his membership of the community of God's chosen people to whom the promises were made. *

I LOVE THE BEAUTY OF GOD'S HOUSE

26

1   Give me justice, O LORD,
             for I have lived my life without reproach,
             and put unfaltering trust in the LORD.

2   Test me, O LORD, and try me;
             put my heart and mind to the proof.

3   For thy constant love is before my eyes,
               and I live in thy truth.

4   I have not sat among worthless men,
               nor do I mix with hypocrites;

5   I hate the company of evildoers
             and will not sit among the ungodly.

I wash my hands in innocence 6
to join in procession round thy altar, O LORD,
singing of thy marvellous acts, 7
recounting them all with thankful voice.
O LORD, I love the beauty*a* of thy house, 8
the place where thy glory dwells.

Do not sweep me away with sinners, 9
nor cast me out with men who thirst for blood,
whose fingers are active in mischief, 10
and their hands are full of bribes.
But I live my life without reproach; 11
redeem me, O LORD,*b* and show me thy favour.
When once my feet are planted on firm ground, 12
I will bless the LORD in the full assembly.

✻ It is sometimes argued that this psalm, along with Pss. 7 and 17 which also contain an appeal for justice and protestation of innocence, is the prayer of an accused man facing trial. Whilst such use cannot be excluded, a much wider application is indicated by the psalmist's expressions of delight in worship and the presence of God (verses 6–8), features found in other psalms, such as 5 and 27, where the temple is a place of refuge and encounter with God. The psalmist's plea is less of legalistic innocence than of loyalty to God (verses 1–8) and it is on these grounds that he appeals for a kind of justice that is not normally extended to sinners (verses 9–12). This psalm is a companion to Ps. 28 and like it is probably pre-exilic in origin.

1–8. He pleads his loyalty and single-hearted devotion to God.

1. *justice*, as God's response to a *life without reproach*, must

[a] *So Sept.; Heb.* dwelling.
[b] O LORD: *so Sept.; Heb. om.*

be more than legal acquittal (cp. Ps. 17: 1), for the character of that life is not sinlessness, but *unfaltering trust in the LORD* to act in accordance with his 'constant love' (verse 3).

2. Cp. Ps. 17: 3. *Test . . . put . . . to the proof:* as carefully as a silver-smith assessing the value of his metals (Ps. 66: 10). *heart and mind:* literally 'kidneys and heart', here denoting man's whole inner consciousness (see on Pss. 7: 9; 16: 7, 9). Nothing new could possibly be uncovered in such a scrutiny, since God already 'knows the secrets of the heart' (Ps. 44: 21). The psalmist's self-offering must therefore be a declaration of his confidence that his commitment and loyalty are in accordance with God's will.

3. *constant love* and *truth* (see on Ps. 25: 5) are synonyms for God's faithfulness to his promise to protect the godly. Herein lies the psalmist's hope, not that he himself is meritorious, but that God is faithful. He dares to present his appeal only because he holds this promise *before* his *eyes* in trust (verse 1) and seeks to *live* accordingly (verses 4–7).

4–5. Cp. Ps. 1: 1. *sat among:* shared in the life-style of. The various designations of the godless are poetic synonyms and do not denote four different classes in society. *the company of evildoers:* contrast 'the full assembly' of the faithful to which the psalmist belongs (verse 12).

6. *I wash my hands in innocence:* the priests washed their hands and feet before entering the sanctuary or offering sacrifice (Exod. 30: 17–21), but as in Ps. 73: 13, the expression may be interpreted metaphorically, here denoting spiritual preparation for worship. *join in procession round thy altar:* take his place amongst the faithful at worship, in contrast to sitting 'among the ungodly' (verse 5).

7. The celebration of God's *marvellous acts*, his redemptive miracles in history and in the lives of his people (Ps. 9: 1), frequently features in the *thankful* praise of the psalms (e.g. Pss. 40: 5; 71: 17).

8. This is both the climax and the transition-point of the psalm. The entire protestation of loyalty is expressed in this

cry of love, as also is the heart-felt yearning that evokes the ensuing prayers. *I love:* contrast 'I hate' in verse 5. *the beauty of thy house:* so the Septuagint; the Hebrew reads 'the habitation of thy house', that is, as the parallelism suggests, 'the house where God *dwells*'. God cannot, of course, be contained in any building (see on Ps. 11: 4), but it is not so much the temple that the psalmist loves as what it betokens, namely God's presence with his people (cp. Ps. 27: 4). Likewise, God's *glory* is a symbol of his presence (see on Ps. 19: 1); cp. the tradition, strongly reflected in this verse, about the glory of the LORD dwelling in the Tent of the Presence in the wilderness (Exod. 40: 34–8).

9–12. He prays to be spared the fate of those whose company he shuns.

9. *sinners:* those who deliberately choose the way that is not God's (Ps. 1: 1). *men who thirst for blood:* literally 'men of blood' (cp. Ps. 5: 6), men who would not shrink from violence to obtain their ends.

10. They also make free use of *bribes* to pervert justice for their own advantage (cp. Ps. 15: 5).

11. *But I live my life without reproach:* to emphasize the contrast between himself and the ungodly, he resumes his opening protestation (verse 1).

12. *When once:* these words are not represented in the Hebrew and their addition gives the erroneous impression that the psalmist intends to reserve his praise till after restoration. But verses 6–8 clearly indicate that he already does *bless the LORD in the full assembly*, even in his misfortune. His praise is not offered conditionally, but in confidence that he already stands *on firm ground*, having 'put unfaltering trust in the LORD' (verse 1, cp. Ps. 13: 5). *

ONE THING I SEEK: TO GAZE ON THE BEAUTY
OF THE LORD

27

1   The LORD is my light and my salvation;
        whom should I fear?
    The LORD is the refuge of my life;
        of whom then should I go in dread?

2 When evildoers close in on me to devour me,
        it is my enemies, my assailants,
        who stumble and fall.

3   If an army should encamp against me,
        my heart would feel no fear;
    if armed men should fall upon me,
    even then I should be undismayed.

4   One thing I ask of the LORD,
        one thing I seek:
        that I may be constant in the house of the LORD
        all the days of my life,
        to gaze upon the beauty of the LORD
        and to seek him*a* in his temple.

5   For he will keep me safe beneath his roof*b*
        in the day of misfortune;
    he will hide me under the cover of his tent;
    he will raise me beyond reach of distress.

6 Now I can raise my head high
        above the enemy all about me;
    so will I acclaim him with sacrifice before his tent
    and sing a psalm of praise to the LORD.

[a] *Or* and to pay my morning worship.
[b] *Lit.* in his arbour.

Hear, O LORD, when I call aloud;   7
    show me favour and answer me.
  'Come,' my heart has said,   8
    'seek his face.'[a]
  I will seek thy face, O LORD;
  do not hide it from me,   9
  nor in thy anger turn away thy servant,
    whose help thou hast been;
do not cast me off or forsake me, O God my saviour.
  Though my father and my mother forsake me,   10
    the LORD will take me into his care.
  Teach me thy way, O LORD;   11-12
  do not give me up to the greed of my enemies;
lead me by a level path
    to escape my watchful foes;
  liars stand up to give evidence against me,
    breathing malice.
  Well I know[b] that I shall see the goodness of the LORD 13
    in the land of the living.

Wait for the LORD; be strong, take courage,   14
    and wait for the LORD.

* It has often been argued that this psalm comprises two
originally independent units, a psalm of confidence (verses
1–6) and a prayer for help (verses 7–13). Apart from the
change in tone, each section is self-contained. The first refers
to the LORD in the third person, the second addresses him in the
second person. Furthermore, verse 14 may be seen as an
address to the psalmist by a third party, perhaps a priest. Even

[a] seek his face: *prob. rdg.; Heb.* seek ye my face.
[b] Well I know: *so some MSS.; others* Had I not well known.

so, the whole psalm may still be used as an integrated unit. Its structure is not unlike that of Ps. 22 and a number of other psalms, though the more commonly observed order of supplication and confidence is reversed. Like these its plea for succour is enfolded in a profound expression of faith that God continues to protect the worshipper, even amid his distress, and that soon he will bring him relief. The prayer therefore suitably ends in a firm resolve to wait for the LORD. This psalm is also akin to Ps. 5 and several others that are suitable for use in a night vigil. To the psalmist the approaching dawn (see on verse 4) symbolizes God's coming in victory to dispel the hostile forces that beset him. But it would appear that his greatest expectation is the restoration of an awareness of God's presence that has been temporarily lost (verses 4, 8–10, 13). There is nothing in this psalm that would help us to date it.

1–3. He expresses his confidence that he will pass through any storms unscathed because God shelters him.

1. *my light*: illuminating the darkness and dispelling all anxiety, hence synonymous with *my salvation*; an appropriate metaphor for a vigil setting and for renewal of hope through the gloom of depression. As surely as the sunrise ends the night, so God will put to flight the powers of darkness. The further characterization of God as his *refuge* is also apt, since it is in the temple that he seeks shelter (verses 4–5).

2. *evildoers . . . enemies . . . assailants*: portrayed not as human foes, but as terrifying animal figures that *close in on me to devour me* (literally 'my flesh'). Nevertheless, it is they that *stumble and fall*, because the psalmist is in God's care. In a vigil setting this kind of imagery would naturally suggest association with the terrifying forces of night (cp. on Ps. 5: 3, 9).

3. A statement of utter confidence. Irrespective of the magnitude of the threat, be it even like the onslaught of a whole army, he has no cause for fear. On the change of metaphor see on Pss. 7: 15; 17: 12.

4–6. He seeks to draw near to God and vows that he will offer sacrifice and praise when his vision comes.

4. The *one thing* he seeks is God's abiding presence, but he describes his expectation in three ways. First, he seeks to be *constant in the house of the LORD*, that is to live in a continuing fellowship with God that will find concrete expression in his regular attendance at worship (cp. Ps. 23: 6). Second, he looks for a lasting vision of God's *beauty*, his splendour and his goodness, upon which he may *gaze* with the eye of his soul lost in wonder (cp. Ps. 17: 15). Third, he expects his illumination to come to him like the morning light which will end his night of watching. The verb rendered *to seek* has been interpreted in many different ways, but it can be translated as in the N.E.B. footnote, 'to pay my morning worship', or perhaps better, 'to watch for the morning'. The appearance of the dawn is thus synonymous with the vision of God's beauty and both are symbols of entry into his presence, or into a communion with him that will last as long as *life* endures. This imagery gains an added dramatic quality in the context of a vigil in the temple.

5. He will be kept *safe* because he has sought sanctuary in the very dwelling-place of God. The word *tent* is an archaic term dating from the period before the temple was built (Exod. 36: 8–38). *beyond reach of distress:* the Hebrew reads 'upon a rock', an expression which suggests defensibility and security (see on Ps. 18: 2).

6. *Now:* consequently, because of God's protection. He will hold his *head high* in triumph (cp. Ps. 3: 3) and celebrate God's help with *sacrifice* and *a psalm of praise*. The picture is one of confidence and rejoicing, for his vow is made in a spirit of complete trust that God will answer his prayer.

7–13. But the triumph is still to come. In the meantime he must pray that God will not take away the comfort of his presence, but will lead him to safety from his enemies.

7. Pleas for hearing are a common feature in prayers for help (cp. Ps. 28: 1f.). They amount to appeals for active intervention, for a positive demonstration of God's *favour*, for an *answer* that is not in words only.

8. The psalmist dedicates himself to his purpose of seeking God's presence. The N.E.B. translation of this difficult verse depends on emendations and gives the impression that the psalmist is motivated by some form of inner compulsion of the *heart*. The Hebrew, as it is literally translated in the N.E.B. footnote, implies that it is a commandment of God that jogs his heart. Perhaps the priest in ancient Israel would advise individuals in certain kinds of trouble or spiritual distress to keep vigil and would support his recommendation by referring them to some oracular command that read 'seek ye my face'. As the first element in this verse can be translated 'my heart recites your (command)', the implication is that the suppliant has been meditating on this divine injunction. God's *face* is an anthropomorphic symbol of his presence or his self-manifestation (cp. Ps. 17: 15).

9. When God blesses, he makes his face shine upon the worshipper (Num. 6: 25), but if he hides his face, he expresses his displeasure and *anger* (cp. on Ps. 13: 1). Such language suggests that the psalmist feels his suffering is partly the result of his own sin. However, he does not dwell on this, for his mind is fixed on God. He recalls the comfort of God's *help* in the past and prays that he be not deprived of the joy of his presence now (cp. Ps. 51: 11f.).

10. This verse should not be used to identify the psalmist or his physical or spiritual condition. His case is hypothetical: 'if everyone were to forsake me, even *my father and my mother*, then . . .' The picture is one of complete dereliction.

11–12. The N.E.B. has somewhat unnecessarily rearranged the word ordering in these verses, but the sense of the Hebrew is unchanged. The psalmist asks not to be abandoned to his enemies, but to be shown the *way* that is right and acceptable in God's eyes, the *level path* where he may walk at peace with God unhindered by any obstacles to his faith. The enemies, who were wild beasts in verse 2, are now likened to malicious slanderers whose venom and spite is well portrayed in the words *greed*, *watchful* and *breathing malice*.

13. This strong concluding statement of confidence is typical of the vigil psalms (cp. Pss. 5: 12; 17: 15). *the land of the living* is this world, in contrast to Sheol which is the land of death (Ps. 6: 5). It is not in the hereafter that the psalmist wants his vision, but now. To *see the goodness of the LORD* is to draw near to him and enjoy his presence, to 'gaze upon' his 'beauty', and this is the 'one thing' (verse 4) that he seeks in his present distress.

14. The resolve to wait. This may be a priestly word of encouragement to the suppliant as he begins his vigil in the temple, but it could equally be the psalmist exhorting himself to patience and hope. Man in his weakness finds it hard to wait for God and such encouragement to his faith is necessary, despite the strength of conviction expressed in the rest of the psalm. The prophet Habakkuk received similar assurance: 'there is still a vision for the appointed time . . . it will not fail. If it delays, wait for it' (Hab. 2: 3). ✻

HEAR MY CRY FOR MERCY

28

To thee, O LORD, I call;   1
O my Rock, be not deaf to my cry,
  lest, if thou answer me with silence,
I become like those who go down to the abyss.
  Hear my cry for mercy   2
  when I call to thee for help,
when I lift my hands to thy holy shrine.
Do not drag me away with the ungodly, with evildoers, 3
who speak civilly to neighbours, with malice in their
    hearts.
Reward them for their works, their evil deeds;   4
  reward them for what their hands have done;

give them their deserts.

5   Because they pay no heed to the works of the LORD
     or to what his hands have done,
       may he tear them down and never build them up!

6   Blessed be the LORD,
     for he has heard my cry for mercy.

7   The LORD is my strength, my shield,
     in him my heart trusts;
     so I am sustained, and my heart leaps for joy,
       and I praise him with my whole body.[a]

8   The LORD is strength to his people,[b]
     a safe refuge for his anointed king.

9   O save thy people and bless thy own,
     shepherd them, carry them for ever.

* This is a companion psalm to Ps. 26. Both plead for
deliverance from the fate of the ungodly (28: 3; 26: 9) and
focus attention on the temple as the symbol of God's saving
presence (28: 2; 26: 6–8), but whereas Ps. 26 is a prayer for
justice based on a protestation of loyalty, Ps. 28 is an appeal
for mercy. The passage from petition to praise is abrupt and
decisive, but it is possible only because the psalmist 'trusts' in
God (verse 7) that 'he has heard' (verse 6; cp. Ps. 6: 8). The
basis for this trust is his membership of the people of God, and
so it is with prayer for their vindication and blessing that he
closes his song (verse 9). This psalm is probably of pre-exilic
origin.

   1–5. His prayer for hearing leads into a curse on the ungodly, but his central plea is to be spared their fate.

   1. *O my Rock:* this figure, suggesting stability and strength

[a] with my whole body: *prob. rdg.; Heb.* from my song.
[b] *So some MSS.; others* to them.

126

(Ps. 18: 2), foreshadows the confidence of verses 6–8. Yet
abandonment is his greatest dread. His prayer, *be not deaf to my
cry*, may be compared with the more familiar cry of dereliction 'hide not thy face from me' (cp. Pss. 13: 1; 27: 9). He
likens the experience to sinking into *the abyss* or Sheol, the
place of the dead, the land of *silence*, and this simile forcefully
conveys his fear of the empty, comfortless, purposeless
existence that must be lived when God's life-giving presence
is no longer felt (cp. Ps. 6: 5).

2. *my cry for mercy:* the psalmist complains of no suffering
or persecution. He merely pleads that he may continue to find
favour with God. The psalm may therefore be used in a wide
variety of settings of physical, mental or spiritual distress, or
even in times of security as a prayer for continued blessing.
I lift my hands: this traditional posture sometimes expresses
adoration (Ps. 134: 2), but here is the token of a heart reaching
out to God in supplication. *thy holy shrine:* for the temple as a
symbol of God's presence, see on Pss. 11: 4; 26: 8.

3. His plea to be distinguished from *the ungodly* and not be
dragged off with them as it were to execution, is not based on
any presupposition of sinlessness. His claim is simply that he is
not one of them. The difference lies in the inner man, in the
motivation of the heart. Outwardly their behaviour may
appear civil enough, but they are essentially *evildoers*, for they
act *with malice in their hearts*. In contradistinction, the pre-
occupation of his heart is his trust and joy in the LORD (verse 7).

4–5. The basis of this prayer is not sheer vindictiveness. God
sets a choice of two ways before men, one leading to blessing,
the other to doom (Ps. 1: 3, 6). But so often it is the ungodly
that seem to prosper in this life while the faithful suffer (cp.
Ps. 10: 2–11). The curse here must therefore be taken together
with the prayer for blessing on the godly (verse 9) as a plea to
God to uphold his promises and vindicate the faithful. The
ungodly are self-centred, concerned about *their works, what
their hands have done*, and show an atheistic disregard for God
and his *works, what his hands have done*. The contrast is explicit:

they have no need for God because they have proudly deified themselves.

6–8. His prayer gives way to praise in anticipation of deliverance.

6. *he has heard . . .:* cp. verse 2. This assurance need not presuppose an act of healing or the utterance of an oracle. It is much rather a statement made in trust (verse 7).

7. *my strength, my shield:* or 'my strong shield', affording protection against all physical and spiritual ills (cp. Ps. 18: 35). *my heart trusts; so I am sustained:* God is the psalmist's 'Rock' (verse 1) and 'Those who trust in the LORD are like' the temple-Rock, 'Mount Zion, which cannot be shaken but stands fast for ever' (Ps. 125: 1). It is this faith in God that permits such *joy* even in times of trouble (see on Ps. 13: 5). *with my whole body:* so the Septuagint, but the Hebrew 'with my song' (N.E.B. footnote 'from my song') makes perfectly good sense.

8. It is because he is one of the faithful, not one of the ungodly, that he can rest in confidence on the promises of blessing or *strength* and protection or *refuge* God has given to *his people* firstly through Moses (Deut. 30: 15–20) and secondly through *his anointed king*, David (2 Sam. 7: 8–16).

9. This invocation of blessing on God's *people* is the counterpart of the curse on the ungodly in verses 4–5 and completes the psalmist's prayer for vindication. *thy own:* God's people, his personal and most valuable possession. It is the closeness of this relationship that enables the worshipper to use the strongly personal 'my' in addressing God (verse 1). *shepherd them:* on the protective warmth of this figure, see Ps. 23. *carry them:* in safety, as a shepherd would carry the little lambs in his arms (Isa. 40: 11). ✻

THE VOICE OF THE LORD AND HIS GLORY

29

Ascribe to the LORD, you gods,   1
ascribe to the LORD glory and might.

Ascribe to the LORD the glory due to his name;   2
bow down to the LORD in the splendour of holiness.[a]

The God of glory thunders: 3
the voice of the LORD echoes over the waters,
the LORD is over the mighty waters.

The voice of the LORD is power.   4
The voice of the LORD is majesty.

The voice of the LORD breaks the cedars,   5
the LORD splinters the cedars of Lebanon.

He makes Lebanon skip like a calf,   6
Sirion like a young wild ox.

The voice of the LORD makes flames of fire burst forth,   7
the voice of the LORD makes the wilderness writhe in 8
    travail;
the LORD makes the wilderness of Kadesh writhe.

The voice of the LORD makes the hinds calve   9
    and brings kids early to birth;
and in his temple all cry, 'Glory!'

The LORD is king above[b] the flood,   10
the LORD has taken his royal seat as king for ever.

The LORD will give strength to his people;   11
the LORD will bless his people with peace.

[a] the splendour of holiness: *or* holy vestments.
[b] *Or* since

* The psalmist, like the author of Ps. 8 or Ps. 19, finds God's glory revealed in nature, but here in the fury of the storm, not in the peaceful calm of the night sky or beneficence of the sun's warmth. His is a picture of an unspeakable majesty that summons the heavens to worship (verses 1–2) and causes the earth and all in it to tremble (verses 3–9). Yet to God's people the roar of his thunder inspires confidence, for it manifests the power of their divine king (verses 10–11). The repetitious style is reminiscent of early Canaanite and Hebrew poetry (cp. Judg. 5), perhaps indicating the great antiquity of this psalm. It has indeed been suggested that we have here an older Canaanite psalm modified by Israel. Its opening verses appear in a further modified form in Ps. 96: 7–9.

1–2. The psalmist summons the celestial host to worship.

1. *you gods:* literally 'sons of gods', that is, heavenly beings. In Old Testament faith there is only one God (Exod. 20: 3), but he is attended by divine beings whose function is to do his bidding (Ps. 82; see on Ps. 58: 1) and to render him praise (Pss. 89: 5; 103: 20f.).

2. *holiness:* describes God's nature, his purity and majesty; his *glory* is this holiness made manifest before men in radiant and kingly *splendour* (cp. Ps. 19: 1). Repeatedly glory and holiness are the themes of praise, as in the seraphim's song in Isa. 6: 3, for in the love and wonder of true worship they are ascribed or reflected back to God. *his name:* himself as men know him. 'holy vestments' (N.E.B. footnote): a possible translation, though less literal, likening the heavenly host to priests at worship, a natural metaphor if the psalm's setting is in the temple (see on verse 9 and cp. the comments at Ps. 96: 9).

3–9. The storm. The seven-fold repetition of *the voice of the LORD* poetically suggests successive peals of thunder. The imagery of these verses has a double significance, for attention is fixed first and foremost on the action of God, the tempest itself being little more than his medium of revelation or the symbol of his activity. Four main spheres of action may be delimited.

3–4. First, God silences the powers of disorder. It is not simply because of its awesome appearance that the thunderstorm speaks of God's *glory* as it approaches over the Mediterranean. His *voice*, now heard in the thunder (cp. Ps. 18: 13; Job 37: 2–5), reminds the worshipper of the creative *power* and *majesty* of his word that brought an ordered universe out of the formless deep at the beginning of time (Gen. 1: 1–10). *the waters* are the repository of all earth's turbulent forces over which God continues to exercise kingly authority (cp. Ps. 93; see on Ps. 24: 2).

5–6. Second, God rebukes the proud. *the cedars of Lebanon:* proverbial for their strength and grandeur, and thus, together with the lofty mountains of the north, a suitable metaphor for all that would vaunt itself against God (cp. Isa. 2: 13f.). *Sirion:* the Phoenician name for Mount Hermon (Deut. 3: 9), part of the Anti-Lebanon range of mountains. *skip like a calf:* not with the vigour of renewed youth, but in terror before God (cp. Ps. 114: 6).

7–8. Third, God stirs up *the wilderness*, and so all that is lifeless. As the *flames of fire* (lightning) *burst forth* over the southern wilderness and the tempest raises a whirling and writhing dust-storm, the worshipper is reminded of the wind and fire that accompanied Elijah's revitalizing encounter with God in the same region (1 Kings 19: 11f.) or the thunder and lightning at his appearance on Mount Sinai (Exod. 19: 16). In this connection it is perhaps also significant that in Acts 2: 1–4 wind and fire were attendant upon the coming of the Spirit at Pentecost, the feast for which this became the appointed psalm in later Judaism.

9. Fourth, as the thunder causes premature birth amongst the animals, so God's *voice* evokes a spontaneous outburst of praise, *and in his temple all cry, 'Glory!'*. Hence the worship of earth becomes united with the song of the angels in the temple of heaven (verses 1–2). The psalmist may have in mind a pic-

ture of the temple crowded at festival time, which is perhaps
the occasion when this psalm was originally used in ancient
Israel.

10–11. The calm after the storm. The voice of God may be
terrible, but it speaks peace and blessing to his people.

10. *The LORD is king* because he has conquered *the flood*
(see on verse 3). The Hebrew word here is used elsewhere
only in Gen. 6–11 of Noah's flood. The storm has reminded
the poet of the supreme occasion when the destructive forces
of the cosmic sea were unleashed on earth, but also the occasion that supremely exhibited God's kingship and his mercy
that are *for ever* (Gen. 9: 8–17).

11. This powerful God of the universe is also the God of
his people, bound to them by the obligations he has laid on
himself in his covenant. Herein lies their confidence and their
hope of *peace*. ✵

JOY COMES IN THE MORNING

30

1   I will exalt thee, O LORD;
        thou hast lifted me up
    and hast not let my enemies make merry over me.
2   O LORD my God, I cried to thee and thou didst heal me.
3   O LORD, thou hast brought me up from Sheol
        and saved my life as I was sinking into the abyss.[a]
4   Sing a psalm to the LORD, all you his loyal servants,
        and give thanks to his holy name.
5   In his anger is disquiet, in his favour there is life.
    Tears may linger at nightfall,
        but joy comes in the morning.

[a] and saved . . . abyss: *or* and rescued me alive from among those who
go down to the abyss.

Carefree as I was, I had said, 6
  'I can never be shaken.'
But, LORD, it was thy will to shake my mountain refuge; 7
thou didst hide thy face, and I was struck with dismay.
  I called unto thee, O LORD, 8
    and I pleaded with thee, Lord,*a* for mercy:
'What profit in my death if I go down into the pit? 9
Can the dust confess thee or proclaim thy truth?
  Hear, O LORD, and be gracious to me; 10
  LORD, be my helper.'
  Thou hast turned my laments into dancing; 11
thou hast stripped off my sackcloth and clothed me with
    joy,
that my*b* spirit may sing psalms to thee and never cease. 12
I will confess thee for ever, O LORD my God.

* In the Hebrew this psalm bears the title 'A song at the dedication of the temple', which is probably a later addition pointing to its use at the Feast of Dedication, *Hanukkah*, after the purification of the temple by Judas Maccabaeus in 164 B.C. (1 Macc. 4: 36–59). It is no longer possible to determine how it came to have this association, for the psalm itself is doubtless many centuries older and in content would seem unrelated to the theme of temple-dedication. It is an ascription of praise and thanksgiving which must originally have been compiled for use by one restored from distress. His was a spiritual torment, because his adopted life-style, in which there was little room for God, had proved to be joyless, purposeless and even death-like. But he had turned to God and was clothed with great joy. And so he praises God, calling on his fellow

[a] with thee, Lord: *lit.* with the Lord.
[b] my: *so Sept.; Heb. om.*

worshippers to join his song. The allusion to a night of weeping and the joy of morning in verse 5 shows that the psalm is suitable for use at the end of a night vigil (see p. 14, sect. C).

1-3. Praise and thanksgiving for restoration.

1. *I will exalt thee:* God is exalted when men lift up his praises and declare his blessing before their brethren. In this instance the blessing is that God has raised the psalmist from the depths of his trouble. The verb translated *lifted . . . up* can be used of drawing water from a well and suggests the same metaphor of rescue from the pit of Sheol as in verse 3. If this image is sustained, the *enemies* must be pictured as angels of death who have been cheated of their victim, though possibly representing human persecutors whose mockery has failed to break the psalmist's faith (see also on Ps. 5: 3).

2-3. *thou didst heal me:* the psalmist tells mostly of delivery from spiritual distress, of 'Tears' (verse 5) and 'dismay' (verse 7) turned into 'dancing' and 'joy' (verse 11). His anguish is so severe, perhaps even affecting his bodily health, that he likens his condition to being in *Sheol* or *the abyss* (cp. Ps. 6: 5). These synonyms for the world of death suggest his strong awareness of the absence of God and the consequent futility of his existence (see further on verses 5, 9).

4-5. He calls on the faithful to join his song of praise.

4. *his loyal servants:* the *ḥasīdīm*, those who are faithfully obedient to God's covenant demands and are the recipients of his love or *ḥesed* (see on Ps. 5: 7). Here the expression probably refers to fellow-worshippers, perhaps persons who have kept vigil with him or who have assembled for the morning sacrifice in the temple. *his holy name:* that is, God himself; literally 'the remembrance of his holiness'. God's name calls to remembrance all that he is and all that he has done.

5. *In his anger is disquiet:* some older translations read 'his anger is but for a moment', but the N.E.B. translation suits the parallelism better. *disquiet* expresses the deathliness of existence without God (verses 3, 9) in contrast to the fullness of *life* in his presence. *Tears* and *joy* illustrate the contrast fur-

ther. The psalmist's concern is clearly with his spiritual rather than his physical well-being, although one may affect the other, and since he regards his distress as a manifestation of God's *anger*, it must be partly a consequence of his own sin. *but joy comes in the morning:* just as darkness is dispelled by morning light, so sin and suffering must yield to God (see on Ps. 27: 1). The intervention appears to be sudden, but this is what the vigil psalms seek (cp. Ps. 17: 15).

6–10. He tells how he was brought to his knees pleading for God's help.

6. *Carefree:* that is, in a state of wealth and security. He felt self-sufficient and saw no need for God; he had virtually deified himself (cp. Deut. 8: 11–20; Luke 12: 16–21).

7. God brought him to see that his self-made security, his *mountain refuge*, was illusory. The N.E.B. suggests that he went through some kind of conversion experience, but the Hebrew is difficult and it is possible to translate 'it was thy will to set my feet on a strong mountain' (cp. the Authorized Version and the Revised Standard Version), implying that his security was spiritual and God-given from the start, but that it was withdrawn for a space when God hid his *face*, probably because of sin (verse 5).

9. *What profit in my death:* how do I profit, what advantage is there for me in this death-like existence? He recognizes the futility of his life without God (cp. verses 3, 5). *Can the dust confess thee:* praise is virtually impossible when the feeling of God's nearness is lost (cp. Ps. 6: 5).

11–12. He is filled with an overwhelming sense of joy and sings out God's praises.

11. He has exchanged beating the breast in lamentation for the festive dance, and has replaced clothing of penitence and mourning, *my sackcloth*, with the festal garments of *joy*.

12. *my spirit:* that is simply 'I'. The N.E.B. has slightly altered the Hebrew which reads 'glory' (cp. Ps. 16: 9), a term that is perhaps intended to convey some notion of the overwhelming nature of the worshipper's experience as God's

presence in glory clothes or fills him with a joy that spills over
in songs of seemingly endless praise. Cp. the similar experience
of the overflow of the Holy Spirit described in John 7:
37–9. ✳

I COMMIT MY SPIRIT INTO GOD'S KEEPING

31

1   With thee, O LORD, I have sought shelter,
     let me never be put to shame.
     Deliver me in thy righteousness;
2   bow down and hear me,
     come quickly to my rescue;
   be thou my rock of refuge,
     a stronghold to keep me safe.
3   Thou art to me both rock and stronghold;
     lead me and guide me for the honour of thy name.
4 Set me free from the net men have hidden for me;
     thou art my refuge,
5   into thy keeping I commit my spirit.
  Thou hast redeemed me, O LORD thou God of truth.
6   Thou hatest*ᵃ* all who worship useless idols,
     but I put my trust in the LORD.
7   I will rejoice and be glad in thy unfailing love;
     for thou hast seen my affliction
     and hast cared for me in my distress.
8   Thou hast not abandoned me to the power of the
       enemy
   but hast set me free to range at will.
9   Be gracious to me, O LORD, for I am in distress,
   and my eyes are dimmed with grief.*ᵇ*

       [a] *So Sept.; Heb.* I hate.
       [b] *Prob. rdg.; Heb. adds* my soul and my body.

136

My life is worn away with sorrow   10
    and my years with sighing;
strong as I am, I stumble under my load of misery;[a]
    there is disease in all my bones.

I have such enemies that all men scorn me;[b]   11
    my neighbours find me a burden,
    my friends shudder at me;
when they see me in the street they turn quickly away.

I am forgotten, like a dead man out of mind;   12
I have come to be like something lost.

For I hear many men whispering   13
    threats from every side,
in league against me as they are
and plotting to take my life.

But, LORD, I put my trust in thee;   14
I say, 'Thou art my God.'

    My fortunes are in thy hand;   15
rescue me from my enemies and those who persecute
    me.

Make thy face shine upon thy servant;   16
    save me in thy unfailing love.

O LORD, do not put me to shame when I call upon thee;   17
let the wicked be ashamed, let them sink into Sheol.

    Strike dumb the lying lips   18
which speak with contempt against the righteous
    in pride and arrogance.

    How great is thy goodness,   19
    stored up for those who fear thee,
made manifest before the eyes of men

[a] *Prob. rdg., cp. Sept.; Heb.* iniquity.
[b] I have . . . scorn me: *or* I am scorned by all my enemies.

for all who turn to thee for shelter.

20   Thou wilt hide them under the cover of thy presence
      from men in league together;
      thou keepest them beneath thy roof,[a]
      safe from contentious men.

21   Blessed be the LORD,
      who worked a miracle of unfailing love for me
      when I was in sore straits.[b]

22   In sudden alarm I said,
      'I am shut out from thy sight.'
      But thou didst hear my cry for mercy
      when I called to thee for help.

23   Love the LORD, all you his loyal servants.
      The LORD protects the faithful
      but pays the arrogant in full.

24   Be strong and take courage,
      all you whose hope is in the LORD.

＊ One of the surprising features of Hebrew poetry, well exemplified in this psalm, is its ability to express intensely personal sentiment in stereotyped words and formulae. The result is by no means artificial, but points to a rich, shared tradition of prayer in Israelite worship from which the poet can freely draw, thus ensuring that his composition is both personal and adaptable for use by other worshippers throughout the ages. This characteristic is particularly noticeable here in the opening verses which are almost identical with Ps. 71: 1–3 and in verses 9–13 which contain much that resembles the very personal poetic compositions in Jeremiah commonly referred to as his 'confessions' (see E. W. Nicholson, *Jeremiah*

[a] *Lit.* in an arbour.
[b] when . . . straits: *prob. rdg.; Heb.* like a city besieged.

1–25, pp. 111f., in this series; note that there is no evidence of direct borrowing and the psalm could be much older than Jeremiah's time). The structure of the psalm is also surprising because of the alternation of supplication and thanksgiving: prayer for help (verses 1–4), statement of confidence (verses 5–8), lamentation in distress (verses 9–13), appeal for vindication (verses 14–18), praise of God's goodness (verses 19–20) and concluding testimony before the congregation (verses 21–4). Some scholars have therefore thought that it must be composite or that it has been poorly constructed, but it is more likely that its complexity expresses the inner conflict that arises from the dilemma of faith (see on Pss. 9–10 and 13). The psalmist's suffering calls forth his pleas for help and his lamentation, but his knowledge of God's protecting presence upholds and strengthens him and evokes his expressions of confidence and praise. The interweaving of these two elements is a product of the tension between faith and experience in the life of the man of God.

1–4. The psalmist prays for help with expressions of confidence and commitment to God.

1. *With thee, O LORD, I have sought shelter:* see on Ps. 7: 1; the spiritual interpretation is perhaps more appropriate here. *in thy righteousness:* in faithfulness to your promises of protection (see on Ps. 5: 7f.).

2–3. *be thou my rock . . . stronghold . . . Thou art to me both rock and stronghold:* show yourself in experience to be what by faith I know you are already. For the titles, see Ps. 18: 2.

3. The sufferer's hope cannot lie in his own imperfect attempts to persuade God, but only in God's 'righteousness' (verse 1) and in his self-revelation (*name*), in the promises which he is *honour*-bound to uphold (cp. Ps. 23: 3).

4. He pictures his enemies as hunters who *have hidden* a *net* to trap him (cp. Ps. 9: 15).

5–8. As he commits himself in trust to God and thinks of his unfailing love, he knows the comfort and assurance of the divine presence.

5. *into thy keeping I commit my spirit:* whether these words are read, as traditionally, with what follows, or as in the N.E.B., with what precedes, they form part of an affirmation of confident trust in God and it is with this sense that Jesus uttered them in his dying breath (Luke 23: 46; cp. Acts 7: 59). It would seem, however, that the psalmist is hoping for deliverance from suffering and oppression in this life rather than committing himself to God's care in the next, but the belief that God 'will take me from the power of Sheol' (Ps. 49: 15) and will 'afterwards . . . receive me with glory' (Ps. 73: 24) makes Jesus' use perfectly legitimate. *my spirit:* that is, 'my life', or simply 'me' (see on Ps. 6: 3). *Thou hast redeemed:* or 'thou wilt surely redeem'; the perfect tense expresses the psalmist's absolute certainty that deliverance will come. After all, the LORD is *God of truth*, the God who is true to his promises (see on Ps. 25: 5).

6. *Thou hatest:* so the Septuagint; the Hebrew reads 'I hate', making this verse a solemn renunciation of other gods and a renewal of exclusive allegiance to the LORD (cp. Ps. 16: 4–5).

7. Having committed and rededicated himself to God, he need no longer fear. Since God's *unfailing love* (see on Ps. 5: 7), expressed in his covenant promises, is completely trustworthy, the suppliant has real cause to *rejoice and be glad*, even though he has not yet emerged from his *affliction* and *distress*.

8. Resuming the metaphor of verse 4, the psalmist now likens himself to a hunted animal *set . . . free to range at will. the enemy:* a collective term for all that oppresses the sufferer, be its *power* human (verse 11) or demonic (verse 13; see also on Ps. 5: 3).

9–13. As he renews his plea for help, he tells how he is worn out by his burden of grief. Scorned, shunned and abandoned by his friends, he feels as though he is surrounded by threatening, whispering voices.

9. *Be gracious:* an appeal for mercy without consideration of merit or justification. *my eyes are dimmed with grief:* the joy

of life has left him, his *distress* has taken the sparkle from his eyes (cp. Ps. 6: 7).

10. *sorrow* and *sighing* suggest emotional distress, whereas *disease in all my bones* means physical affliction. Also for *misery* the Hebrew reads 'iniquity', suggesting spiritual torment. But none of these pictures should be interpreted literally, for the language is stereotyped (cp. Pss. 6:6; 22: 14) and adaptable for use in different kinds of suffering.

11. At a time when he seeks sympathy, he finds only rejection. Men *scorn* him, either because they believe his God is impotent (Ps. 42: 3) or because they think his suffering is a sign of divine disfavour (see on Ps. 38: 12). Some find him an irksome *burden* and others *shudder* in abhorrence at the sight of his pain or disfigurement (cp. on Ps. 22: 8). These attitudes probably express fairly natural human reactions to his condition, especially in a society where men fear the curse of God and would hesitate to associate with one apparently under judgement. *I have such enemies that . . .*: this translation implies that his enemies have incited others to scorn; the translation in the footnote suggests that the scorn comes from the enemies themselves.

12. *I am forgotten*: that is, by his friends, though clearly not by his enemies; these words express the psalmist's own feelings of forsakenness. *like something lost*: the more usual translation is 'like a broken vessel', that is, like a useless pot no longer needed by anyone (cp. Jer. 22: 28).

13. Though the enemies continue to be human, they take on a more sinister, almost demonic quality. They are now an unseen multitude whose voices are heard *whispering* from all directions, inundating the sufferer's soul with *threats* full of hatred and murder. *threats from every side*: a favourite expression of Jeremiah's, see especially Jer. 20: 10.

14–18. Though his friends have let him down, he can still trust in God, and so he calls for blessing and for vindication in the sight of his foes.

14. With this statement he reiterates the declaration of trust and allegiance made in verse 6.

15. *My fortunes:* literally 'my times', every moment of my life. *in thy hand:* in God's power or under his control.

16. *Make thy face shine:* that is in blessing to restore health and joy (see Ps. 4: 6–7); contrast the 'alarm' experienced when God's presence is not felt (verse 22). It is in the context of reaffirmed commitment, as in verses 6–7, that the appeal to God's *unfailing love* is repeated.

17. Cp. Jer. 17: 18. The psalmist renews his prayer for vindication (verse 1). *the wicked:* those who do not walk in God's ways (Ps. 1: 1). *let them sink:* the Hebrew reads 'let them be silent'; *Sheol*, the final home of the wicked (Ps. 49: 13f.), is the land of silence (Pss. 94: 17; 115: 17) where their 'scorn' must cease for ever.

18. The worshipper himself is *the righteous*, not because he is sinless, but because he has committed himself to God, unlike the wicked who act in their own *pride and arrogance*.

19–20. With the vision of unfailing love before him he praises God for his goodness and for the protection he offers to the faithful.

19. *those who fear* God or show him reverence are the faithful. When they turn to him *for shelter*, as the psalmist himself has done (verse 1), they find an abundant store of *goodness*. But God's grace is not a private gift; it is *made manifest before the eyes of men* for the vindication of his honour (verse 3) and the strengthening of his people (verse 24).

20. Cp. Ps. 27: 5. *the cover of thy presence:* a compressed expression which, like the phrase 'the shadow of thy wings' (see on Ps. 17: 8), suggests both the complete protection and also the embracing warmth of God's personal presence. The same double notion is conveyed by the image of oriental hospitality contained in the parallel phrase *beneath thy roof* (cp. Ps. 23: 5f.).

21–4. The psalmist ends by sharing his testimony and encouraging the congregation to strengthen their trust in God.

21. The *miracle* is not that the psalmist's well-being has been suddenly restored, but that he once more knows the comforting nearness of God (verses 16, 22) renewing his trust and confidence (verses 5–8, 14). It would therefore be less misleading to translate 'who has taught me how wonderful is his unfailing love' (cp. the Authorized Version and the Revised Standard Version). Even in his suffering he now has assurance and hope, because he once more sees that God is faithful and will grant ultimate restoration. This knowledge in itself gives healing (cp. on Ps. 22: 1–3).

22. Faith brings assurance and the comfort of God's presence, but this can be shattered by the *sudden alarm* that rises inside when a man turns from God to view his distressing environment (Pss. 11, 12, 14); but even then God restores confidence when man turns again and calls to him *for help*.

23. *Love the LORD*, for 'perfect love banishes fear' (1 John 4: 18). *his loyal servants:* the *ḥasīdīm* (cp. Ps. 30: 4), for whom the only real ground of hope is God's *ḥesed* or 'unfailing love' (verses 7, 16, 21).

24. Man discovers through suffering how hard it can be to *hope . . . in the LORD* when all is not well, but repeatedly this psalm reminds the worshipper that God is faithful (cp. 2 Tim. 2: 13). It is therefore fitting that it should end with this exhortation. See further on Ps. 27: 14. ✳

HAPPY THE MAN WHOSE SIN IS FORGIVEN

32

Happy the man whose disobedience is forgiven,   1
  whose sin is put away!
Happy is a man when the LORD lays no guilt to his 2
  account,
  and in his spirit there is no deceit.

While I refused to speak, my body wasted away   3
  with moaning all day long.

4   For day and night
       thy hand was heavy upon me,
       the sap in me dried up as in summer drought.
5 Then I declared my sin, I did not conceal my guilt.
   I said, 'With sorrow I will confess
       my disobedience to the LORD';
   then thou didst remit the penalty of my sin.
6 So every faithful heart shall pray to thee
   in the hour of anxiety,[a] when great floods threaten.
   Thou art a refuge for me from distress
       so that it cannot touch me;[b]
7   thou dost guard me[c] and enfold me in salvation
       beyond all reach of harm.[d]

8 I will teach you, and guide you in the way you should go.
   I will keep you under my eye.
9 Do not behave like horse or mule, unreasoning creatures,
   whose course must be checked with bit and bridle.
10   Many are the torments of the ungodly;
   but unfailing love enfolds him who trusts in the LORD.
11 Rejoice in the LORD and be glad, you righteous men,
   and sing aloud, all men of upright heart.

⁎ This is a song of praise expressing the joy of forgiveness,
though in Christian tradition it is one of the seven 'Penitential
Psalms' (see p. 14, sect. C). The style is at times reminiscent of
wisdom teaching, as in the beatitudes of verses 1–2 or the
instructions of verses 8–11, but the language has a vitality of
its own that clearly reflects the living experience of the

[a] of anxiety: *prob. rdg.; Heb. unintelligible.*
[b] *Prob. rdg.; Heb.* him.
[c] *Prob. rdg.; Heb. adds an unintelligible word.*
[d] beyond . . . harm: *transposed from end of verse 9.*

psalmist and the sentiment it expresses is far from artificial. Verses 1–7 are a testimony to the blessedness and reality of God's forgiveness and protection, offered as a prayer of praise and thanksgiving. This must have been rehearsed before the assembled congregation, to whom the oracular instruction of verses 8–11 are addressed, probably by a priest. Traces of wisdom influence are often taken as a sign of late writing, but it is impossible to date this psalm.

1–2. The joy of forgiveness. *Happy:* more a cry of exuberant rejoicing than in Ps. 1:1. *disobedience . . . sin . . . guilt:* three different aspects of sin, namely rebellion against God, wandering from the way and crooked depravity. Likewise *forgiven . . . put away . . . lays* not *to his account* indicate three aspects of forgiveness, which in the Hebrew suggest that God lifts the burden, covers up the offensive sight and now holds nothing against the sinner. The use of these terms is probably governed by stylistic rather than doctrinal considerations. They simply represent three parallel or synonymous ways of expressing the fact of forgiveness, but the triplication suggests the thoroughness and completeness of the experience. *in his spirit there is no deceit:* this expresses both the precondition and the consequence of forgiveness: God pardons only if the worshipper's confession is sincere, and once forgiven the penitent feels cleansed from all deceit. These verses are cited in Rom. 4: 7f.

3–5. He testifies to his experience of forgiveness.

3. *I refused to speak:* at first he would not admit the truth about himself and repent. But his stubborn attitude only caused him to suffer from a tortured conscience which in its turn caused bodily languor. His *moaning all day long* was an expression, not of sorrow for sin, but of self-pity.

4. *thy hand:* here a figure of judgement or punishment (cp. Ps. 38: 2). *sap* symbolizes vitality; as a plant wilts for lack of moisture, so he became enervated and lost his zest for life.

5. *declared . . . did not conceal:* that is, not that he informed God of his sin, for God already knew and was punishing him, but that he decided to give up his deception and admit his

folly before God. The consequence was heart-felt relief, for God lifted *the penalty* (literally 'the guilt') *of* his *sin*; that is, his feelings of guilt were removed together with their physical and emotional effects.

6–7. He offers praise because he now knows the comfort of God's salvation.

6. *So:* because this has happened to me. He feels that his experience should serve to encourage *every faithful* worshipper to *pray* for and expect God's help in his *hour of anxiety* (Authorized Version, 'in a time when thou mayest be found'; the Hebrew is difficult). *when great floods threaten:* comparing the onslaught of distress with the raging torrents that storm down the Palestinian wadis in winter (cp. Ps. 42: 7). The description of God as *a refuge* (literally 'hiding-place') may partly reflect feelings of security that result from being in the temple (see next verse; cp. on Ps. 17: 7).

7. *enfold me in salvation:* the Hebrew reads 'enfold me with shouts of salvation', suggesting that his embracing sense of security is enhanced by the presence of worshippers encompassing him and praising God for his salvation.

8–11. Concluding oracle and priestly instruction.

8. The *you* is singular and must refer to the recent penitent; the *I* must be God who alone has the authority to speak in this fashion. This oracular promise, 'God will *guide* and look after you', is intended for the encouragement of the newly pardoned sinner, but would have a similar heartening effect on his fellow worshippers who are also addressed, as is shown by the plural form of the imperative in the Hebrew of the next verse; cp. 'you righteous men' in verse 11.

9. This is a summary of the teaching in verses 1–5 that it is better to submit willingly to God than to require the discipline of his 'heavy hand' (verse 4). If a man will not freely draw near to God, then he behaves like the *unreasoning creatures* that must be subdued by brute force. The N.E.B. has transposed the Hebrew ending of this verse to verse 7 where it is thought to suit the context better.

10. This verse summarizes the doctrine of the two ways (see more fully in Ps. 1) which is central to Israel's covenant faith (cp. Exod. 20: 5f.). It is noteworthy that the measure of judgement is not human virtue, but man's response to God's *unfailing love* (see on Ps. 5: 7).

11. *you righteous men:* the faithful (see on Ps. 1: 5). They are commanded to *Rejoice in the LORD*, for joy is of the very essence of worship (Neh. 8: 10; Phil. 4: 4). ✳

THE LORD'S WORD HOLDS TRUE, HE IS OUR HELP

33

Shout for joy before the LORD, you who are righteous; 1
praise comes well from the upright.
Give thanks to the LORD on the harp; 2
sing him psalms to the ten-stringed lute.
Sing to him a new song; 3
strike up with all your art and shout in triumph.
The word of the LORD holds true, 4
and all his work endures.
The LORD loves righteousness and justice, 5
his love unfailing fills the earth.
The LORD's word made the heavens, 6
all the host of heaven was made at his command.
He gathered the sea like water in a goatskin;[a] 7
he laid up the deep in his store-chambers.
Let the whole world fear the LORD 8
and all men on earth stand in awe of him.
For he spoke, and it was; 9
he commanded, and it stood firm.
The LORD brings the plans of nations to nothing; 10
he frustrates the counsel of the peoples.

[a] *So Sept.; Heb.* heap.

11   But the LORD's own plans shall stand for ever,
        and his counsel endure for all generations.
12 Happy is the nation whose God is the LORD,
        the people he has chosen for his own possession.
13   The LORD looks out from heaven,
        he sees the whole race of men;
14   he surveys from his dwelling-place
        all the inhabitants of earth.
15   It is he who fashions the hearts of all men alike,
        who discerns all that they do.
16   A king is not saved by a great army,
        nor a warrior delivered by great strength.
17   A man cannot trust his horse to save him,
        nor can it deliver him for all its strength.
18   The LORD's eyes are turned towards those who fear
        him,
        towards those who hope for his unfailing love
19   to deliver them from death,
        to keep them alive in famine.
20   We have waited eagerly for the LORD;
        he is our help and our shield.
21   For in him our hearts are glad,
        because we have trusted in his holy name.
22 Let thy unfailing love, O LORD, rest upon us,
        as we have put our hope in thee.

✳ This is a hymn calling the congregation to offer joyous
praise to God (verses 1–3) for what he is and does, firstly that
he is faithful to his word and, as creator and ruler of the
world, has the strength to uphold it (verses 4–11), secondly
that he sees man's needs and, as lord and protector of Israel, is

able, in a way that no earthly power is, to fulfil the hopes of
the faithful (verses 12–19). The psalm concludes with an
affirmation of trust and a brief prayer for continued favour
(verses 20–2). The structure is thus symmetrical, the beginning
and end expressing complementary aspects of worship –
jubilant, adoring praise and quiet, expectant dedication – while
the central portion falls into two equal parts on the themes of
God's faithfulness and his salvation. There is nothing to
indicate the date of composition.

1–3. The worshippers are invited to rejoice, give thanks and
sing.

1. This verse takes up the call with which the preceding
psalm ended. The *righteous* and *upright* are again the faithful.
praise comes well from them, indeed it is their duty and their
privilege, for they are 'the people he has chosen' (verse 12),
over whom he watches with protecting eye (verses 18f.) and
on whom his 'unfailing love' rests (verse 22).

2. *the harp* and *lute* are probably to be regarded as representative of all musical instruments used to accompany congregational singing. For a fuller list, see Ps. 150.

3. *a new song:* an expression of gratitude reflecting the inner
renewal of those who have experienced the transforming and
life-giving action of God (cp. Pss. 40: 3; 96: 1). *shout in triumph:*
the Hebrew word is sometimes used in connection with the
acclamation of God as king (cp. Ps. 47: 5).

4–11. The LORD's word is trustworthy; it is expressed in
creation and will stand for ever.

4. God's *word* and *his work* are virtually identical, for when
he speaks his will is done; he is God and his word does 'not
return . . . without accomplishing (his) purpose' (Isa. 55: 11).

5. *righteousness, justice* and *love unfailing* are used here as
synonyms to express the utter dependability of God's promises (see on Ps. 5: 7f.). Though his *love unfailing* embraces his
chosen people with a special intimacy (verse 18), it also *fills
the earth*, as it must, since it is inseparable from him (cp. Ps.
36: 5f.).

6. Creation is a common theme in the Psalter's hymns of praise, but here, as in Ps. 8, the psalmist's thoughts dwell especially on Gen. 1 where also God 'spoke, and it was' (verse 9 below). For him the universe is a tangible proof of the effective power of God's *word*, and hence of his ability to fulfil his promises to Israel (see further on Ps. 147: 15). *his command:* literally 'the breath of his mouth', but correctly interpreted by the N.E.B. as a synonym for his *word. the host of heaven:* the sun, moon and stars (Gen. 1: 14–19) likened to an army under God's command (Isa. 40: 26).

7. *the sea . . . the deep:* the cosmic waters that existed before God uttered his first creative word (Gen. 1: 1–2). According to ancient Hebrew cosmology, which was very different from our own (see on Ps. 24: 2), these waters were separated and partly stored above the solid vault of heaven (Gen. 1: 6–8), partly *gathered* into earth's oceans (Gen. 1: 9–10) and the subterranean abyss (Gen. 7: 11). Despite the immeasurable vastness of this cosmic sea, to God it is *like water* scooped up *in a goatskin* bottle (so most of the ancient versions) and kept *in his store-chambers,* later to be released as rain (Gen. 7: 12), just like the snow and the hail (Job 38: 22).

8–9. The sheer immensity of the universe engendered a sense of humility in the writer of Ps. 8, but here it is the majestic effortlessness of God's action that evokes the response of *fear* (reverence) and *awe,* which should also be the response of *the whole world,* since creation bears witness to his power 'through all the earth' (Ps. 19: 4).

10–11. *the LORD's own plans:* his purposes for his people and for all mankind expressed in promises that must *stand for ever* if his word is trustworthy and powerful. By contrast, *the plans of nations* cannot endure, for there is no power on earth that can thwart God's purposes (cp. Ps. 2).

12–19. Happy is Israel to have such a God, omniscient and almighty, as its protector.

12. *Happy:* both a statement of fact and a cry of joyous praise, as in 1: 1, though here the psalmist concentrates more

on God's action than on man's response (cp. Ps. 144: 15; Deut. 33: 29).

13–14. Cp. Pss. 11: 4; 14: 2, but here the theme that God *surveys . . . all the inhabitants of earth* is introduced to emphasize the unique privilege of Israel. *his dwelling-place:* that is *heaven* (cp. 1 Kings 8: 38), though 'Heaven itself, the highest heaven, cannot contain' him (1 Kings 8: 27).

15. God does not simply observe the earth in a detached way, for he created it and still *fashions* men's *hearts*. Somehow *all men* and *all that they do* must serve his purposes.

16–19. As earthly power is ineffectual to change the course of history (verses 10f.), so it can afford no protection, even to the mighty *king* or the strong *warrior*. 'all men alike' (verse 15) are subject to a will beyond themselves, but those *who fear* the LORD may expect his blessing and find in him a sure *hope* of deliverance (cp. Ps. 20: 7f.).

16. The belief that it is God's strength, not *a great army*, that gives deliverance is illustrated in the stories of battles won by Gideon (Judg. 7) and Jehoshaphat (2 Chron. 20).

17. *his horse:* cavalry and chariotry were the most formidable weapons of ancient warfare (cp. Isa. 31: 1).

18. *The LORD's eyes are turned:* that is in watchful care (cp. Pss. 32: 8; 34: 15). *fear him:* stand before God in the awe and reverence of true worship (verse 8; cp. on Ps. 25: 12). *hope for his unfailing love:* wait and look for the fulfilment of his promises to protect and bless his people (see verse 5).

19. *death . . . famine:* the context suggests that untimely death by military violence and privation in time of siege are meant, but this is hardly an exhaustive list. These are simply two typical examples of extreme urgency presented to illustrate the point that God is able *to deliver* in any circumstances. There is no notion of eternal life in this verse.

20–2. The people profess their faith and offer prayer for continued blessing.

20. *We have waited:* that is, in hope (verse 18) and trust (verse 21). *our help and our shield:* or 'the shield that guards us'

(cp. Deut. 33: 29), offering complete protection against all ills (cp. Ps. 28: 7).

21. *his holy name:* God's revealed character (see also on Ps. 20: 1). The faithful's trust is based, not on some vain hope (contrast verses 16f.), but on God's self-revelation in the lives and history of his people. Here they find ample ground for confidence and so their *hearts are glad.*

22. *Let thy unfailing love . . . rest upon us:* continue to support and protect us in accordance with your promises (see verse 18). This simple prayer gathers up the whole theme of the psalm, God's faithfulness to his word and his power to uphold and bless his people. ✱

TASTE AND SEE THAT THE LORD IS GOOD

34

1 I will bless the LORD continually;
  his praise shall be always on my lips.

2 In the LORD I will glory;
  the humble shall hear and be glad.

3 O glorify the LORD with me,
  and let us exalt his name together.

4 I sought the LORD's help and he answered me;
  he set me free from all my terrors.

5 Look towards him and shine with joy;
  no longer hang your*[a]* heads in shame.

6 Here was a poor wretch who cried to the LORD;
  he heard him and saved him from all his troubles.

7   The angel of the LORD is on guard
  round those who fear him, and rescues them.

8 Taste, then, and see that the LORD is good.
  Happy the man who finds refuge in him!

9 Fear the LORD, all you his holy people;

[a] *So Sept.; Heb.* let them no longer hang their . . .

for those who fear him lack nothing.
Unbelievers suffer want and go hungry, 10
but those who seek the LORD lack no good thing.
Come, my children, listen to me: 11
    I will teach you the fear of the LORD.
Which of you delights in life 12
and desires a long life to enjoy all good things?
Then keep your tongue from evil 13
and your lips from uttering lies;
turn from evil and do good, 14
    seek peace and pursue it.
    The eyes of the LORD are upon the righteous, 15
    and his ears are open to their cries.
The LORD sets his face against evildoers 16
to blot out their memory from the earth.
When men cry for help, the LORD hears them 17
and sets them free from all their troubles.
The LORD is close to those whose courage is broken 18
and he saves those whose spirit is crushed.
The good man's misfortunes may be many, 19
the LORD delivers him out of them all.
    He guards every bone of his body, 20
and not one of them is broken.
Their own misdeeds are death to the wicked, 21
    and those who hate the righteous are brought to ruin.

The LORD ransoms the lives of his servants, 22
and none who seek refuge in him are brought to ruin.

* Here the prayer of Ps. 25 finds its counterpart in a song of
joy. The two psalms are acrostics, but both lack a verse

beginning with *wāw* and have an extra verse at the end. They also exhibit a similar capability of division according to theme into three equal portions of seven verses each. So here, the psalmist opens by giving thanks for deliverance and inviting the faithful to share in his rejoicing (verses 1–7), he continues by encouraging others to 'fear the LORD' and thus experience his goodness and blessing (verses 8–14), and concludes by meditating on the justice of God and his constant nearness to the faithful (verses 15–21). Verse 22 aptly summarizes his faith. There is a title in the Hebrew which ascribes the psalm to David 'when he altered his behaviour before Abimelech who drove him away, and he departed'. The allusion must be to the occasion when David feigned madness before the king of Gath, though in 1 Sam. 21: 10–15 the Philistine king is called Achish. If this is not simply an instance of a copyist's error, Abimelech may have been a dynastic name. However, the psalm's artificial structure and its affinities with the wisdom literature (see comments on the text) may indicate a later date of composition. But the title does suggest that the psalmist believed this hymn, with its thoughts of God's goodness and protecting care, ideally suited for use on occasions of deliverance from danger, like that in which David found himself at the Philistine court.

1–7. He gives personal testimony to God's faithfulness and calls on others to share in his joy.

1. Verse *'ālep. bless:* both give thanks and adore. *continually* (literally 'at all times'), *always:* cp. 1 Thess. 5: 16–18: 'Be always joyful; pray continually; give thanks whatever happens.' *praise* and rejoicing in whatever circumstances are of the essence of a living faith (cp. Ps. 32: 11).

2. Verse *bēt.* The godly man *will* not *glory* or boast in himself, but only *In the LORD* (cp. Gal. 6: 14; contrast Ps. 49: 6). *the humble:* the faithful (cp. Ps. 25: 9).

3. Verse *gīmel. glorify the LORD:* no-one can make God glorious; he is glorified and *his name* exalted when men sing his praise and declare his blessings before the brethren.

4. Verse *dālet*. *I sought:* the 'one thing' the faithful seek is to enter the presence of God himself and there to find blessing and peace (Ps. 27: 4, 8). It would therefore be better to translate, not *the LORD's help*, but, as literally, 'the LORD'. *he answered me:* not with words only, but by setting *me free.*

5. Verse *hē*. The psalmist is saying 'I have cause to rejoice (verses 1–2), join me (verse 3); this was my experience (verse 4), you can enter into it too (verse 5).' *Look towards him:* with trust and confidence; cp. Ps. 27: 4: 'one thing I seek: . . . to gaze upon the beauty of the LORD', that is to enter his presence. Some manuscripts read 'they looked', suggesting the translation 'those who look to him will shine . . .', but the lesson is the same. *shine with joy:* reflecting the light of God's presence when he makes 'his face shine upon you' in blessing (Num. 6: 25; cp. 2 Cor. 3: 18).

6. Verse *zayin*. The psalmist reiterates that he can vouch for the truth of his statements from personal experience.

7. Verse *ḥēt*. *The angel of the LORD:* a picturesque characterization of the power of God protecting the faithful; contrast Ps. 35: 5–6 where this angel appears as his avenging power, a figure of terror to the ungodly. *fear:* stand in awe and reverence before. 'The fear of the LORD' (cp. Prov. 1: 7) is virtually a synonym for true religion.

8–14. He exhorts his fellows to seek God's blessing by living in his fear and faith.

8. Verse *ṭēt*. Cp. 1 Pet. 2: 3. *Taste, then, and see . . . :* well interpreted in the paraphrase of Ps. 34 by seventeenth-century hymn-writers, Tate and Brady:

> O make but trial of his love,
>   Experience will decide
> How blest are they, and only they,
>   Who in his truth confide.

Happy: see on Ps. 1: 1.

9. Verse *yōd*. *Fear the LORD:* see verse 7. *his holy people:*

see on Ps. 16: 3 where the same word is translated 'gods'. *lack nothing:* cp. Ps. 23: 1.

10. Verse *kap. Unbelievers:* a translation based on the observation of a similar word in Arabic, but the older English versions render 'young lions' (also Ps. 35: 17). That the faithful *lack no good thing* is not a statistically verifiable statement, but an expression of faith in the absolute trustworthiness of God, here confirmed by the psalmist's own joyous experience. The same doctrine is found in the teaching of Jesus (Matt. 6: 25–34).

11. Verse *lāmed.* Since such blessings are available to the faithful, men must be taught *the fear of the LORD* (see verse 7). The psalmist therefore casts himself in the role of teacher addressing his *children* after the customary fashion of the wisdom teacher in Prov. 1–8 (e.g. Prov. 4: 1).

12. Verse *mēm.* Verses 12–16 are cited in 1 Pet. 3: 10–12. *Which of you . . .:* this and the next verse should be read together with the sense, 'If you want to delight in life . . . then . . . (verse 13)'. *life:* not simply prolonged existence, but the joyous vitality of the presence of God (see Ps. 16: 11), hence characterized by the enjoyment of *all good things,* that is, God's blessings promised to the faithful (verse 10).

13. Verse *nūn.* The first part of his instruction is negative: cause no hurt to others, avoid malicious talk. On the power of the *tongue* to work *evil,* see Jas. 3: 2–12.

14. Verse *sāmek.* The second part is positive. *evil* and *good* are not simply deeds of malice and kindness, but two ways of life (cp. Ps. 1). The man who would be godly must *turn* decisively *from* his old way and *pursue* the new with single-hearted devotion, seeking to work for the *good* and the *peace* of mankind.

15–21. God is faithful and just, upholding the righteous and judging the wicked.

15. Verse *'ayin. The eyes of the LORD . . . his ears:* poetic symbols of God's vigilant care for his people and his readiness to respond to their prayers (cp. Ps. 33: 18). *the righteous:* the faithful (see on Ps. 1: 5).

16. Verse *pē*. God's *face* commonly signifies his presence, but the poet is also pursuing the human imagery used in verse 15. As the human features display the emotions, so God's face may reflect his love or his wrath. For the faithful who seek his presence there can be only a vision of goodness (Ps. 27: 8, 13), but God cannot look with the same approval on *evildoers*. *blot out their memory:* destroy them so utterly that even the memory of them is lost.

17. Verse *ṣādē*. *men:* literally 'they'. Several versions insert 'the righteous', but the psalmist's exhortations are aimed at encouraging men, presumably even 'evildoers', to become 'the righteous', to turn from evil (verse 14), look to God (verse 5) and make trial of his goodness (verse 8). His constant theme is God's willingness to hear any man who turns to him in sincerity.

18. Verse *qōp*. *courage* (literally 'heart') *is broken . . . spirit is crushed:* in Ps. 51: 17 the same vocabulary expresses sorrow and penitent humility. If such is also the intention here, though that is not evident in the N.E.B. translation, this verse may be read as a comment on the last, that none is beyond God's help so long as he seeks it with the right attitudes.

19. Verse *rēsh*. *The good man* is not exempt from *misfortunes*, but he will have God's help to face and surmount them.

20. Verse *shīn*. Even in the worst possible situations of physical torment or calamity God gives his protection. Perhaps the author of the fourth Gospel had this verse in mind, as well as Exod. 12: 46, when he wrote his account of the crucifixion (see John 19: 36).

21. Verse *tāw*. *Their own misdeeds . . . :* the boomerang effect of sin. But the Hebrew reads literally 'evil shall slay the wicked', which could perhaps suggest more direct punishment by God. *are brought to ruin:* contrast verse 22 where the same verb is used.

22. Concluding summary of the psalm's teaching. *ransoms the lives:* delivers from any troubles that could lead to untimely death. There is nothing here to suggest that the psalmist is

thinking of ultimate delivery from the power of death, as in
Ps. 49: 15 where the same phrase is used. ✳

RESCUE ME FROM MY ENEMIES

35

1   Strive, O LORD, with those who strive against me;
       fight against those who fight me.

2   Grasp shield and buckler,
       and rise up to help me.

3   Uncover the spear and bar the way
      against my pursuers.
      Let me hear thee declare,
       'I am your salvation.'

4 Shame and disgrace be on those who seek my life;
     and may those who plan to hurt me retreat in dismay!

5   May they be like chaff before the wind,
       driven by the angel of the LORD!

6 Let their way be dark and slippery
       as the angel of the LORD pursues them!

7   For unprovoked they have hidden a net[a] for me,
      unprovoked they have dug a pit to trap me.

8   May destruction unforeseen come on him;
      may the net which he hid catch him;
      may he crash headlong into it!

9   Then I shall rejoice in the LORD
       and delight in his salvation.

10   My very bones cry out,
      'LORD, who is like thee? –
    thou saviour of the poor from those too strong for them,

[a] *Prob. rdg., transposing* a pit *from this line to follow* have dug.

the poor and wretched from those who prey on them.'
   Malicious witnesses step forward;   11
     they question me on matters of which I know
       nothing.
   They return me evil for good,   12
     lying in wait*a* to take my life.
And yet when they were sick, I put on sackcloth,   13
   I mortified myself with fasting.
   When my prayer came back unanswered,
   I walked with head bowed in grief as if for a brother; 14
as one in sorrow for his mother I lay prostrate in mourn-
       ing.
   But when I stumbled, they crowded round rejoicing, 15
     they crowded about me;
   nameless ruffians*b* jeered at me
     and nothing would stop them.
When I slipped, brutes who would mock even a hunch- 16
     back
   ground their teeth at me.
   O Lord, how long wilt thou look on   17
     at those who hate me for no reason*c*?
   Rescue me out of their cruel grasp,
     save my precious life from the unbelievers.
   Then I will praise thee before a great assembly,   18
   I will extol thee where many people meet.
   Let no treacherous enemy gloat over me   19
     nor leer at me in triumph.*d*

[a] lying in wait: *prob. rdg.; Heb.* bereavement.
[b] nameless ruffians: *or* ruffians who give me no rest.
[c] *Line transposed from verse 19.*
[d] *See note on verse 17.*

20   No friendly greeting do they give
         to peaceable folk.
     They invent lie upon lie,
21 they open their mouths at me:
         'Hurrah!' they shout in their joy,
         feasting their eyes on me.
22   Thou hast seen all this, O LORD, do not keep silence;
     O Lord, be not far from me.
23   Awake, bestir thyself, to do me justice,
         to plead my cause, my Lord and my God.
24 Judge me, O LORD my God, as thou art true;
         do not let them gloat over me.
25 Do not let them say to themselves, 'Hurrah!
         We have swallowed him up at one gulp.'[a]
26 Let them all be disgraced and dismayed
         who rejoice at my fall;
     let them be covered with shame and dishonour
         who glory over me.
27   But let all who would see me righted shout for joy,
         let them cry continually,
         'All glory to the LORD
     who would see his servant thrive!'
28   So shall I talk of thy justice
         and of thy praise all the day long.

* It has been argued that this is the prayer of an accused man
facing trial, like Ps. 7 to which it is very similar in theme and
phraseology, but the metaphors are mixed and there is no
reason why it should not have been used in a more general
way. It is made up of three extended pleas for deliverance from

[a] *So Pesh.; Heb. adds* let them not say.

oppression, each concluding in words of praise. In Ps. 31, with which there are also several points of contact, supplication and praise alternate in a similar fashion, but in the present psalm the former element predominates and the theme is developed somewhat differently. Ps. 31 also lacks the strongly emotional expressions of anger and hurt and the protestations of personal innocence. This is a plea for justice, for vindication in the face of unwarranted enmity. The suppliant repeatedly claims that he has acted with integrity and with a genuine concern for his fellows. But they have responded with unaccountable bitterness. Indeed their vicious behaviour reveals more than personal enmity; it shows a hostility that is ultimately directed against God himself. Hence the psalmist does not hesitate to describe them with quasi-demonic pictures and to pray for their complete overthrow. They are God's enemies, but he is loyal and so looks to God for rescue, trusting in his promise of protection to the faithful. According to John 15: 23–5, Jesus also saw such 'hate . . . for no reason' (verse 17) as directed against his Father and as his own predestined lot. The date of composition cannot now be determined.

1–10. The psalmist prays for God's help against his enemies, using military and hunting metaphors, and anticipates the joy of deliverance.

1. *Strive:* or perhaps 'plead my cause', as it were in a lawsuit (cp. verse 23). Though the verb is more frequently used in the forensic sense, the N.E.B.'s translation suits the martial context of verses 1–3 better.

2. The description of the LORD as a 'warrior' (Exod. 15: 3) bearing weapons is entirely metaphorical (cp. Ps. 7: 12f.), and not to be compared with the anthropomorphic depictions of the war-gods of paganism. *shield and buckler:* such use of synonyms is a poetic device to convey the notion of completeness, here of complete protection.

3. *Let me hear thee declare:* feeling partly that God has abandoned him to the devices of his enemies (verse 22; cp. Ps. 71: 9–12), he seeks some reassurance, some tangible evidence,

perhaps in the form of an oracle, that God's protection has not been withdrawn. *salvation:* victory over his enemies, vindication of his trust and freedom of spirit to sing God's praise (cp. on Ps. 3: 2).

4. Cp. Pss. 40: 14; 70: 2; 71: 13. Continuing the military metaphor, he prays for the rout of his foes, picturing them as an army retreating in *Shame, disgrace* and *dismay.*

5. Helpless as *chaff before the wind* (cp. Ps. 1: 4), the enemy are *driven* headlong in ignominious and uncontrolled retreat. To them *the angel of the LORD*, who 'is on guard round those who fear him' (Ps. 34: 7), has become the terrifying and avenging power of God. The image is apt, considering the demonic portrayal of the enemy (verses 15–17, 19–21), but the language is poetic, and the parallelism suggests some degree of synonymity between the terms *wind* and *angel of the LORD*; cp. Ps. 104: 4, where the winds are described as God's 'messengers' or angels (the same word is used in the Hebrew).

6. The picture assumes a dimension of terror as he envisages the retreating army in *dark and slippery* places where confusion and stumbling hinder the speed of flight from the pursuing *angel.*

7. The metaphor changes; the enemy is now a hunter laying traps (cp. Ps. 7: 15). The slight rearrangement suggested by the N.E.B. is required by both the sense and the parallelism. *unprovoked:* cp. verses 11–16 where he complains that his kindnesses have been repaid with evil. It is because he can make this protestation of innocence that his plea in verses 23–8 is for justice rather than mercy.

8. May his mischief recoil upon his own head and prove self-destructive (cp. Pss. 7: 15; 9: 15; 57: 6).

9. Somewhat abruptly the psalm turns to rejoicing. The N.E.B.'s *Then* tries to soften the transition, but it introduces the notion, absent from the Hebrew, that the psalmist intends to reserve his praise for a thank-offering after his *salvation* (see verse 3) is complete; but the very utterance of verses 9–10 is in itself an offering of praise and is perhaps best regarded as an

act of faith and an expression of trust in the midst of suffering (cp. on Ps. 13 : 5). To *rejoice in the LORD* is to offer true worship (Ps. 32 : 11).

10. *My very bones:* his bodily frame, through which there runs a thrill of joy in God's presence (cp. Ps. 51 : 8). *who is like thee?:* cp. Ps. 71 : 19; the LORD is incomparable in power and righteousness, and therefore a strong and trustworthy *saviour. the poor:* the godly man who lacks the protection from the buffeting of society that wealth affords (see on Ps. 9 : 12).

11–18. His suffering is made doubly bitter by the ingratitude of those for whom he had shown sympathy in the past, for they now repay him with mockery and insult.

11. The metaphoric setting is now the law-court, with the psalmist in the dock called to account for crimes about which he claims to have no knowledge (cp. Matt. 26 : 59f.).

12. *evil for good:* ingratitude for kindness (verses 13–16; cp. Ps. 38 : 20). It is not personal enmity that evokes such a response, but a natural abhorrence of pain coupled with a belief that suffering is a sign of divine disfavour (see on Pss. 31 : 11; 38 : 11f.). *lying in wait to take:* the Hebrew reads 'bereavement for', likening his feelings of desolation at the loss of former friends to the forlornness of one mourning for the dead.

13. His display of concern was no mere affectation. He wore *sackcloth*, the garments of sorrow, as an outward token of sympathy, and he pleaded with God for their recovery *with fasting* and *prayer*.

13c–14. *When my prayer . . .:* his *grief* and *mourning* are not signs of defeat, but of intensified prayer (cp. 2 Sam. 12 : 16). Had the afflicted been his own *brother* or *mother* he could not have shown greater concern for them in their troubles. *unanswered:* literally 'to my bosom'. The text of verses 14–17 has suffered badly in transmission, but the N.E.B. introduces a minimum of emendation. *in mourning:* that is, in the dark attire of a mourner.

15. But now that he has met with misfortune (*stumbled*), he is surrounded by a faceless, jeering mob. There is no historical

situation in mind. The pictures are conventional (cp. Ps. 22: 6f., 16), portraying the nightmarish horror of desertion and betrayal in suffering. *nameless ruffians:* literally, 'smiters and I did not know (them)'. A slight vowel-change is required to obtain this reading; the Hebrew has 'smitten ones and . . .' (cp. the Revised Standard Version's 'cripples').

16. The N.E.B.'s translation depends on considerable vowel changes, but most commentators resort to emendation to make sense of the difficult Hebrew. A possible literal rendering would be 'With the profanest mockers of the circle, they grind . . .' and this would retain the image of the encircling, mocking crowd in verse 15. *ground their teeth at me:* in cruel hatred (cp. Ps. 37: 12).

17. The real stigma of his plight is that, despite all his pro-testations of innocence, he feels that the God whom he has acknowledged as his 'saviour' (verses 9–10) is simply looking on with indifference. He needs to see God's promised salvation in operation (verse 3), to see justice done (verse 23). *my precious life:* the only thing left to him (see on Ps. 22: 20). *the unbelievers:* the more usual translation is 'young lions' (see on Ps. 34: 10). There is no apparent reason why the transposed words should be thought to fit this verse better than their original context.

18. *Then:* not in the Hebrew (see on verse 9). *a great assembly . . . where many people meet:* the gathering of the faithful for worship in the sanctuary (cp. Ps. 22: 22, 25). The public offering of *praise* leads to an increase of faith and joy amongst the brethren (verse 27).

19–28. His enemies must not be allowed to gloat in triumph; God must act and execute justice so that the faithful may rejoice.

19. The transposition of part of this verse to verse 17 re-moves from this final section the statement, found in each of the other two parts, that the enmity directed against the psalmist is unmerited (verses 7, 11–12).

20. There is no clear reason why the N.E.B. should wish to

divide this verse differently from the Hebrew: '. . . *give*. But against *peaceable folk they invent* . . .' The conduct of his enemies is the exact opposite of that required from those who 'fear the LORD' (Ps. 34: 13f.).

21. They surround him with gaping mouths like ravenous monsters of the night (cp. Ps. 22: 12f.) and they show a perverted glee at his misfortune. These pictures of horror portray the sufferer's inner feelings of insecurity and fear rather than any actual activity of his contemporaries.

22. His persecutors may be 'feasting their eyes' (verse 21), but he knows that the LORD is also watching. He therefore resumes his prayer for intervention. *do not keep silence:* cp. verse 3, 'Let me hear . . .' *be not far from me:* see on Ps. 22: 2, 11, 19.

23. *Awake, bestir thyself:* see on Ps. 17: 15. He prays for *justice* because he claims that his suffering is unmerited (see on verse 7); contrast Ps. 6 where the plea is for mercy. *plead my cause:* perhaps resuming his prayer of verse 1 where the same Hebrew verb is used.

24. *as thou art true:* literally 'according to thy righteousness'. The expression contains the double notion that God is a reliable, indeed the only reliable judge, and that in his judgement he will be true to his promise to uphold the faithful.

25. See verse 21.

26. He prays for a reversal of fortunes in words that echo the theme of verse 4. He envisages his enemies *covered* (literally 'clothed') *with shame and dishonour*, the garments of defeat and humiliation (cp. Ps. 71: 13), very much in contrast with God the victorious creator who is 'clothed in majesty and splendour, and wrapped in a robe of light' (Ps. 104: 1–2).

27. *all who would see me righted:* not his friends, for they have betrayed him, but any who long to see righteousness prevail. Just as his vindication will bring disgrace to his enemies, so it will be a source of continual *joy* to the upright and faithful.

28. And finally, to the worshipper himself salvation will

provide an impetus to witness publicly to God's *justice* (verse
18) and will be a cause for the perpetual expression of grateful
praise. This concluding vow, like the closing words of the first
two parts of this psalm (verses 9–10, 18), is a profound expression of trust in God and hence in itself an act of praise, even
though the suffering is not yet ended. ✻

MAINTAIN THY LOVE UNFAILING

36

1   Deep in his*a* heart, sin whispers to the wicked man
     who cherishes no fear of God.

2   For he flatters himself in his own opinion
     and, when he is found out, he does not mend his ways.*b*

3   All that he says is mischievous and false;
     he has turned his back on wisdom;

4   in his bed he plots how best to do mischief.
     So set is he on his wrong courses
       that he rejects nothing evil.

5   But thy unfailing love, O Lord, reaches to heaven,
     thy faithfulness to the skies.

6   Thy righteousness is like the lofty mountains,*c*
     thy judgements are like the great abyss;
  O Lord, who savest man and beast,

7   how precious is thy unfailing love!
  Gods and men seek refuge in the shadow of thy wings.

8   They are filled with the rich plenty of thy house,
      and thou givest them water from the flowing stream
        of thy delights;

9   for with thee is the fountain of life,

[a] *So some MSS.; others* my.
[b] he does . . . ways: *prob. rdg.; Heb. unintelligible.*
[c] *Lit.* the mountains of God.

166

and in thy light we are bathed with light.

Maintain thy love unfailing over those who know thee,   10
    and thy justice toward men of honest heart.

Let not the foot of pride come near me,   11
    no wicked hand disturb me.

There they lie, the evildoers,   12
they are hurled down and cannot rise. '

---

* The theme of this psalm is one that is common to several in
the Psalter (see p. 14, sect. E), namely the contrast between the
godlessness of the wicked (verses 1–4) and the infinite goodness of God (verses 5–9). But there is no expression of anguish
at the apparent triumph of the wicked, as, for instance, in Ps. 10:
1–11. On the contrary, the mood is confident and trustful, as in
Ps. 1, and the psalmist's meditation flows naturally into a prayer
for protection (verses 10–11) culminating in a cry of victory
(verse 12). The language and thought of this psalm find many
parallels in the New Testament. The date of writing is unknown.

1–4. Godlessness leading to utter perversity.

1. *sin whispers:* literally 'oracle of sin'. These, the opening
words of the psalm in Hebrew, present a startling contrast
with the common Old Testament formula 'oracle of the
LORD' (usually translated 'says the LORD'). It is as though Sin
were a demonic figure that has become *the wicked man*'s god
(cp. Gen. 4: 7; Rom. 6: 12f.). *cherishes* is a misleading translation of the Hebrew 'before his eyes', since *fear* in this instance
is not reverence for God, as in Pss. 33: 8 or 34: 9, but dread or
terror inspired by God. The wicked man is not afraid of God's
judgements because for him God is simply irrelevant (cp. Ps.
14: 1). Paul cites from this verse in Rom. 3: 18.

2. Translation of this verse must depend partly on conjecture, and the N.E.B.'s interpretation, that the self-opinionated,
godless man will not accept correction even when it comes
(cp. Ps. 10: 5), is as good as any.

3. *wisdom:* the pursuit, not of intellectual erudition, but of

knowledge of God and his ways (cp. Ps. 14: 2). The Hebrew adds 'and goodness' and there is no apparent reason why it should be omitted by the N.E.B.

4. The godly man spends the silent hours of the night reading his scriptures (Ps. 1: 2), or recalling God's mercies and singing his praises (Ps. 63: 6f.), but the wicked man restlessly occupies himself with planning his crimes (cp. Mic. 2: 1). But the man who *rejects* God and so thinks that he is a free agent in fact becomes a slave to *evil* in the end.

5–9. Turning away from this picture of depravity, the psalmist enters into adoring contemplation of the immensity and the intimacy of God's love.

5. Cp. Ps. 57: 10; 108: 4. *thy faithfulness:* here a synonym of *thy unfailing love*, which is God's fidelity to his promises of protection (see on Ps. 5: 7). Like God himself, it is beyond measure and human comprehension; it *reaches to heaven . . . to the skies* (cp. Rom. 11: 33; Eph. 3: 18).

6. Comparison with *the lofty mountains* and *the great abyss* (the unfathomable depth of the sea) again suggests the immeasurable and inexhaustible nature of God's grace. His *righteousness* is his faithfulness to the obligation he has laid on himself in the covenant and his *judgements* are his interventions to uphold that obligation and bring about his promised salvation (*who savest*, see on Ps. 3: 2). All nature is included in his care, both *man and beast* (Ps. 104; Isa. 11: 1–9).

7. *how precious:* the psalmist's thoughts now turn from the vastness to the intimate and personal experience of God's love. It is for him a treasure beyond comparison (cp. Matt. 13: 44). It is a love that embraces the whole universe of created things, supernatural and human (*Gods and men*), and yet offers the warmth of security that a fledgeling knows as it shelters under its mother's *wings* (cp. Ps. 17: 8).

8. God is also the bountiful host (cp. Ps. 23: 5–6). The metaphor may derive from the sacrificial meal in which God receives the worshippers at his table, but it signifies blessings of a spiritual kind as the parallelism shows. *the flowing stream*

of thy delights is a phrase rich with spiritual implications. The Hebrew word for *delights*, '*ēden*, calls to mind the primaeval Eden from which there also flowed a river to water the garden (Gen. 2: 10). Furthermore, it was part of Israel's and later the Christian Church's hope that this life-giving stream would flow from the temple or the throne of God himself (Ezek. 47: 1–12; Rev. 22: 1f.). The river therefore represents God's original purpose and man's ultimate hope that the 'life' of God (verse 9) should flow over the earth bringing health and joy to mankind. According to John 4: 8–15; 7: 37–9, Jesus used the same symbols when he invited men to drink of the 'living water' that he provides.

9. *fountain of life:* cp. Jer. 2: 13, where God as the 'spring of living water' is contrasted with false gods that are leaking cisterns. When the *light* of God's presence (Ps. 4: 6) falls on the faithful, he is *bathed with* (literally 'sees') the *light* of divine blessing and knows overflowing happiness (Ps. 4: 7).

10–12. The psalmist's praise and adoration gives him the strength to pray with assurance of victory.

10. Firstly, he asks that the *love unfailing* and *justice*, which he so highly esteems (verses 5f.), be maintained toward the community of the faithful.

11. Secondly, he prays for personal protection from 'the wicked man' of verses 1–4 who might arrogantly 'trample upon the poor' (Amos 5: 11, Revised Standard Version) or seize his property and drive (*disturb*) him from his home (Mic. 2: 2).

12. *There:* the scene is one viewed with the eye of faith and portrays the overthrow of *the evildoers* at the appearing of God (cp. Ps. 14: 5). Their end will be final, for they *cannot rise.* ✻

COMMIT YOUR LIFE TO THE LORD

37

✻ This psalm is like Ps. 9–10 in that it is an acrostic and its theme is the contrasting fates of the wicked and the godly, but unlike it in that it contains no cry of distress in the face of oppression and offers no prayer to God. Like Ps. 1 it is addressed to men, not to God. In the manner of the wisdom literature, it gives instruction as from an elderly sage (verse 25) in twenty-two proverbs, alphabetically arranged. This style of writing is often taken to indicate a post-exilic date. But its theme is recompense and retribution and that could have been topical at any stage in Israel's history, for the doctrine of just rewards and punishments undergirds the Old Testament's legal, prophetic and historical teaching as well as its proverbial tradition. It must have caused serious problems for the Israelite in every age, particularly when he saw the wicked prosper and the godly suffer, for he did not have a sufficiently developed notion of a life hereafter to conceive of retribution beyond the grave. Hence the divorce between creed and experience could evoke an anguished 'Why?' (Ps. 10: 1, 13) or result in near loss of faith (Ps. 73: 13f.). As a solution to the problem of human injustice and suffering the doctrine is inadequate, as Job discovered. But Ps. 37 is not a reasoned doctrinal statement; it is a call to trust (verses 3, 5), commitment (verse 5) and expectant hope (verses 7, 9, 34). Like the beatitudes of Matt. 5: 3-12, it presents a basis for living in complete dependence on and faith in God, rather than for understanding the mechanics of the universe. The ultimate lesson Job learned was that it is not in a theology, but in the experience of God's presence, that man finds peace and understanding (Job 42: 5), and this is achieved through faith, not by human reasoning. Ps. 37 invites men to have this faith. For the purposes of this commentary the psalm has been divided into convenient sections, but there is no marked division of thought and it should be read as a continuous whole. *

1   Do not strive to outdo the evildoers
       or emulate those who do wrong.
2   For like grass they soon wither,

and fade like the green of spring.
Trust in the LORD and do good;   3
settle in the land and find safe pasture.

Depend upon the LORD,   4
and he will grant you your heart's desire.

Commit your life to the LORD;   5
trust in him and he will act.

He will make your righteousness shine clear as the day 6
and the justice of your cause like the sun at noon.

Wait quietly for the LORD, be patient till he comes;   7
do not strive to outdo the successful
nor envy him who gains his ends.

Be angry no more, have done with wrath;   8
strive not to outdo in evildoing.

For evildoers will be destroyed,   9
but they who hope in the LORD shall possess the land.

A little while, and the wicked will be no more;   10
look well, and you will find their place is empty.

But the humble shall possess the land   11
and enjoy untold prosperity.

⋆ 1–11. The psalmist calls for trust in God.

1. Stanza *'ālep*. Cp. Prov. 24: 19. *Do not strive to outdo:*
literally, 'do not become heated about'. The man of God must
'Wait quietly for the LORD, be patient' and not become heated
with envy and fits of rage (verse 7; cp. Gal. 5: 20, 22). It is the
prosperity of *those who do wrong* that arouses envy and entices
the faithful to *emulate* them (Ps. 73: 2f., 10).

2. *grass . . . green of spring:* common symbols of that which
is transient and perishable (cp. Ps. 90: 5f.; Isa. 40: 6–8).

3. Stanza *bēt*. *Trust in the LORD:* that is instead of emulating
wrongdoers as if they were God (verse 1). *the land:* the place of
God's promised blessing for his people, historically the land of

Israel, but the blessing was always more than territorial possession (cp. Deut. 28: 1–14), and users of this psalm in places far removed from Palestine in post-exilic times would doubtless have interpreted this verse in terms of the spiritual aspects of the promise. Since these are obtainable only by obedient trust, the invitation to *settle in the land* may be compared to the invitation extended to the faithful servant in Matt. 25: 23: 'enter into the joy of your master' (Revised Standard Version).

4. Cp. Matt. 6: 33: 'Set your mind on God's kingdom and his justice before everything else, and all the rest will come to you as well.' *Depend upon:* more commonly translated 'delight in', characterizing the nature of the experience of dependence as one of joy (cp. Ps. 4: 7).

5. Stanza *gīmel. Commit:* literally, 'roll', as though getting rid of a burden (cp. 1 Pet. 5: 7). Wherever there is *trust*, God will *act*, but where it is lacking, his working is inhibited (Jas. 1: 5–8; Matt. 13: 58).

6. The *righteousness* of the faithful and *the justice of* their *cause* is obscured in this present age, but the psalmist reaffirms that God will honour his promises and openly vindicate his people. For the simile, cp. Job 11: 17; Matt. 13: 43.

7. Stanza *dālet. Wait quietly:* literally, 'be silent'. Since the solution to man's problems will come from God alone, the heated, feverish activity that arises from insecurity (verse 1) must give way to a positive attitude of *patient* and trustful waiting for the LORD. *the successful . . . who gains his ends,* that is by wicked scheming.

8. Stanza *hē.* The warning of verses 1–2 is now reiterated. The suffering of the righteous may lead to anger and *wrath* when he contrasts his lot with that of the prosperous wicked, but his indignation only shows his lack of trust in God and may encourage him to join them *in evildoing.*

9. Just as the nations who lived in Canaan before the conquest were *destroyed* (literally 'cut off') that Israel might *possess the land,* so the *evildoers will be destroyed* that the faithful may enjoy their inheritance (see verse 3).

10. Stanza *wāw*, expanding on verses 8–9. Despite all their prosperity, *the wicked will* soon *be no more* (cp. verse 36). *their place:* their abode.

11. Cp. Matt. 5: 5. *the humble,* the godly, who is now afflicted and poor (see on Ps. 9: 12), will see a reversal of conditions. *untold prosperity:* not just material wealth, but bodily and spiritual well-being that comes from God (cp. on verse 3). ✻

The wicked mutter against the righteous man	12
and grind their teeth at the sight of him;	
the Lord shall laugh at them,	13
for he sees that their time is coming.	
The wicked have drawn their swords	14
and strung their bows	
to bring low the poor and needy	
and to slaughter honest men.	
Their swords shall pierce their own hearts	15
and their bows be broken.	
Better is the little which the righteous has	16
than the great wealth of the wicked.	
For the strong arm of the wicked shall be broken,	17
but the LORD upholds the righteous.	
The LORD knows each day of the good man's life,	18
and his inheritance shall last for ever.	
When times are bad, he shall not be distressed,	19
and in days of famine he shall have enough.	
But the wicked shall perish,	20
and their children shall beg their bread.[a]	
The enemies of the LORD, like fuel in a furnace,[b]	
are consumed in smoke.	

[a] *Line transposed from verse 25.*
[b] like . . . furnace: *prob. rdg.; Heb.* like the worth of rams.

✻ 12–20. To encourage the faithful in their response to his call for commitment and faith, the psalmist reminds them that the decreed destiny of the wicked is destruction, but the LORD upholds the righteous.

12. Stanza *zayin*. *mutter . . . grind their teeth:* in fanatical hatred. *The wicked*, being the persecutors of God's people and therefore the rebellious enemies of God (Ps. 1: 1), are commonly depicted in the psalms as arrogant, utterly reprobate and even cruel.

13. *the LORD shall laugh:* (cp. Ps. 2: 4) because the futile arrogance of the wicked is so ridiculous. They reckon God to be powerless (Pss. 14: 1; 36: 1), but it is they who are impotent. *their time* of reckoning and judgement is at hand and is inevitable.

14. Stanza *ḥēt*. *swords . . . bows:* used metaphorically to symbolize oppression, but in a corrupt society this would often take the form of physical violence.

15. Sin ultimately recoils upon the sinner and destroys him (cp. Ps. 7: 16).

16. Stanza *ṭēt*. *great wealth* could be a sign of divine favour (cp. verse 11; Job 42: 9f.), but poverty is more blessed than ill-gotten riches (cp. Luke 6: 20–6).

17. True wealth is durable. The power *of the wicked* (his *strong arm*) has no permanence, but the power of *the righteous* is *the LORD* who *upholds* him and so cannot *be broken*.

18. Stanza *yōd*. *The LORD knows each day:* he is concerned about our daily needs as well as our ultimate destiny (cp. Matt. 6: 8, 11). There is durability in the blessing *the good man* secures. It passes to his children and is reflected in their lives, whereas the heritage bequeathed by the wicked is death and destruction (verses 28, 38).

19. Cp. Matt. 6: 25–34. God's provision for the faithful is witnessed repeatedly in biblical history; for example, Elijah was fed miraculously *in days of famine* (1 Kings 17: 1–16).

20. Stanza *kap*. *like fuel in a furnace:* this rendering is based on emendation. The Hebrew may be translated 'like the best

of the he-lambs' (cp. Authorized Version), a simile from the consumption of the sacrifice on the altar, or 'like the glory of the pastures' (Revised Standard Version), suggesting comparison with the greenery of spring around Jerusalem, all traces of which are gone by summer (cp. Matt. 6: 30). *consumed in smoke:* a common figure of that which is ephemeral (Pss. 68: 2; 102: 3). ✻

The wicked man borrows and does not pay back,	21
but the righteous is a generous giver.	
All whom the LORD has blessed shall possess the land,	22
and all who are cursed by him shall be destroyed.	
It is the LORD who directs a man's steps,	23
he holds him firm and watches over his path.	
Though he may fall, he will not go headlong,	24
for the LORD grasps him by the hand.	
I have been young and am now grown old,	25
and never have I seen a righteous man forsaken.[a]	
Day in, day out, he lends generously,	26
and his children become a blessing.	
Turn from evil and do good,	27
and live at peace for ever;	
for the LORD is a lover of justice	28
and will not forsake his loyal servants.	
The lawless[b] are banished for ever	
and the children of the wicked destroyed.	
The righteous shall possess the land	29
and shall live there at peace for ever.	
The righteous man utters words of wisdom	30
and justice is always on his lips.	

[a] *See note on verse 20.*
[b] *The lawless: prob. rdg., cp. Sept.; Heb. om.*

31   The law of his God is in his heart,
        his steps do not falter.

✻ 21-31. In contrast to the worthlessness of the wicked, there
is an abiding value in the way of the righteous. Their reward
is sure; it is with God.

21. Stanza *lāmed*. There is no suggestion here that *The
wicked man* is poor or *the righteous* wealthy, though verse 22
could imply that they will become so. It is his dishonest and
oppressive ways, not his wealth, that brings judgement on the
wicked (verses 7, 12-16). In contrast, the faithful often show
extreme generosity, even in the depths of poverty (cp. 2 Cor.
8: 1-4).

22. Cp. verses 9-11. Enrichment and ruin are not brought
about by the working of an impersonal principle in nature,
but by the blessing and curse of God that are written into his
covenant with his people (Deut. 28; 30: 15-20).

23. Stanza *mēm*. Cp. Ps. 1: 6 and Prov. 16: 9. *watches over*:
better 'delights in'. As a man depends upon the LORD, so he
finds guidance, protection and bountiful care (verse 4; Matt.
6: 33).

24. The faithful may certainly experience hardship and
suffering in his life, but even then God *grasps him by the hand*
to steady him and protect him from *headlong* ruin (cp. Isa. 41:13).

25. Stanza *nūn. never . . . forsaken*: it is the repeated theme
of this psalm that the faithful do suffer at the hands of the
wicked, but the psalmist has just affirmed in verse 24 that God
upholds his servants at such times. He now reinforces this
affirmation by appealing to lifelong experience (cp. Job 8: 8).

26. See verse 21. *his children become a blessing* to society
because they are reared in an upright and generous home.

27. Stanza *sāmek*. The psalmist renews his call for commitment to the ways of God (verses 1-8). *live at peace*: on the
imperative form, see verse 3. *for ever*: not to eternity, but in
security, without fear of being uprooted. There is no notion
of eternal life contained in this verse or verse 29. In both places

the N.E.B. suitably introduces the words *at peace* to convey
this impression of security.

28a–b. lover of justice: God is himself just and demands justice of *his loyal servants. will not forsake:* see verse 25.

28c–d. Stanza *'ayin.* Cp. verses 9–10. *The lawless are
banished:* an emended reading supported by the Septuagint;
the Hebrew, which reads 'they (his loyal servants) will be
preserved', appears to lack the opening word required by the
alphabetic structure.

29. live . . . at peace for ever: see verse 27.

30. Stanza *pē.* True *wisdom* is grounded in the fear (reverence) of the LORD (Prov. 1: 7) and since *The righteous man*
lives in a right relationship with God, wisdom flows from his
mouth (Prov. 10: 31).

31. *The law of his God is in his heart,* where God wants it to
be (Deut. 6: 6; Jer. 31: 33). It is not sufficient to have the law
of God written in a book (2 Cor. 3: 3, 6), it must become the
governing principle and the inner motivation of a man's
whole life. Then *his steps* are firm because he walks with God
(contrast Ps. 73: 2). ✳

The wicked watch for the righteous man	32
and seek to take his life;	
but the LORD will not leave him in their power	33
nor let him be condemned before his judges.	
Wait for the LORD and hold to his way;	34
he will keep you*ᵃ* safe from wicked men*ᵇ*	
and will raise you to be master of the land.	
When the wicked are destroyed, you shall be there to see.	
I have watched a wicked man at his work,	35
rank as a spreading tree in its native soil.	
I*ᶜ* passed by one day, and he was gone;	36

[a] *Prob. rdg.; Heb.* them.
[b] he will . . . wicked men: *transposed from verse 40.*
[c] *So Sept.; Heb.* He.

I searched for him, but he could not be found.

37 Now look at the good man, watch him who is honest,
    for the man of peace leaves descendants;

38   but transgressors are wiped out one and all,
      and the descendants of the wicked are destroyed.

39 Deliverance for the righteous comes from the LORD,
    their refuge in time of trouble.

40   The LORD will help them and deliver them;[a]
    he will save them because they seek shelter with him.

✻ 32-40. Reiterating his exhortation to wait for the LORD,
the psalmist draws a final contrast between the fate of the
wicked and the recompense of the faithful.

32. Stanza *ṣādē*. *seek to take his life:* by judicial as well as by
violent means (verse 33. See also on Ps. 10: 8).

33. *will not leave him:* cp. verses 25, 28. Release from the
power of the courts is instanced several times in the New
Testament; cp. Acts 4: 1–22.

34. Stanza *qōp*. *Wait:* that is in trust and expectant hope
(cp. Ps. 27: 14). On God's *way*, see Ps. 1: 1–3, 6. *you shall be
there to see:* not to gloat vindictively over the fate of *the
wicked*, but to witness the fulfilment of God's promises. It is
consideration of the metre that has prompted the N.E.B.
translators to transpose the second clause of verse 40 to this
point, but the reordering is of questionable value and what is
transposed has also to be emended to suit its new context.

35. Stanza *rēsh*. In a style reminiscent of Job 5: 3–4, the
psalmist renews his appeal to experience (cp. verse 25). The
tree simile suggests security and opulence, but unlike the tree
in Ps. 1: 3, which was 'planted' and watered by God, this one
is *in its native soil* without protection against drought. The
wicked man's security is illusory.

[a] *See note on verse 34.*

37. Stanza *shīn. the good man:* better, 'the man of integrity'. *the man of peace leaves descendants:* his destiny is not to be forgotten, lost in oblivion, but to leave an 'inheritance' (verse 18) and children that 'become a blessing' (verse 26).

38. The continuance of his name and family in future generations approximates to immortality for the ancient Israelite. Hence childlessness or the death of his *descendants* was a great disaster, virtually amounting to personal annihilation.

39–40. Stanza *tāw. Deliverance:* or 'salvation' (see on Ps. 3: 2). Since the psalm is essentially a call to renewed trust and commitment, the psalmist concludes with a word of encouragement, reaffirming that God will help and protect those who take refuge in him. The clause which the N.E.B. has removed to verse 34 adds emphasis to this concluding point. ✳

DO NOT REBUKE ME, BUT HASTEN TO MY HELP

38

O Lord, do not rebuke me in thy anger,   1
   nor punish me in thy wrath.

For thou hast aimed thy arrows[a] at me,   2
   and thy hand weighs heavy upon me.

Thy indignation has left no part of my body unscarred;   3
   there is no health in my whole frame because of my sin.

For my iniquities have poured over my head;   4
they are a load heavier than I can bear.

My wounds fester and stink because of my folly.   5

I am bowed down and utterly prostrate.   6

All day long I go about as if in mourning,
for my loins burn with fever,   7
   and there is no wholesome flesh in me.

[a] thou ... arrows: *prob. rdg.; Heb.* thy arrows have come down.

8   All battered and benumbed,
        I groan aloud in my heart's longing.
9   O Lord, all my lament lies open before thee
        and my sighing is no secret to thee.
10 My heart beats fast, my strength has ebbed away,
        and the light has gone out of my eyes.
11 My friends and my companions shun me in my sickness,
        and my kinsfolk keep far away.
12   Those who wish me dead defame me,
        those who mean to injure me spread cruel gossip
        and mutter slanders all day long.
13 But I am deaf, I do not listen;
        I am like a dumb man who cannot open his mouth.
14 I behave like a man who cannot hear
        and whose tongue offers no defence.
15 On thee, O Lord, I fix my hope;
    thou wilt answer, O Lord my God.
16 I said, 'Let them never rejoice over me
        who exult when my foot slips.'
17 I am indeed prone to stumble,
        and suffering is never far away.
18   I make no secret of my iniquity
        and am anxious at the thought of my sin.
19 But many are my enemies, all without cause,[a]
        and many those who hate me wrongfully.
20 Those who repay good with evil
        oppose me because my purpose is good.
21   But, Lord, do not thou forsake me;
        keep not far from me, my God.
22 Hasten to my help, O Lord my salvation.

[a] all . . . cause: *prob. rdg.; Heb.* living.

✻ This is the third of the seven 'Penitential Psalms' in Christian tradition (see p. 14, sect. C). The psalmist portrays his suffering, which he believes to be the consequence of his sin, in terms of the most appalling physical affliction (verses 2–10), rejection by friends (verses 11–12) and oppression by enemies (verses 19–20). But it must be obvious to any reader that no-one in the terrible condition he describes would be fit to recite this psalm as a prayer, let alone to compose it. However, much of the language and imagery is simply the stereotyped material of Hebrew lamentations and the poem itself, though not an acrostic like Ps. 37, is an artificial creation containing twenty-two verses, which is the number of the letters in the Hebrew alphabet. The psalmist's sin is never specified, his unfaithful friends and his enemies lack definition and his illness cannot be medically diagnosed. The psalm has been composed for general use at any time of inward or bodily suffering by the individual whose total commitment to God (verses 13–15) has evoked hostile criticism (verses 11–17, 19–20), and who is also conscious of his own sin as a cause of his distress (verses 1–10, 16–18). Apart from this consciousness of sin, his plight could be compared with the sufferings of Job, Jeremiah or Jesus. His prayer is that God will not desert him, but will forgive and come to his aid (verses 1, 21–2); hence the Hebrew text has the title 'to bring to remembrance' (cp. also Ps. 70), that is, to set the situation before God and ask for his help. The date of authorship is uncertain.

1–10. Chastised by God, he pleads for mercy and recounts his agony of soul and body.

1. In words almost identical with Ps. 6: 1 he prays for the alleviation of his punishment. It is only here and in the concluding verses that he directly petitions God.

2. God's chastisement is compared to pain inflicted by the piercing of his *arrows* or the pressure of his *hand* (cp. Ps. 32: 4). It is doubtful whether these parallel images signify anything more specific than punishment in general. God is pictured as an archer on several other occasions (cp. Ps. 7: 12f.).

3. *body* and *frame* are flesh and bones respectively. The parallelism suggests that both words are simply a poetic circumlocution for 'me', that is, me in the outer and inner man. God's *indignation* is here his just wrath provoked by *sin*, which itself leaves the psalmist without *health* (or 'peace'). While God's wrath attacks from without, his own sin torments him from within.

4. His sin is too great simply to be shrugged off; it is like an overwhelming flood or an unbearable burden.

5. *My wounds:* that is, stripes, inflicted as it were by God's lash in punishment for his *folly*. Sin is essentially foolishness (cp. Ps. 107: 17).

6. *bowed down and utterly prostrate:* as one doubled up and laid low by pain. That this picture is not literal, but metaphorical of an inner anguish caused by guilt, is suggested by the parallel comparison with a man going about in *mourning* garments, presumably betokening sorrow for sin.

7. *my loins . . . flesh:* the inner and the outer man, both of which suffer torment (see verse 3). The loins are the seat of procreative power and a symbol of strength and vitality. But his strength has been sapped by the internal *fever* of sin.

8. *benumbed:* better 'crushed'. The same verb is used of the broken bones and the broken spirit in Ps. 51: 8, 17. The verb translated *groan aloud* denotes the roaring of lions and here suitably suggests the magnitude of the anguish that issues from the sufferer's *heart*.

9. *lament:* the Hebrew could also be translated 'longing'; God knows all the psalmist's needs (Ps. 10: 17; cp. Matt. 6: 8).

10. As his heart races with the fever, the vitality leaves his body and his vision fails. He is approaching death. The picture appropriately describes one whose zeal for life has gone (cp. Ps. 6: 2–5).

11–22. Rejected by friends and despised by foes, he clings to his faith in God and renews his plea for help.

11. *sickness:* the Hebrew word may denote illness in general or some malignant skin-disease (Lev. 13–14). His friends cer-

tainly treat him as unclean, but the picture is metaphorical, for the use of this psalm is not restricted to persons with a bodily affliction.

12. What the psalmist regards as *cruel gossip* and *slanders* may be the suggestions of his former 'friends' and 'kinsfolk' concerning the nature of his sin. Somewhat like Job's comforters, their intention would be to determine the cause of his suffering so that appropriate punishment or remedy could be applied. There was certainly little room for love or pity in their theology (cp. Luke 10: 31f.), and doubtless they would have held that the psalmist's faith must be misguided before he had to endure such pain.

13. But he refuses to listen. He is only too conscious of his sin and believes that he is already being punished. Furthermore, he does trust in God completely, and so he offers no defence, but leaves the judgement to him, resigning himself to bear the insults in silence.

14. Unlike Job, he does not plead innocence and *offers no defence* (contrast Job 23: 4).

15. *I fix my hope:* or 'I wait'. Patient waiting and hope are inseparable and Hebrew uses the same verb for both. God is the psalmist's only hope and his *answer* will be both a refutation of the enemies' taunts and an act of saving intervention (verse 22; see on Ps. 27: 7).

16. He now gives a series of reasons why he hopes God will act soon. The first is that he has constantly prayed (*said*) that final victory be not granted to his enemies who exult over his suffering because they see in it a proof of God's displeasure. *when my foot slips:* a metaphor for misfortune of any kind.

17. The second reason why he seeks prompt intervention is that he is *prone to stumble*, or rather is on the point of total collapse. The situation is more serious than the N.E.B. suggests, and *suffering*, even death, *is never far away*.

18. Thirdly, his confession is a motive for God to act. He is not simply upset at being found out, nor is he merely reciting

a prescribed formula; he is deeply *anxious* and seeks to turn to a new life with God.

19. A fourth argument for speedy hearing is the number of his enemies. He has not provoked their malicious opposition (most commentators accept the reading *without cause*). He certainly knows that he is not faultless himself, but he is convinced that the enemies are wrong in what they say about him.

20. Finally, *my purpose is good*. It is for his loyalty to God and his care for his fellows that he suffers persecution.

21. As he began, so he ends with an appeal to God. By punishing him, God has in a sense already forsaken him, but not so irrevocably that he cannot ask for help (cp. Ps. 22: 1).

22. In these last words the psalmist expresses the urgency of his need (*Hasten*) and confesses his faith in God to save. Without faith in God to forgive and restore there can be no true repentance. ✻

MY HOPE IS IN GOD

39

1 I said: I will keep close watch over myself
    that all I say may be free from sin.
I will keep a muzzle on my mouth,
    so long as wicked men confront me.
2 In dumb silence I held my peace.
So my agony was quickened,
3   and my heart burned within me.
My mind wandered as the fever grew,
    and I began to speak:
4 LORD, let me know my end
    and the number of my days;
tell me how short my life must be.
5 I know thou hast made my days a mere span long,
    and my whole life is nothing in thy sight.

Man, though he stands, upright, is but a puff of wind,
he moves like a phantom;   6
the riches[a] he piles up are no more than vapour,
he does not know who will enjoy them.

And now, Lord, what do I wait for?   7
My hope is in thee.

Deliver me from all who do me wrong,   8
make me no longer the butt of fools.

I am dumb, I will not open my mouth,   9
because it is thy doing.

Plague me no more;   10
I am exhausted by thy blows.

When thou dost rebuke a man to punish his sin,   11
all his charm festers and drains away;
indeed man is only a puff of wind.

Hear my prayer, O LORD;   12
listen to my cry,
hold not thy peace at my tears;
for I find shelter with thee,
I am thy guest, as all my fathers were.

Frown on me no more and let me smile again,   13
before I go away and cease to be.

☆ The purpose of life is the theme of a number of psalms (see p. 14, sect. E), but always the psalmist's handling of this topic is more personal than philosophical (see introduction to Ps. 73). So here his presentation takes the form of a testimony and a prayer, relating his own involvement in the universal dilemma of human suffering. His own problem is two-fold. Firstly, he sees that suffering is not diminished by the effort to live without sin (verses 1–3). Secondly, he feels that the

[a] the riches: *prob. rdg.; Heb.* they murmur.

transience of man makes any attempt to improve his earthly lot futile (verses 4–6). In effect he has realized that a religion of human effort is one without hope, a mere humanism that deifies man, who is 'but a puff of wind' (verses 5, 11), in place of God. He therefore turns to God for help (verses 7–8), repenting of his folly (verses 9–11) and seeking a speedy restoration of joy (verses 12–13). It is often thought that the psalmist's problem has only arisen because he has no doctrine of a life after death, but it is doubtful whether such a doctrine would have made a great deal of difference to his prayer, which is not about ultimate recompense or the justice of God, but about a right attitude to God and the enjoyment of his presence in this life. Anyhow, it is only a misguided belief in life after death that sees in it the solution to the problem of evil here and now, a mere escapism. The date of this psalm's composition is a matter of conjecture.

1–3. In a time of distress he determined to redouble his efforts to be free from sin, but his agony only increased.

1. *myself:* literally 'my ways', that is 'my behaviour'. This verse reveals mixed feelings of fear and bitterness. There is no suggestion that the psalmist was tempted like Job to curse God (Job 1: 22; 2: 10) or his enemies (Job 31: 29f.), but knowing himself to be in the grips of an overriding emotion (verses 2–3), he was afraid that an unguarded word might add to his burden of *sin* and sorrow (see verse 11) or provide *wicked men* with an occasion for scorn. And so with bitter determination he refused to speak, presumably hoping that his attempts to avoid sin would secure God's favour, as well as avert derision. But this is a negative stance, a religion of fear, not faith.

2. All his efforts led nowhere and his troubles worsened. The total negativeness of his policy of *dumb silence* is more fully emphasized in the Hebrew which reads '*I held my peace from good*'.

3. *My mind wandered as the fever grew:* this translation implies that his prayer was the feverish raving of a sick man, but the Hebrew is perhaps better represented by the Authorized

Version's 'while I was musing the fire burned', suggesting the flaring of an exasperated passion that could no longer be restrained from verbal expression (cp. Jer. 20: 9).

4–6. He cries out in anguish; all human effort, all life seems so futile.

4. It is not intellectual knowledge the psalmist seeks, for he is well aware *how short* his *life must be* (verse 5). His question is rhetorical, a stylistic device to convey the depth of his agony and frustration. What he wants is not enlightenment, but an end to suffering (verse 8) and freedom to enjoy what time remains to him (verses 12–13).

5. Man's *life* is like *a mere span* of the hand, virtually *nothing* in the *sight* of God who is eternal. *though he stands upright* and so has the appearance of stability, he is no more durable than *a puff of wind*.

6. He is *like a phantom* or 'a shadow', fleeting and of no real consequence (cp. Ps. 73: 20). All his efforts to obtain some sense of security by piling up *riches* cannot alter this fact, for he has no control over these possessions when he has gone (cp. Ps. 49: 11, 17).

7–8. Confronted thus with failure and futility, he turns to God for help.

7. *And now, Lord, what do I wait for?*: this question sums up his sense of complete hopelessness. He now stands right where Job stood (Job 17: 15), but suddenly, and quite unlike Job, he reaches out for God with a *hope* that, in his dead-end situation, can be based on nothing other than the mercy of God himself.

8. *who do me wrong*: this represents an emended text and links the verse with the theme of the wicked, but the Hebrew reads 'my transgression' and there is no good reason why that should have been changed. What he seeks is deliverance not from the hands of men, but from the power of sin that holds him and is the cause of his suffering (verses 10–11). *fools*: the ungodly (see Ps. 14: 1).

9–11. In faith and penitence he seeks relief.

9. The contrast with verses 1–2*a* is obvious. No longer does he act in negative fear, but in positive faith. What was needed was not a change from silence to speech, but an inner change of heart. Formerly his dumbness had signified a grim struggle to save himself, but now a patient trust and resignation to the will of God in recognition that salvation *is* his *doing*.

10. *Plague me:* the Hebrew uses the same word as that translated 'my sickness' in Ps. 38: 11.

11. The three words for *sin* in verses 1, 8 and 11 are the same as those found in Ps. 32: 1–2, but they are probably used as poetic synonyms. *all his charm festers and drains away:* this line is more commonly rendered 'thou dost consume his beauty like a moth', giving a simile that describes the destructive power of God's anger.

12–13. Finally he pleads for hearing, protection and restoration.

12. *Hear . . . listen:* his prayer is for active help, not just for a sympathetic ear. *I find shelter . . . I am thy guest:* the two Hebrew words denote resident aliens, persons living more or less permanently in a country to which they did not belong. They were usually poor, they had no rights of citizenship and they depended much on the goodwill of the state and its inhabitants. Like an alien the psalmist can make no demands on God, but only entrust himself to his protection and care.

13. *Frown on me no more:* literally 'look away from me', an unusual phrase that must be interpreted as a prayer that God look no more in anger. *before I go away:* that is, to Sheol. *and cease to be:* death is the cessation of life, though not of all existence, but in Sheol man, cut off from the living and from God, ceases to exist in any fashion known on this earth (see on Ps. 6: 5). ✳

40

I waited, waited for the LORD,   1
he bent down to me and heard my cry.
He brought me up out of the muddy pit,   2
    out of the mire and the clay;
  he set my feet on a rock
    and gave me a firm footing;
and on my lips he put a new song,   3
    a song of praise to our God.
  Many when they see will be filled with awe
    and will learn to trust in the LORD:
    happy is the man   4
  who makes the LORD his trust,
and does not look to brutal and treacherous men.
  Great things thou hast done,   5
    O LORD my God;
  thy wonderful purposes are all for our good;
    none can compare with thee;
  I would proclaim them and speak of them,
    but they are more than I can tell.
If thou hadst desired sacrifice and offering   6
    thou wouldst have given me ears to hear.
If thou hadst asked for whole-offering and sin-offering
    I would have said, 'Here I am.'[a]   7
My desire is to do thy will, O God,   8
    and thy law is in my heart.
In the great assembly I have proclaimed what is right,   9
  I do not hold back my words,

[a] *Prob. rdg.; Heb. adds* in a scroll of a book it is prescribed for me.

as thou knowest, O LORD.

10   I have not kept thy goodness hidden in my heart;
    I have proclaimed thy faithfulness and saving power,
      and not concealed thy unfailing love and truth
        from the great assembly.

11   Thou, O LORD, dost not withhold
      thy tender care from me;
    thy unfailing love and truth for ever guard me.

12   For misfortunes beyond counting
      press on me from all sides;
      my iniquities have overtaken me,
      and my sight fails;
    they are more than the hairs of my head,
      and my courage forsakes me.

13[a] Show me favour, O LORD, and save me;
      hasten to help me, O LORD.

14   Let those who seek to take my life
    be put to shame and dismayed one and all;
   let all who love to hurt me shrink back disgraced;

15   let those who cry 'Hurrah!' at my downfall
    be horrified at their reward of shame.

16   But let all those who seek thee
      be jubilant and rejoice in thee;
   and let those who long for thy saving help ever cry,
      'All glory to the LORD!'

17   But I am poor and needy;
    O Lord, think of me.[b]
    Thou art my help and my salvation;
      O my God, make no delay.

[a] *Verses 13–17: cp. Ps. 70: 1–5.*
[b] O Lord . . . me: *prob. rdg.; Heb.* may the Lord think of me.

* It is usually held that this psalm consists of two distinct elements, a hymn of thanksgiving for past deliverance (verses 1–11) and a prayer for help in present troubles (verses 12–17). Verses 13–17 are indeed preserved as an independent unit in Ps. 70, but the two parts are firmly joined together here by verse 12 which sets the scene for the prayer, though not itself part of it, being more closely linked to verse 11 by the introductory 'For'. Though the more common sequence in the Psalter is supplication followed by thanksgiving, the order here is not unique. It has already been found in Pss. 9–10 and 27 and is therefore no argument for treating the two parts in isolation from each other. This is the prayer of a man in whom realization of the healing reality of God's presence has inspired an overflow of praise (verses 1–4) and called forth a response of heart-felt dedication (verses 5–8). He has testified to these blessings in the congregation of the faithful (verses 9–11), and strengthened with the knowledge of God's unfailing love, he now offers prayer for a speedy release from the troubles that still beset him (verses 12–17). Here is reflected the truth that amid suffering there is joy in God's presence and that amid joy there is continuing human need on earth. The theme is timeless; the psalm cannot be dated. There may be an allusion to verse 8 in John 4: 34, in a passage which speaks of the passion of Christ. The writer to the Hebrews certainly uses verses 6–8 in Heb. 10: 5–10 to explain the fundamental character of Christ's sacrifice on the cross, and it is doubtless for this reason that the psalm is traditionally used on Good Friday in the Christian Church.

1–4. The psalmist rejoices in his knowledge of God's saving presence.

1. *I waited, waited:* not with defeated resignation, but with expectant hope and patient trust in the LORD's faithfulness to bring his promised blessing. *bent down . . . and heard:* cp. Ps. 31: 2.

2. *the muddy pit:* Sheol, the underworld of the dead, here picturesquely described as an abhorrent place of *mire* and *clay*.

The notion of sinking into a swamp (cp. Ps. 30: 3) aptly characterizes the encroachment of the power of death or the sapping of vital energy that accompanies distress or sickness (see on Ps. 13: 3) and it suggests terror and complete helplessness. In contrast, the picture of *a rock* suggests strength and security; cp. Ps. 31: 2 where God himself is that rock.

3. *a new song:* not just a new form of words. His encounter with God has brought release and has filled him with a spirit of joy that overflows in a thankful *song of praise.* God has 'turned (his) laments into dancing' (Ps. 30: 11f.). *Many:* cp. 'the great assembly' (verse 9); his public praise and testimony inspire the faithful to deeper *awe* and stronger *trust in the LORD* (cp. Ps. 22: 22–6).

4. The message of this verse is identical with that of Ps. 1. *happy is the man:* see on Ps. 1: 1. The allure of materialism is a constant danger to faith, even though those who possess wealth and power are often *brutal and treacherous men* (cp. Ps. 73: 2–12).

5–8. Inspired by his awareness of God's incomparable mercy, he offers himself in complete dedication.

5. *Great things . . . thy wonderful purposes:* it is doubtless intended that the worshipper should think both of the great salvation events of his people's history and of the outworking of God's grace in his own life (cp. Ps. 9: 1). *none can compare with thee:* though the mind cannot comprehend nor the voice *proclaim* the wonder of God, yet the heart can respond to him in love and praise (verses 3, 8; cp. Ps. 71: 19).

6. There is no implied repudiation of the Israelite sacrificial system in this or other similar verses in the Psalter (see on Ps. 51: 16f.). The psalmist's desire is to express his total, heart-felt dedication to God and he realizes that his self-offering is a truer form of service than any ritual sacrifice can ever be. Several technical terms are used here, probably as poetic synonyms. *sacrifice (zebaḥ):* a sacrifice in which the roasted flesh was shared amongst the priests and worshippers. *offering (minḥā):* any kind of offering, but in post-exilic times the term was reserved mainly for cereal-offerings. *whole-*

offering (*'ōlā*): an offering completely burnt on the altar. *sin-offering* (*ḥaṭā'ā*): an expiatory sacrifice for cleansing from sin. *ears to hear:* the reading 'a body for me' in Heb. 10: 5 follows the Septuagint.

7. The N.E.B. relegates the second half of this verse to the footnotes on the assumption that it is a later scribal insertion. Though it cannot be identified, the 'book' must be one that calls for a response of commitment, such as the Mosaic law, for the implication of the omitted words is that the psalmist offers himself in obedience to God's will as declared in this written prescription.

8. *My desire:* or 'my delight'. The service of God is not restrictive, but liberating and full of joy (cp. Ps. 1: 2). *thy law is in my heart:* where it ought to be (see on Ps. 37: 31).

9–11. He tells how he has testified to God's unfailing love amongst the faithful.

9. *the great assembly:* the congregation of the faithful (cp. Pss. 22: 22; 35: 18). Public testimony to God's saving acts is important because it strengthens faith and inspires joy amongst the brethren (verse 3). *what is right:* or 'righteousness'; this is not moral teaching, but God's faithfulness to his promise to bring deliverance, as is clearly shown by the parallel expressions in verse 10 (cp. Pss. 5: 8; 71: 2).

10. *goodness* (literally 'righteousness'; see verse 9), *faithfulness* (Ps. 36: 5), *saving power* (Ps. 35: 3), *unfailing love* (Ps. 5: 7) and *truth* (Ps. 25: 5) appear here as synonyms expressing the trustworthiness of God as seen in his care for the loyal worshipper who now testifies to his saving intervention.

11. Having borne witness to God's faithfulness, he can now make this confident assertion that God on his part will not fail him in what remains. He has not held back his words (verse 9), so God will *not withhold* his *tender care* or loving action. It is also possible to render this verse as the opening of the prayer that follows: 'Do not...withhold...' (so the Revised Standard Version). On the presentation of *unfailing love and truth* as guardian angels, cp. Pss. 43: 3; 57: 3.

12–17. The psalmist reminds God that he still has many troubles and he prays for their speedy alleviation.

12. *my iniquities have overtaken me:* this must not be regarded as a belated plea for forgiveness. Sin sets a barrier between man and God, isolating him from his source of life and well-being. But the praise-filled statements of God's faithfulness and saving power in the preceding verses clearly indicate that a close relationship with God has already been restored. The psalmist's concern is with the consequences of his sin, with the *misfortunes* that have followed in its wake. Furthermore, not all of his suffering is a direct result of his actions, though some in Israel would doubtless have thought this to be the case (Job 4: 7f.; Luke 13: 1–5), for the activity of oppressors is also mentioned in verse 14. *my sight fails:* a symbol of ebbing vitality (cp. Pss. 6: 7; 38: 10). *more than the hairs of my head:* a poetic hyperbole (cp. Ps. 69: 4).

13. Verses 13–17 recur as Ps. 70 with some minor variations and verses 14–16 are very similar to Ps. 35: 25–7. *Show me favour:* literally 'be pleased', a verb which in the Hebrew echoes and suggests an appeal to God's 'will' (verse 8). *hasten:* because the need is urgent (cp. Ps. 38: 22).

14. As in Pss. 35: 4, 26; 71: 13, which are variants of this verse, those *who seek* his *life* and his *hurt* are probably being compared with defeated warriors shrinking back in dismay and disgrace.

15. As in Ps. 35: 21, 25, this picture of perverted glee at his misfortunes is probably intended to convey an impression of the psalmist's own feelings of terror rather than describe anything his enemies actually do or say. *be horrified:* Ps. 70: 3 reads 'turn back', more positively suggesting the figure of a routed army (see verse 14), but the two verbs could very easily be confused in Hebrew.

16. Cp. Ps. 35: 27. Just as his vindication must bring shame to his persecutors and silence their spiteful jeers (verse 15), so it will give the faithful cause to *be jubilant and rejoice*. A new and happier sound will be heard, an unending *cry* of praise: '*All*

glory to the LORD!', a cry not unlike the song of heaven itself (Isa. 6: 3; Rev. 5: 13). *who seek thee:* perhaps in the temple, but more probably in spiritual experience, as the parallel *who long for* (literally 'love') *thy saving help* implies.

17. *I am poor and needy:* though a godly man, he recognizes that he lacks the physical, material and spiritual strength to stand alone against the buffeting of the world; he knows his continuing need of God (see also on Ps. 9: 12; cp. Matt. 5: 3). But he makes his final appeal in the strong assurance that God is veritably his *help* and *salvation. think of me:* Ps. 70: 5 reads 'hasten to my aid', which offers a better parallel to *make no delay,* stressing again in conclusion the urgency of his need (see verse 13). *Lord:* the common word meaning 'master', not God's name, LORD. ✳

THE LORD PROTECTS THE MERCIFUL

41

Happy the man who has a concern for the helpless!   1
The LORD will save him in time of trouble.

The LORD protects him and gives him life,   2
    making him secure in the land;
    the LORD never leaves him*a* to the greed of his enemies.

    He nurses him on his sick-bed;   3
he turns*b* his bed when he is ill.

But I said, 'LORD, be gracious to me;   4
heal me, for I have sinned against thee.'
'His case is desperate,' my enemies say;   5
'when will he die, and his line become extinct?'
All who visit me speak from an empty heart,   6
alert to gather bad news;

[a] never leaves him: *prob. rdg.; Heb.* do thou not give him up . . .
[b] *Prob. rdg., cp. Pesh.; Heb.* thou hast turned.

then they go out to spread it abroad.

7 All who hate me whisper together about me
and love to make the worst of everything:

8 'An evil spell is cast upon him;
he is laid on his bed, and will rise no more.'

9 Even the friend whom I trusted, who ate at my table,*a*
exults over my misfortune.

10 O LORD, be gracious and restore me,
that I may pay them out to the full.*b*

11 Then I shall know that thou delightest in me
and that my enemy will not triumph over me.

12 But I am upheld by thee because of my innocence;
thou keepest me for ever in thy sight.

13   Blessed be the LORD, the God of Israel,
from everlasting to everlasting.
Amen, Amen.

＊ This is a psalm for use in time of suffering and dereliction.
It presents a picture of desperate, possibly fatal, illness which
can be accepted as the due reward for sin, but which is made
unbearable through the unsympathetic, even hostile, attitudes
of associates and former friends (verses 4–9). The irony is that
the sufferer, having comforted others, is now shown no
comfort. But his trust in God is unshaken, for he rejoices in the
knowledge of his care (verses 1–3) and confidently looks to him
for restoration (verses 10–12). The date of composition cannot
be determined. Verse 13 does not belong to the psalm; it is the
doxology concluding the first book of the Psalter.

1–3. 'How blest are those who show mercy; mercy shall be
shown to them' (Matt. 5: 7).

[a] who . . . table: *or* slanders me.
[b] to the full: *transposed from end of verse 9.*

1. *Happy* . . . : the last psalm in Book 1, like the first, opens with a beatitude, which is both a statement of belief and a cry of joy. The psalmist has learned to rejoice even in his sufferings (see on Ps. 13). But he can only do so in faith and in the knowledge that he is himself one *who has a concern for the helpless* (cp. verse 12).

2. *gives . . . life:* restores both the body and the spirit with vigour and joy (cp. Ps. 23: 3). *making him secure:* rather 'he will be counted happy' (cp. A.V.); the verb is from the same root as 'Happy' in verse 1. *never leaves him:* so several ancient versions; the passage from promise to prayer in the Hebrew (see N.E.B. footnote) is less suited to the context, but may be prompted by the psalmist's own need.

3. This metaphor of a nurse adjusting the mattress to give ease and relief contrasts sharply with the picture of unsympathetic rejection and scorn that follows in verses 5–9. God's promise to the faithful is not exemption from all human suffering, but the sustaining comfort of his presence.

4–9. As he pleads for healing, he tells of the enmity and mockery that surround him.

4. *I said:* or 'I say'. A past tense implies that the psalmist's suffering lies in the past and that here, by rehearsing this prayer as one he once used, he is testifying, perhaps before the congregation, to his experience of the truth of the beatitude. A present tense suggests that he is calling attention to his urgent need for fulfilment of the beatitude's promise in present suffering. This latter interpretation is preferred here, for it seems unnatural to regard the prayer of verse 10 as simply part of a report from the past. *I have sinned:* this does not annul his ground of hope in verses 1–3. He lays no claim to sinless perfection, but pleads that, unlike his heartless acquaintances, he has shown some humanitarian concern. He therefore prays *be gracious*, asking for mercy, as he himself has shown mercy.

5. This is a fairly free rendering of the Hebrew, but it neatly depicts the eager speculation of those who are impatient to lay greedy hands on his possessions (cp. Ps. 22: 17f.).

6. His visitors bring no real comfort, for they have none in their *heart* to offer. But they are alert to pick up gossip.

7. A further free translation, but accurately portraying the gossips after their visit as they secretively share their impressions and speculate maliciously on his condition.

8. *An evil spell . . .:* better 'an evil thing has taken hold of him'; literally 'a thing (or word) of Belial . . .' (cp. on Ps. 101: 3). The Hebrew certainly suggests something sinister. The gossips appear to be more interested in the effects of this supposed spell than in its causes.

9. More bitter than all else is betrayal by his most trusted friend (cp. Ps. 55: 12-15). In the N.E.B. translation this is no longer recognizable as the verse cited in John 13: 18 as being fulfilled in the treachery of Judas. In the Hebrew it reads '. . . who ate my bread, has raised his heel against me', perhaps suggesting physical violence, but the N.E.B. has transposed the word for 'his heel' to verse 10 and altered it to mean 'to the full'.

10-12. He resumes his prayer and expresses his trust in God's protection.

10. *be gracious:* see verse 4. *that I may pay them out:* this is an unusual prayer, for the psalmists mostly ask God to exact the vengeance. Perhaps the phrase means no more than 'that my recovery may prove their evil predictions wrong'. *to the full:* see on verse 9.

11. *Then I shall know:* better 'By this I know' (Authorized Version); the Hebrew verb is more correctly represented by a past or a present tense. The psalmist is not hoping that God might delight in him, but expressing confidence that God already does, *and that his enemy will not triumph.*

12. *my innocence:* not sinlessness (see verse 4), but the pure intention of the heart to be loyal to God and walk blamelessly before him. It is to men of such purpose that God promises to show himself loyal and blameless (Ps. 18: 25), and this is the whole basis of his confidence. *for ever in thy sight:* the highest expectation of the faithful is the abiding presence of God himself (cp. Ps. 27: 4).

13. The doxology to mark the close of Book 1 (see p. 3). *from everlasting to everlasting:* from eternity past to eternity future; that is, in God's eternal present. Cp. the New Testament formula: 'God, who is and who was and who is to come' (Rev. 1: 8). *Amen:* 'surely', 'truly'; an affirmation of approval, usually uttered by the congregation as a response (see Ps. 106: 48). ✳

BOOK 2

I LONG FOR GOD'S PRESENCE

42–43

As a hind longs for the running streams,   1
so do I long for thee, O God.

With my whole being I thirst for God, the living God. 2
When shall I come to God and appear in his presence?
Day and night, tears are my food;   3
'Where is your God?' they ask me all day long.

As I pour out my soul in distress, I call to mind   4
how I marched in the ranks of the great*a* to the house of
      God,

among exultant shouts of praise, the clamour of the
      pilgrims.

How deep I am sunk in misery,   5
groaning in my distress:
yet I will wait for God;
I will praise him continually,
my*b* deliverer, my God.

I am sunk in misery, therefore will I remember thee,   6
though from the Hermons and the springs of Jordan,
      and from the hill of Mizar,

[a] of the great: *so some MSS.; others have an obscure word.*
[b] *So some MSS.; others* his.

199

7 deep calls to deep in the roar of thy cataracts,
 and all thy waves, all thy breakers, pass over me.
8   The LORD makes his unfailing love shine forth[a]
        alike by day and night;
      his praise on my lips is a prayer
        to the God of my life.
9 I will say to God my rock, 'Why hast thou forgotten
        me?'
10 Why must I go like a mourner because my foes oppress
        me?
11 My enemies taunt me, jeering[b] at my misfortunes;
   'Where is your God?' they ask me all day long.
      How deep I am sunk in misery,
      groaning in my distress:
      yet I will wait for God;
      I will praise him continually,
      my deliverer, my God.

43 Plead my cause and give me judgement against an impious
        race;
   save me from malignant men and liars, O God.
2 Thou, O God, art my refuge; why hast thou rejected me?
   Why must I go like a mourner because my foes oppress
        me?
3 Send forth thy light and thy truth to be my guide
   and lead me to thy holy hill, to thy tabernacle,
4 then shall I come to the altar of God, the God of my[c] joy,
   and praise thee on the harp, O God, thou God of my
        delight.

[a] makes . . . forth: *or* entrusts me to his unfailing love.
[b] jeering: *prob. rdg.; Heb. obscure.*
[c] my: *so one MS.; others om.*

How deep I am sunk in misery,   5
groaning in my distress:
yet I will wait for God;
I will praise him continually,
my deliverer, my God.

✻ Though these appear as independent psalms in all the
ancient versions, there are several good reasons for believing
that they, like Pss. 9 and 10, were originally one. There is
continuity of thought, style and metre throughout and the
whole poem falls into three parts, each ending in the same
refrain (42: 5, 11; 43: 5). Furthermore Ps. 43, like Ps. 10, bears
no title in the Hebrew. Some commentators argue that this
composition is exilic, since the psalmist describes his condition
in terms of geographical distance from the temple (42: 6;
43: 3). But the spatial language may well be entirely symbolic
of the more profound inner feeling of separation from God
that is the burden of his lament (42: 3, 9, 10; 43: 2). And so he
speaks of his longing for God's presence (42: 1–2) and of his
faithful determination to wait for God, singing his praises as he
recalls past blessings (42: 4–5) and anticipates the restoration of
joy (43: 4–5).

42: 1–5. Overwhelmed by sorrows and surrounded by
scoffers, he longs for the comfort of God's presence, and yet
finds courage to hope and give praise.

1. *running streams:* watercourses that do not go dry in
summer, hence a suitable and frequent symbol of divine
refreshment (see on Pss. 23: 2; 36: 8).

2. *thirst for . . . the living God:* an apt parallel to 'longs for the
running streams', for God himself is 'the fountain of living
water' (Jer. 17: 13). With him is 'the fountain of life' and the
thirsty may drink freely from its 'flowing streams' (Ps. 36: 8f.;
cp. Rev. 21: 6; 22: 17). *come to God and appear in his presence:*
perhaps in the temple where he seeks to sing God's praise
(43: 3–4) as in former times (42: 4), but a spiritual interpreta-

tion is strongly implied by the language of longing and *thirst*. The two notions are not incompatible, for the temple was an earthly symbol of God's presence with his people (see on Pss. 2: 6 and 11: 4).

3. *tears are my food:* a poetic hyperbole suggesting the depth of sorrow. '*Where is your God?*': cp. the gibe of the nations in Pss. 79: 10; 115: 2 and the sarcasm hurled at Jesus on the cross in Matt. 27: 43. The taunt, which implies that God is either unconcerned or powerless to help, is particularly bitter, for it almost echoes the question the psalmist himself is asking (verses 9–10; cp. Matt. 27: 46).

4. *I marched:* better 'I used to march', recalling the regular festival celebrations when he walked in processions with the faithful whom he regarded as *the great*, the true nobility of this earth (cp. on Ps. 16: 3). He remembers these occasions for their mood of *exultant* joy that found its expression in *shouts of praise* and *the clamour of the pilgrims*, all of which forms a stark contrast with his present feelings of emptiness.

5. *How deep . . .:* this strong expression of lamentation makes an excellent conclusion to verses 1–4, but is less appropriate as an ending to Ps. 43. According to the older, more familiar translation, the psalmist rebukes himself for his self-pity: 'Why are you cast down, O my soul, and why are you disquieted within me?' This gives a refrain that is well suited to each context and it coheres better with the following expressions of determination to *wait for God* (see on Ps. 27: 14), to offer *praise* in anticipation of deliverance and to do so *continually* in faith, even amid his suffering (cp. on Ps. 13: 5).

6–11. Though distant from God and immersed in his sea of misery, the thought of God's unfailing love encourages him to repeat his plea and reiterate his expression of hope and confidence.

6. *therefore will I remember thee:* it is as a man looks away from himself to God that strength and healing come, but the initial act of remembering requires a conscious effort of will. *the hill of Mizar*, or 'the little hill', is unknown, but *the*

Hermons and *the springs* (the text actually has 'land') *of Jordan* lie in the Anti-Lebanon mountains beyond the northern borders of Israel. However, it is not to be thought that the psalm was composed for the exclusive use of some community exiled in those regions. Their distance from Jerusalem makes them apt symbols of the psalmist's feeling of separation from God, which is the whole theme of this psalm.

7. Dereliction is a nightmarish experience. It is not on some pleasant hillside that he finds himself, but amid the raging torrents that cascade down the mountain slopes in winter. He feels as though God has unleashed the very powers of hell from the vast subterranean *deep* and the *roar* of their voice reverberates round his valley of isolation as he is engulfed in their onrushing flood of misery. In ancient mythology the ocean depths are the repository of earth's destructive and death-bearing forces (cp. Ps. 71: 20; Jonah 2: 6).

8. The Hebrew of this verse is problematic and many different interpretations have been offered, but the N.E.B.'s translation implies that the psalmist, following his decision in verse 6, now turns his thoughts away from himself to God, seeking comfort in the knowledge that he gives of himself *day and night* in his *unfailing love* (see on Ps. 5: 7). *God of my life:* who grants freely to drink from the water-springs of life (verse 2).

9. *my rock:* a figure of strength and security (cp. Ps. 18:2). His faith in the promise of God's love (verse 8) restores assurance, but sadly he is still *like a mourner* and his prayer must continue to be a cry of desolation. *Why . . . Why:* it is not answers he seeks, but restoration (Ps. 43: 2–3; cp. Pss. 10 :1; 22: 1).

10. *jeering at my misfortunes:* the Hebrew could also be rendered 'while (I feel) death in my bones'. Neither translation suggests that the enemies' *taunt* is the cause of his misfortune, though it adds greatly to his suffering (cp. verse 3).

11. See verse 5.

43: 1–5. The psalmist now offers direct prayer for vindication and restoration to the joy of God's presence.

1. Using the image of the heavenly court (cp. Ps. 7: 7f.), he appeals to God as both his defence-counsel and his judge to uphold his case *against* the ungodly, his tormentors, whose *malignant* and lying accusations that his faith is without foundation (Ps. 42: 3, 10) cannot be true since God's promises are completely trustworthy. Collectively they are *an impious race* and therefore enemies of God.

2. Cp. Ps. 42: 9. Knowing that his protection lies with God, he repeats his cry of dereliction for the last time, still wondering *why* God has *rejected* him.

3. *thy light and thy truth:* God's blessing and his faithfulness to his covenant promises (see on Pss. 36: 9 and 25: 5), here poetically personified as angels of mercy (cp. Ps. 57: 3). Since the temple (*tabernacle*, see Ps. 15: 1) on God's *holy hill*, Mount Zion (Ps. 2: 6), represented his presence, this verse and the next are susceptible to spiritual interpretation (cp. Ps. 42: 2).

4. Mention of the sacrificial *altar* and the music of the *harp* recalls the psalmist's picture of former *joy*-filled times in God's house (Ps. 42: 4). In a moment of inspiration he has captured the vision of release into the presence of God and he sings out: *God of my joy*, I shall *praise thee, O God, thou God of my delight*. Following upon these exuberant words, the final refrain is a cry of triumph.

5. See Ps. 42: 5. ✻

DO NOT REJECT US FOR EVER

44

1   O God, we have heard for ourselves,
     our fathers have told us
  all the deeds which thou didst in their days,
2 all the work of thy hand in days of old.
  Thou didst plant them in the land and drive the nations
     out,

thou didst make them strike root, breaking up the
    peoples;
it was not our fathers' swords won them the land,   3
nor their arm that gave them victory,
    but thy right hand and thy arm
    and the light of thy presence; such was thy favour to
      them.

Thou art my king and my God;   4
at thy bidding Jacob is victorious.

By thy help we will throw back our enemies,   5
in thy name we will trample down our adversaries.

I will not trust in my bow,   6
nor will my sword win me the victory;
for thou dost deliver us from our foes   7
and put all our enemies to shame.

In God have we gloried all day long,   8
and we will praise thy name for ever.

But now thou hast rejected and humbled us   9
and dost no longer lead our armies into battle.

Thou hast hurled us back before the enemy,   10
and our foes plunder us as they will.

Thou hast given us up to be butchered like sheep   11
    and hast scattered us among the nations.

Thou hast sold thy people for next to nothing   12
and had no profit from the sale.

Thou hast exposed us to the taunts of our neighbours, 13
to the mockery and contempt of all around.

Thou hast made us a byword among the nations,   14
    and the peoples shake their heads at us;
so my disgrace confronts me all day long,   15
and I am covered with shame

16   at the shouts of those who taunt and abuse me
        as the enemy takes his revenge.
17 All this has befallen us, but we do not forget thee
        and have not betrayed thy covenant;
18 we have not gone back on our purpose,
        nor have our feet strayed from thy path.
19 Yet thou hast crushed us as the sea-serpent[a] was crushed
        and covered us with the darkness of death.
20 If we had forgotten the name of our God
        and spread our hands in prayer to any other,
21 would not God find this out,
        for he knows the secrets of the heart?
22 Because of thee we are done to death all day long,
        and are treated as sheep for slaughter.
23 Bestir thyself, Lord; why dost thou sleep?
        Awake, do not reject us for ever.
24   Why dost thou hide thy face,
        heedless of our misery and our sufferings?
25   For we sink down to the dust
        and lie prone on the earth.
26   Arise and come to our help;
            for thy love's sake set us free.

* In times of national distress the people could be enjoined to observe a fast in the temple in order to seek God's guidance or protection (cp. Joel 1: 14) and on such occasions a psalm like this would have been recited by their religious leader, perhaps usually the king, as in 2 Chron. 20. The psalm is unique in its confident assertion of national fidelity (verses 17–22). More commonly Israel's suffering is seen as punishment for sin (cp.

[a] *So Pesh.; Heb.* the jackals.

Lam. 3), but here, with a Job-like persistence, the psalmist seeks some other explanation. Pleading the basic faithfulness – but not sinless perfection – of his people and the apparent injustice of God, his lament reaches its climax in the anguished perplexity of verse 22: 'Because of thee we are done to death ...', where he glimpses something of the truth that the way of faith is also the way of suffering. This lesson was to be more fully learned in the experience of exile and to find vivid expression in the crucifixion of Jesus and the death of the Christian martyrs.

1–3. The psalmist recalls God's past help and care for his people.

1. *our fathers have told us:* handing on the story of God's mighty *deeds* in the exodus and settlement was a religious duty incumbent on all parents (Exod. 13: 14–16; Deut. 6: 20–5; cp. Ps. 78: 3).

2. *plant them ... make them strike root:* see more fully Ps. 80: 8f. where God as master-gardener (cp. Pss. 1: 3; 65: 9f.) clears the Canaanites (*the nations*) from the ground like weeds in preparation for the planting and cultivation of Israel like a vine.

3. The thought is not that Israel did no fighting, but that she could have won no *victory* had it not been granted by God. It became an article of faith in Israel that the land was God's gift (Deut. 26: 5–10) and it was regarded as a dangerous sign of pride to claim that it had been won solely by human might (Deut. 8: 11–18). *thy right hand and thy arm:* metaphorical symbols of God's power and strength. *the light of thy presence:* God's *favour* and blessing (cp. Ps. 4: 6).

4–8. The psalmist expresses confidence that God's strength, so manifest in the past, must still avail for the deliverance of his people who continue to trust in him alone.

4. *my king:* singular pronouns also appear in verses 6 and 15f., otherwise plurals are used throughout. The alternation may indicate that the psalm was normally recited by a leader of worship on behalf of the community. *my king and my God:* the notion of strength and the will to victory conveyed by these

titles is well illustrated in Ps. 68 where they recur in verse 24.
Jacob: a synonym for Israel (Ps. 14: 7).

5. *we will throw back:* like a wild ox goring its adversaries
(Deut. 33 : 17). *in thy name:* synonymous with *By thy help* (literally 'by you'). God's name is his revealed character, but that
includes his favour towards Israel and his power to uphold it.

6–7. *the victory* depends on the will and power of God, not
on human strength (cp. verse 3 and see on Ps. 33: 16).

8. The godly will glory *In God* alone and will not boast
proudly in their own prowess (cp. Ps. 20: 7 and see on verse 3
above).

9–16. Present suffering and disaster appear to contradict this
faith that seems so surely founded on God's mighty acts in
Israel's past.

9. *But now:* the transition is abrupt, emphasizing how stark
is the contrast between the hope loyally maintained by the
faithful and the reality of their experience. The strength of
their feeling, almost one of betrayal, is further expressed in a
series of accusations hurled at God, each beginning with *thou
hast. rejected:* if the victories of the past were a consequence of
God's favour (verse 3), then present defeat must betoken its
withdrawal. *lead our armies:* as LORD of Hosts (see on Ps. 24: 10)
God accompanied Israel *into battle,* his presence sometimes
symbolized by the Ark (Num. 10: 35; 1 Sam. 4: 3).

11. *hast scattered us among the nations:* as refugees and
prisoners of war. These words would have assumed an added
poignancy during the exile.

12. *Thou hast sold thy people:* God has handed them over
completely to the disposal of their enemies, like slaves, and that
for next to nothing, as though they were worthless in his
estimation.

13. Cp. Pss. 79: 4; 80: 6. *the taunts of our neighbours:* the
transjordanian peoples in Edom, Moab and Ammon were
always jealous of Israel and only too ready to gloat over her
misfortunes (cp. Obad. 11–14).

14. *a byword:* such is the extent of Israel's calamity that she

could well serve as a proverbial example of a people abandoned by God. *shake their heads:* a gesture of derision (cp. Ps. 22: 7).

15–16. These verses are the antithesis to verse 9, drawing sharply the contrast between the people's experience and their hope. Instead of glorying in God and continually thanking him for victory, they must endure *disgrace* and *shame*, while the praise of God's name gives place to the vengeful *shouts* and abusive taunts of their enemies.

17–22. The real bitterness for Israel lies in her knowledge that the calamity is unmerited; she can find no good reason for her plight, for she has been basically faithful to God's covenant.

17–18. *not forget . . . not betrayed:* the psalmist does not plead national innocence or moral purity, for that would be unrealistic. His plea is loyalty. The people, imperfect though their service may be, have not played false to their covenanted word or withdrawn from their *purpose* to be faithful. *thy covenant:* the allusion is probably to the agreement established through Moses on Mount Sinai (Exod. 19–23), though the covenants with Abraham (Gen. 15) and David (2 Sam. 7) may also be in mind.

19. *as the sea-serpent was crushed:* this translation is based on the Syriac and seems to make better sense than the Hebrew reading 'in the place of the jackals'. The sea was thought to be the home of all earth's inimical and disruptive forces and in the ancient myths it is sometimes personified as a monstrous dragon that was subdued and slain by God at creation (cp. Pss. 68: 22; 74: 13f.). *the darkness of death:* a metaphor signifying severe distress; see more fully on Ps. 23: 4 where the same Hebrew word is used.

20. *forgotten:* the psalmist is concerned not about accidental lapses of memory, but about conscious unfaithfulness, as the parallelism clearly shows. *spread our hands:* a gesture used both in supplication (Ps. 28: 2) and adoration (Ps. 134: 2).

21. The theme of God's insight into men's secret thoughts is more fully expressed in Ps. 139: 1–6.

22. *Because of thee:* not only are the people suffering *despite* their loyalty (verse 17), but *because* of it. Perhaps this accusa-

tion reflects a mood of anguish, or even bitterness, but it is bold
and marks a significant step away from any mechanistic
doctrine of reward and punishment, for it implies some
recognition that suffering is an inevitable consequence of faith,
the price of loyalty to God in a world at war with him. It is
doubtful whether the author of the psalm himself had religious
persecution, let alone martyrdom, in mind, but in such a
context his words are bound to assume a deeper significance
(see Rom. 8: 36). *all day long:* unceasingly, cp. verse 15 and
contrast verse 8.

23–6. An urgent appeal for immediate help.

23. *Bestir thyself . . . Awake:* the psalmists frequently call
God to action with similar invocations (e.g. Ps. 7: 6), but the
cry *why dost thou sleep?* makes the challenge here much more
daring in its expression than is usual elsewhere. The language
is clearly metaphorical (cp. Ps. 78: 65). The author would have
agreed that 'The guardian of Israel never slumbers, never
sleeps' (Ps. 121: 4), but his words are intended to show that
from the point of view of the faithful it would appear that he
does.

24. *hide thy face:* in indifference or displeasure; the phrase
implies the withdrawal of God's blessing (cp. Ps. 13: 1).

25. Prostration could be a sign of humiliation in prayer
before God, but here the thought is more probably of the
people lying crushed and helpless in their distress.

26. *Arise:* perhaps more than a simple repetition of the
summons to 'Awake' (verse 23); this invocation is reminiscent
of the ancient war-cry of the Israelites calling God to battle
against their foes (Num. 10: 35). *for thy love's sake:* it is God's
own reputation that is ultimately at stake in the continued
oppression of the faithful. His *love* (see on Ps. 5: 7) is expressed
in his trustworthy promise to uphold and bless his people, but
herein lies their hope. Behind all the appearance of aloofness
and inactivity there stands the essential reality of God's eternal
nature expressed to them in a pledge of abiding love (cp. Rom.
8: 35–9). ✳

IN A KING'S HONOUR I UTTER THE SONG

I HAVE MADE

45

My heart is stirred by a noble theme,   1
in a king's honour I utter the song I have made,
   and my tongue runs like the pen of an expert scribe.

   You surpass all mankind in beauty,   2
   your lips are moulded in grace,
so you are blessed by God for ever.
With your sword ready at your side, warrior king,   3
your limbs resplendent*[a]* in their royal armour,   4
ride on to execute true sentence and just judgement.
   Your right hand shall show you a scene of terror:
   your sharp arrows flying, nations beneath your feet,   5
      the courage of the king's foes melting away!*[b]*

Your throne is like God's throne, eternal,   6
   your royal sceptre a sceptre of righteousness.
You have loved right and hated wrong;   7
so God, your God, has anointed you
   above your fellows with oil, the token of joy.
Your robes are all fragrant with myrrh and powder of aloes,   8
   and the music of strings greets you
   from a palace panelled with ivory.
A princess*[c]* takes her place among the noblest of your   9
   women,
   a royal lady at your side in gold of Ophir.

[a] your limbs resplendent: *prob. rdg.; Heb.* and in your pomp prosper.
[b] the courage . . . away: *prob. rdg.; Heb. obscure.*
[c] *So Pesh.; Heb.* daughters of kings.

10 Listen, my daughter, hear my words
        and consider them:
    forget your own people and your father's house;
11 and, when the king desires your beauty,
        remember that he is your lord.
12 Do him obeisance, daughter of Tyre,
    and the richest in the land will court you with
            gifts.

13   In the palace honour awaits her;[a]
        she is a king's daughter,
14   arrayed in cloth-of-gold richly embroidered.
        Virgins shall follow her into the presence of the king;
            her companions shall be brought to her,[b]
15   escorted with the noise of revels and rejoicing
            as they enter the king's palace.

16 You shall have sons, O king, in place of your forefathers
        and will make them rulers over all the land.[c]
17 I will declare your fame to all generations;
    therefore the nations will praise you for ever and
        ever.

* This psalm celebrates the wedding of a king. In contrast
with modern European weddings, where the dress of the bride
is the main point of interest, verses 2–9 address the king in
language abounding in superlatives. When his bride is the
subject, in verses 10–15, only verses 13–15 are devoted to her
appearance; for the rest, she is exhorted to be a loyal wife.

[a] honour awaits her: *prob. rdg.; Heb.* all honoured.
[b] *So some MSS.; others* to you.
[c] over all the land: *or* in all the earth.

It is impossible to identify the king for whose wedding the
psalm was first written, and in any case, it was presumably used
for many royal weddings. A case has sometimes been made for
connecting it originally with the marriage of Ahab to Jezebel
(1 Kings 16: 31). Supporters of this view have pointed to the
phrase 'daughter of Tyre' in verse 12, connecting it with the
fact that Jezebel was a princess from Sidon (1 Kings 16: 31;
Tyre and Sidon were close geographically) and arguing that
verse 10c implies that the bride was a foreigner. Although it is
unlikely that a psalm composed for the wedding of a northern
king who was judged by the biblical tradition to be particularly
evil (1 Kings 16: 30) should have found its way into the Psalter,
this theory draws attention to two points. First, Jerusalem is
not explicitly mentioned in the psalm, and second, the
reference to Tyre in verse 12 constitutes a major problem of
interpretation.

A royal wedding in ancient Israel was a national event,
because the continuation of the royal dynasty depended upon
it (verse 16 and possibly verse 11) and because a harmonious
marriage with a wife loyal to God would help to establish a
happy reign. Thus the king is not merely offered the usual
expressions of good luck in his marriage; he is reminded that
he is to 'execute true sentence and just judgement' (verse 4)
and if he is addressed as God in verse 6 (see commentary) this
is a reminder of his special relationship with God, as the
anointed head of God's chosen people.

The hopes for just and prosperous rule that the people
entertained at the beginning of a reign were often cruelly
disappointed. When there was no Davidic king from the
middle of the sixth century, the psalm came to be interpreted
messianically, looking forward to the reign of the future king
who would establish God's universal rule. In Jewish interpretation, the king Messiah would first defeat the powers of evil
(verses 3–5) and then establish peace. In the New Testament,
verses 6–7 translated 'Thy throne, O God' are referred in Heb.
1: 8f. to Jesus, and taken as proof that he is God and is superior

to the angels. Thus, a psalm whose beginnings are in a royal wedding, becomes the means of expression of man's deepest longings for God's universal rule of justice and peace.

1. *My heart is stirred:* the speaker, probably a priest or prophet, who addresses the king and his bride in the second person in verses 2–12 and 16 (and possibly 17), speaks in the first person about how the great occasion has inspired very many ideas for his psalm. *my tongue runs:* my speech is fluent. *an expert scribe:* although Ezra is similarly described in Ezra 7: 6, the Hebrew word for 'expert' is probably an Egyptian loan-word, indicating the influence of Egyptian scribal schools in ancient Israel. The Israelites may have connected the loan-word with a similar Hebrew verb meaning 'to hasten', and the complete phrase may mean 'my tongue is fluent like the pen of a rapid scribe'.

2–9. The royal bridegroom.

2. *You surpass . . . beauty:* the speaker may be deferentially polite, or expressing a popular belief that the king was always of outstanding physical appearance; cp. also the description of David in 1 Sam. 16: 12. *your lips . . . grace:* either, the king smiles graciously or his manner of speech is gracious. *so you are blessed:* the king is not *blessed . . . for ever* because of his beauty and grace; these are signs that God has blessed him from birth (and cp. Ps. 110: 3). *for ever* means either the whole life-time of the king, or alludes to the divine promise for all time to the house of David (2 Sam. 7: 13, 16).

3. *warrior king:* see on Ps. 18.

4. *true sentence and just judgement:* Hebrew 'for the cause of truth, meekness (and) right'. This wish is not that the king should win victory for Israel, but that he should uphold that justice which is according to God's will. *Your right hand . . . terror:* Hebrew 'your right hand will teach you dread deeds'. The traditional Hebrew order of words takes this with what precedes, possibly meaning that where the king fights for truth and justice, his right hand (power) will certainly bring him victory. The N.E.B. takes the phrase with what follows.

5. Hebrew 'Your arrows are sharp; nations fall beneath your feet; (the arrows fall) into the heart of the king's foes.' The N.E.B. emendation (see the footnote) is probably too radical, and sense can be produced by a simpler re-arrangement of the words, e.g. 'Your arrows are sharp; they fall into the heart of the king's foes. Nations are subject to you.'

6. *Your throne . . . throne:* there has been much discussion about how to translate this phrase. One approach compares 1 Chron. 29: 23 'Solomon sat on the LORD's throne' and proposes 'your throne is God's throne', i.e. you rule as the special servant of God. The N.E.B. takes the Hebrew literally to be 'your throne is God' implying the translation *Your throne is like God's throne.* Yet another line of interpretation renders the Hebrew 'your throne, O God, is eternal', the king being addressed as God. This is the translation in all the ancient versions, but it may have been influenced by the messianic interpretation of the psalm. If the king is addressed as God, this does not mean that the king was regarded as divine in ancient Israel. The king was 'adopted' as the son of God (Ps. 2: 7) and stood in a special relation to him as king of the chosen people; but he was never regarded as divine. *sceptre of righteousness:* the sceptre or staff that symbolizes the king's power also symbolizes that his power is exercised for the sake of true justice.

7. *You have loved:* or 'you love right and hate wrong'. *so God . . . has anointed you:* cp. verse 2 'so you are blessed'. In the present verse (unlike verse 2) the *so* indicates God's response to the king who has proved his loyalty. Kings were *anointed . . . with oil* in ancient Israel (1 Sam. 10: 1) but *token of joy* may indicate that the whole phrase denotes blessings in general.

8. *myrrh:* sweet-smelling resin taken from a thorny shrub, which could be compounded into an oil. *powder of aloes:* Hebrew 'and aloes (and) cassia'. N.E.B. has taken 'cassia' to mean *powder.* Both aloes and cassia were derived from the wood or bark of exotic trees.

9. *A princess:* Hebrew 'daughters of kings are among your precious women; a queen takes her place at your right hand in

gold of Ophir'. The N.E.B. assumes that the bride is referred
to in the words *princess* and *royal lady*; she will take an honoured place in the king's harem (the *noblest . . . women*). It is
also possible to translate *noblest of your women* as 'adorned with
your precious jewels'. If the Hebrew is correct, and if the
noble women are the harem, then the harem is said to contain
princesses, indicating how powerful the king is. The *royal lady*
may be either the queen mother, or the bride herself. If it is the
bride, then her place at the king's right hand indicates her
superiority to all other women in the realm. If the bride is not
referred to in the verse, then it describes the king's entourage
as he waits to meet his bride (and see verses 13–15).

10–12. Advice to the bride.

10. *Listen, my daughter:* the bride is addressed in words typical
of wisdom instruction (cp. Prov. 4: 20–1). *own people . . .
father's house:* it is not certain that this phrase implies that the
bride is a foreigner. The word translated *people* need not mean
'nation' (cp. 1 Sam. 9: 13 where it means people of the city).
The bride is urged to have exclusive loyalty for her husband.

11. *when the king desires your beauty:* this may counsel
obedience whenever the king desires marital intercourse, since
the continuance of the dynasty and the making of alliances will
depend upon a marriage blessed by many children. Cp. these
verses with Esther 2: 13–14.

12. *daughter of Tyre:* experts disagree on whether the
Hebrew means a Tyrian princess, or whether it must mean the
people of Tyre (e.g. 'daughter of Zion', Isa. 1: 8, means Zion
and its inhabitants). The N.E.B. seems to imply that the bride
is a Tyrian princess, and if this is correct, we are perhaps
puzzled as to whether the psalm was used regularly, and if so,
what the users made of the reference. The Hebrew division of
verses 11–12 is (11*b*) 'for he is your lord; do him obeisance.
(12) And the people of Tyre (will be there) with a gift; the
richest in the land will court you with gifts.' In the Hebrew
'people of Tyre' represents the world's rich trading nations
either presenting a wedding gift, or honouring the queen

throughout her reign. See the description of the riches of Tyre in Ezek. 27.

13–15. Unless verse 9 refers to the bride, we are to assume that these verses describe the bride's procession as it prepares to accompany the princess to meet her future husband, perhaps for the first time. Whether a palace is mentioned is uncertain, and many commentators emend the Hebrew *penīmā* (lit. 'within' but paraphrased by the N.E.B. as *in the palace*) to *penīnīm*, meaning 'corals', and producing the phrase 'the princess is richly adorned with corals' which provides good parallelism with *arrayed in cloth-of-gold*. *shall follow her:* Hebrew 'she is conducted to the king; her virgin companions are brought (or with some Hebrew manuscripts: bring her) to you.'

16–17. Promise of blessing.

16. The king is now addressed, and assured that soon he will no longer be thought of as the son of his father and his *forefathers*, but as the father of *sons* who will be *rulers over all the land*. *land* could mean either the kingdom or the whole earth.

17. It is not certain whether the psalmist, speaking in the name of God, promises undying *fame* to the king, or whether the king now addresses God, pledging to him loyal service that will glorify God among *the nations*. If the king addresses God, then *fame* should be translated as 'name', and the psalm closes by asserting that the greatest task laid upon the servant of God in every age is that he should make known the character and will of God, in action and in word (cp. John 17:6: 'I have made thy name known'). ✳

THE LORD OF HOSTS IS WITH US

46

God is our shelter and our refuge,   1
a timely help in trouble;
so we are not afraid when the earth heaves   2
and the mountains are hurled into the sea,

3   when its waters seethe in tumult
       and the mountains quake before his majesty.
4 There is a river whose streams gladden the city of God,[a]
       which the Most High has made his holy dwelling;[b]
5   God is in that city; she will not be overthrown,
       and he will help her at the break of day.
6 Nations are in tumult, kingdoms hurled down;
       when he thunders, the earth surges like the sea.
7   The LORD of Hosts is with us,
       the God of Jacob our high stronghold.

8   Come and see what the LORD has done,
       the devastation he has brought upon earth,
9   from end to end of the earth he stamps out war:
   he breaks the bow, he snaps the spear
       and burns the shield in the fire.

10 Let be then: learn that I am God,
    high over the nations, high above earth.
11   The LORD of Hosts is with us,
       the God of Jacob our high stronghold.

   * This psalm speaks of confidence in God's protecting presence
   even amid the most terrible of life's vicissitudes, when it seems
   that the whole world around is in upheaval (verses 1–3) or that
   the clamour of the nations would threaten the very sanctuary of
   God itself (verses 4–7). The language can suggest a strongly personal and present application, but it also directs the worshipper's
   thoughts to the future, to the final dissolution of the earth and
   the ultimate conquest of the nations. The ensuing stillness

   [a] the city of God: *or* a wondrous city.
   [b] which . . . dwelling: *so Sept.; Heb.* the sanctuary of the dwellings of
   the Most High.

(verses 8–11) is thus life's moments of rest when the faithful are able to reflect that God is ever present through all turmoils working out his purpose, but it is equally the eternal quiet and peace of God's kingdom beyond time. It was this psalm that inspired Luther's magnificent hymn, 'A safe stronghold our God is still'.

Pss. 46, 47 and 48 clearly form a trilogy, for they share the same themes, use the same kind of language and breathe the same atmosphere of confidence in God's protecting power and kingship. Amongst the suggestions put forward to explain their similarity are that they were composed by the same poet, that they derive from the same earlier collection of psalms or from the works of the same group of temple-singers, that they were all written to celebrate the same specific historical event, perhaps the deliverance of Jerusalem in 701 B.C. (2 Kings 19: 35f.), and that they were originally used together in connection with some festival or ritual action celebrating God's kingship in Zion. Unfortunately we lack the necessary historical information to enable us to judge finally between such alternative theories.

1–3. God, our refuge, is lord of the universe.

1. *timely:* literally 'abundantly found'; that is, time and again he has been found to be a reliable *help in trouble.* It is precisely because it is thus anchored in past history and experience that this verse becomes an expression of confident hope for the future.

2–3. *the mountains:* figures of strength and permanence. *the sea:* a symbol of all that fights against God and men. At creation God did 'fix the mountains in their place' and 'calm the rage of the seas' (Ps. 65: 6f.) and he maintains this order in the present by his might (cp. Ps. 89: 9). The picture here of the disintegration of the universe and the resurgence of chaos may refer to natural upheavels such as earthquakes, or it may be metaphorical of the turbulence and insecurity of life in general, but it is also a picture elaborated by the prophets in connection with God's future intervention in judgement (cp. Isa. 24: 19f.; Jer. 4: 23–8).

4-7. God, our stronghold, is lord of history.

4. This image of a gently flowing *river* irrigating the land along distributary *streams* and channels is a metaphor of God's life-giving presence (cp. Ps. 65: 9f.; see more fully on Ps. 36: 8) and in sharp contrast to the tumult of the sea it signifies peace, security and gladness (cp. Isa. 8: 6f.; 33: 21). *the city of God:* Jerusalem, the city chosen by God for *his holy dwelling* (Ps. 68: 16), but, like its temple, it represents to the faithful the spiritual reality of God's abiding presence and protection (verse 5; see also on Pss. 2: 6; 11: 4). *the Most High:* a title that appropriately suggests God's universal sovereignty (see on Ps. 7: 17).

5. It is not in her defences, but in God's presence that the city finds its security and blessing (cp. Mic. 3: 11). *she will not be overthrown:* unlike the mountains (verse 2), or the nations (verse 6). *at the break of day:* as daylight dispels darkness with its attendant fears and nightmares, so God will end earth's turmoil (verses 2-3, 6) and cause a new age of peace to dawn (verses 8-10). This theme has a more personal application in several other psalms that are suited for use in a dawn vigil (see p. 14, sect. C), but perhaps the present psalm was sometimes used in some similar way, possibly at festival time when Israel celebrated in anticipation the coming reign of God.

6. This is a historical counterpart to the more mythological scene in verses 2-3, and it must be interpreted in the same ways, that is as an allusion either factually to international warfare, or metaphorically to the general turbulence in society, or with future reference to the ultimate victory of God. Perhaps all three are in mind, but as in verses 2-3 it is God who subdues *the earth, like the sea.*

7. *LORD of Hosts:* a title suggesting cosmic kingship, authority over all the hosts of heaven and earth (cp. Ps. 24: 10). *God of Jacob:* this title reminds of Israel's unique status as God's covenant people (cp. Ps. 24: 6). *is with us:* the basis of Israel's confidence and hope (verse 5; cp. Isa. 7: 14; 8: 8, 10). The refrain (cp. verse 11) may originally have stood after verse 3 also.

8-11. God is God and Lord for ever; there is no other.

8–9. War is ended and a new day has dawned. In the light of God's eternal morning the faithful look out over the field of battle and survey *the devastation . . . upon earth*, weapons of war lying broken never to be used again. Whilst this is a picture of the end of time, it represents an ever present hope that may be glimpsed and instanced in the events of history or personal experience.

10. *Let be:* a rebuke to this restless and turbulent world (cp. Mark 4: 39), an exhortation to the nations to abandon their hostilities now (cp. Ps. 2: 10), and perhaps also an injunction to the faithful to cease from all human strivings and rely solely on God (cp. Isa. 7: 4; 30: 15).

11. See verse 7. ✷

GOD REIGNS

47

Clap your hands, all you nations;   1
acclaim our God with shouts of joy.
How fearful is the LORD Most High,   2
great sovereign over all the earth!
He lays the nations prostrate beneath us,   3
    he lays peoples under our feet;
he chose our patrimony for us,   4
the pride of Jacob whom he loved.

God has gone up with shouts of acclamation,   5
    the LORD has gone up with a fanfare of trumpets.
Praise God,*a* praise him with psalms;   6
praise our king, praise him with psalms.
God is king of all the earth;   7
    sing psalms with all your art.*b*

[a] Praise God: *or* Praise, you gods.
[b] with all your art: *mng. of Heb. word uncertain.*

8   God reigns over the nations,
     God is seated on his holy throne.
9   The princes of the nations assemble
         with the families of Abraham's line;[a]
     for the mighty ones of earth belong to God,
     and he is raised above them all.

✻ This psalm transports the worshipper into the festivity and
excitement of a coronation-day celebration, though the king
is God himself. It paints the scene so vividly that some scholars
believe it was written to accompany some annual dramatic
celebration of God's enthronement as king and victor over all
creation. But this theory remains without concrete proof (see
more fully on Ps. 93). The psalm takes up and expands upon
the thought of Ps. 46, especially verse 10. Its central message is
that 'God is king of all the earth' (verse 7) and in the strength
of this assurance it invites the congregation to enter in
anticipation into the jubilations of the great day when God
finally ascends his throne to receive the homage of all mankind
(verses 8–9).

1–4. The universal sovereign subdues the earth and cares for
his own.

1. *Clap your hands . . . with shouts:* so the people greeted the
young Joash at his coronation (2 Kings 11: 12). The invitation
to *acclaim* Israel's God as king is extended to all nations for three
reasons.

2. First, he is *the LORD Most High.* This title designates him
'creator of heaven and earth' (Gen. 14: 19, 22) and so *great
sovereign over all the earth,* that is ultimately king of the nations
themselves (cp. Ps. 46: 4).

3. Second, he shows his power over the *peoples* in Israel's
conquests. Perhaps the poet had the occupation of Canaan in
mind, but the Hebrew tenses are difficult to translate and could

[a] the families of Abraham's line: *prob. rdg.; Heb.* the God of Abraham.

equally refer to the future, to the final consummation of God's victory over the world.

4. Third, he shows the effectiveness of his sovereignty in his provision for *Jacob* (= Israel, cp. Gen. 32: 28). Again the tenses can refer to the future, but it accords with the psalmist's purpose to present history as instancing what is to be fully realized in the end. *the pride of Jacob:* Jacob's proud possession, his *patrimony*, the land of Canaan.

5-9. God reigns supreme.

5. *God has gone up:* that is, to his throne (verse 8). If the psalm accompanied a drama, the setting must be the temple where the Ark was a symbol of God's heavenly throne. *with a fanfare of trumpets:* the new-crowned king was regularly thus saluted in ancient Israel (e.g. 1 Kings 1: 39; 2 Kings 9: 13).

6. 'you gods' (N.E.B. footnote): a perfectly possible translation. The heavenly beings are elsewhere summoned to praise God (Ps. 29: 1) and are even coupled with the nations as rebellious subjects (Ps. 82).

7. *God is king:* to this history attests, on this man's hope is founded. Though God's total rule is not yet consummate, it is already assured (note the ambiguity of the tenses in verses 3-4) and is therefore a present reality to faith.

8. *God reigns:* that is, actively exercises his kingly power. Those who give the psalm a dramatic setting prefer some such rendering as 'God has become king' or 'God has ascended his throne as king'. The Hebrew phrase, similar to that translated 'the LORD is king' in Pss. 93, 96-99, is also reminiscent of the cry 'X is king' heard at Israelite coronation ceremonies (cp. 2 Kings 9: 13). *his holy throne:* see on verse 5.

9. The outworking of the process of election in history may look like unfair favouritism (verses 3-4), but its culmination is the day when *The princes of the nations* stand before God together with the elect. The Hebrew actually suggests a closer union than the N.E.B.'s emended reading, *with the families of Abraham's line,* for it describes the nations as 'the people of the God of Abraham', suggesting their incorporation and identi-

fication with the community that God loves (verse 4). This is
the fulfilment of the promise to Abraham (Gen. 12: 3) and the
goal of history (cp. Rom. 11: 13–32). If the psalm did have a
ritual setting, *the mighty ones* (literally 'shields') *of earth* may
have been represented in the drama. ✻

THE CITY OF OUR GOD

48

1 The LORD is great and worthy of our praise
     in the city of our God, upon his holy hill.
2   Fair and lofty, the joy of the whole earth
     is Zion's hill, like the farthest reaches of the north,*a*
     the hill of the great King's city.
3 In her palaces God is known for a tower of strength.
4   See how the kings all gather round her,
     marching on in company.
5 They are struck with amazement when they see her,
     they are filled with alarm and panic;
6 they are seized with trembling,
     they toss in pain like a woman in labour,
7   like the ships of Tarshish
     when an east wind*b* wrecks them.
8 All we had heard we saw with our own eyes
     in the city of the LORD of Hosts,
     in the city of our God,
     the city which God plants firm for evermore.
9 O God, we re-enact the story of thy true love
     within thy temple;
10   the praise thy name deserves, O God,

[a] Or of Zaphon.
[b] when . . . wind: *so some MSS.; others* with an east wind which . . .

is heard at earth's farthest bounds.
Thy hand is charged with justice,
　　and the hill of Zion rejoices,　　　　　　11
Judah's daughter-cities exult
　　in thy judgements.

　　　　　　　　　　　　　　　　　　　　　12
Make the round of Zion in procession,
　　count the number of her towers,
take good note of her ramparts,　　　　　　13
　　pass her palaces in review,
that you may tell generations yet to come:
　　Such is God,　　　　　　　　　　　14
our God for ever and ever;
　　he shall be our guide eternally.[a]

✻ This psalm elaborates on the theme of Ps. 46: 5, just as Ps. 47
develops Ps. 46: 10. The atmosphere of elation is also similar,
though the scene is now Jerusalem rejoicing after deliverance.
Some scholars believe the psalm was written to celebrate a
historic deliverance of the city, but others again concentrate
more on theories of dramatic setting at a yearly festival (see on
Ps. 47). The N.E.B. translators leave no doubt where their
sympathies lie (see verses 9 and 12). In any case, the theology is
clear. The city is the place of God's abiding presence and
therefore a symbol of present safety to its faithful inhabitants.
But it also speaks to them of a future glory, of an eternal city
which is to be 'the joy of the whole earth' (verse 2).

1–3. 'God is in that city' (Ps. 46:5).

1. *The LORD is great:* an acclamation of majesty; he is 'the
great King' (verse 2), 'great sovereign over all the earth' (Ps.
47: 2). *the city of our God:* Jerusalem, so called because it is the
site of the temple, 'his holy dwelling' (Ps. 46: 4), thus in a
sense the place where heaven and earth meet.

[a] *Poss. mng.; Heb. word uncertain.*

2. *Zion's hill* is no more prominent than many other Palestinian hills (cp. Ps. 68: 15f.), but to the faithful it is *Fair and lofty, the joy of the whole earth*, partly because it symbolizes God's presence with his people, partly because they await the day when it will 'be set over all other mountains' and 'All the nations shall come streaming to it' (Isa. 2: 2; cp. Ps. 68: 18, 29–31). *the farthest reaches of the north:* the abode of the gods (Isa. 14: 13), usually located by the Canaanites in Northern Syria where stood Mount Zaphon (N.E.B. footnote), the seat of Baal. The psalmist claims that everything these distant northern mountains signify is in fact to be found in Jerusalem. *the great King's city* (cp. Matt. 5: 35): that the city is God's and that he is king are the predominant themes of Pss. 46 and 47.

3. The city's *strength* lies not in her towers and *palaces*, but in God's presence.

4–8. 'kingdoms are hurled down' (Ps. 46: 6).

4. *the kings:* the Septuagint and Vulgate read 'the kings of the earth', thus recalling the world-wide conspiracy of Ps. 2 and further emphasizing that this is no ordinary battle-scene, but a glimpse of the continuing war against God's city, its king and his people which must ultimately lead to the defeat of the nations.

5. The Hebrew does not say what *they see*. Perhaps their *alarm and panic* would result more readily from an encounter with God himself (cp. Ps. 77: 16), especially since it is in him alone that the city's strength lies (verse 3).

7. *the ships of Tarshish:* perhaps ships built in or trading with the Phoenician colony at Tartessus in Spain. No doubt they were large, stately merchantmen and so apt symbols of pride and defiance against God. A similar metaphor of ship-wreck caused by *an east wind* describes the fall of Tyre in Ezek. 27: 25f.

8. *All we had heard:* the tradition of the fathers (Ps. 44: 1–3). *saw with our own eyes:* perhaps an allusion to dramatic action at festival time (see verse 9), but certainly also to living experience that adds confirmation to past history, thus strengthening the foundation for belief that *the city* and the hope of final victory

that it symbolizes are *firm* and eternal. *the LORD of Hosts:* a title denoting power and strength, hence well suited to the context (cp. Ps. 46: 7; see on Ps. 24: 10).

9–11. The people rejoice in their eternal hope.

9. *we re-enact:* literally 'we picture'. Most versions and translations relate this to mental rather than dramatic activity (e.g. 'we reflect on', Jerusalem Bible). The N.E.B.'s interpretation is, however, fairly popular and may be correct, though the evidence for drama and mime in Israelite worship is inferential and tenuous. *thy true love:* God's acts of salvation based on his obligation to protect his covenant-people (see on Ps. 5: 7).

10–11. Since the hope of *Zion* is world-wide (verse 2), so also the acclaim of his self-revelation (*name*) and his power (*hand*) must ultimately reach to *earth's farthest bounds. justice . . . judgements:* the righteous outworking of God's purpose in the vindication of the faithful and the defeat of his and their enemies.

12–14. A concluding appeal to reflect and be edified.

12–13. Those who favour ritual interpretations will see here the priest addressing a *procession* as it waits to begin its *round of Zion*. But the Hebrew reads simply 'Go about Zion, walk round about her' and, as in verse 9, these words may equally relate to mental activity. In that case the would language be more metaphorical, based on a picture of military officers making a tour of inspection round the city's defences. The purpose of these closing verses would then be similar to that of the exhortations that end several other psalms, namely to encourage the worshippers to greater faith, praise or endeavour (cp. Pss. 27, 46, 95).

14. *Such is God:* not 'Such is Zion'! Reviewing the towers, ramparts and palaces brings to mind the message of verse 3 and directs the worshippers' thoughts beyond the city of God to God himself. But the God he then sees is not simply a protecting force, but *our God* who has personally undertaken to uphold his city and its people *for ever* (cp. verses 8–9). ✳

BUT GOD WILL RANSOM MY LIFE

49

1 Hear this, all you nations;
    listen, all who inhabit this world,
2 all mankind, every living man,
    rich and poor alike;
3 for the words that I speak are wise,
        my thoughtful heart is full of understanding.

4 I will set my ear to catch the moral of the story
    and tell on the harp how I read the riddle;
5 why should I be afraid in evil times,
    beset by the wickedness of treacherous foes,
6   who trust in their riches
        and boast of their great wealth?
7 Alas! no man can ever ransom himself
    nor pay God the price of that release;
8 his*a* ransom would cost too much,
        for ever beyond his power to pay,
9 the ransom that would let him live on always
        and never see the pit of death.

10 But remember this:*b* wise men must die;
    stupid men, brutish men, all perish.*c*
11 The grave*d* is their eternal home,
        their dwelling for all time to come;

[a] *So Sept.; Heb.* their.
[b] But remember this: *prob. rdg.; Heb.* But he will remember this.
[c] *Line transposed from here to follow verse 11.*
[d] *So Sept.; Heb.* Their inward parts.

they may give their own names to estates,   12
but they must leave their riches to others.[a]
For men are like oxen whose life cannot last,[b]   13
they are like cattle whose time is short.

Such is the fate of foolish men   14
   and of all who seek to please them:
like sheep they run headlong into Sheol, the land of
     Death;
he is their shepherd and urges them on;
   their flesh must rot away[c]
and their bodies be wasted by Sheol,
   stripped of all honour.

But God will ransom my life,   15
   he will take me from the power of Sheol.

Do not envy a man when he grows rich,   16
   when the wealth of his family increases;
for he will take nothing when he dies,   17
and his wealth will not go with him.

Though in his lifetime he counts himself happy   18
and men praise him in his[d] prosperity,
he[e] will go to join the company of his forefathers   19
who will never again see the light.

For men are like oxen whose life cannot last,[f]   20
they are like cattle whose time is short.

[a] *Line transposed from verse 10.*
[b] whose life cannot last: *Sept. has* who have no understanding (*see note on verse 20*).   [c] and urges . . . rot away: *prob. rdg.; Heb. obscure.*
[d] him . . . his: *prob. rdg.; Heb.* you . . . your.
[e] he: *prob. rdg.; Heb.* you.
[f] whose life cannot last: *so many MSS.; others* who have no understanding.

✻ Like Ps. 37 and several others, this psalm is addressed to men, not God, giving instruction about the inequalities of life (see p. 14, sect. E). The style is that of the wisdom teacher, and the teaching about the futility of worldliness, summed up in the refrain in verses 12 and 20, is reminiscent of the teaching of Ecclesiastes with its frequent emphasis on the 'emptiness' of human experience. Some scholars are therefore of the opinion that, though no certain conclusions are possible, this may be one of the latest psalms in the Psalter. We have already seen in various psalms different approaches to the problem raised by the prosperity of the wicked and the suffering of the faithful. Sometimes it is asserted that the life of wickedness is ephemeral, leaving no heritage (Pss. 1, 37), or that God does care and will judge (Pss. 9–10, 14, 36), or that even amid suffering God is present upholding his servants (Pss. 11, 12, 37). Always the life of godliness is presented as the superior way, leading to peace and happiness (especially Ps. 1), and the worshipper is called to renewed commitment (Ps. 37) or to prayer (Pss. 9–10). Some of these themes reappear in Ps. 49, but here the psalmist is almost entirely intent on stressing the worthlessness of wealth that cannot buy God's favour (verses 7–9) and the futility of a life-style that leads nowhere but to the grave (verses 10–14, 16–20). Then briefly, but powerfully, he declares his own faith that God will do for him what all the wealth in the world cannot do for the wicked (verse 15; contrast verse 7). Their fate is emphatically death, but his destiny is to be ransomed from the power of Sheol. This statement marks a significant step forward towards the hope of resurrection and recompense in a life after death (contrast Ps. 37, p. 170), and so it is that Jesus' parables about the rich fool (Luke 12: 16–21) and about the rich man and Lazarus (Luke 16: 19–31) present basically the same message as Ps. 49.

1–3. The solemnity of these verses emphasizes the importance of the psalmist's theme.

1. *Hear this:* a common opening for wisdom speeches (cp. Prov. 4: 1, 10). The psalmist addresses *all you nations* or 'all

mankind' (verse 2) because his theme, like most wisdom themes, is one of universal interest. *this world:* this translates a Hebrew word that may suggest transitoriness.

2. Unlike most other psalms on the same subject, this one is not simply a word of encouragement to the *poor*. It is also intended as a warning to the *rich* who must learn the limitations of their wealth.

3. Such emphasis on the value and profundity of his words is characteristic of the wise man's prologue to his instruction (cp. Prov. 4: 2, 11).

4–9. There is no need to fear the wicked, for their riches, no matter how great, cannot buy God's favour.

4. *to catch the moral:* the injustice of life presents an enigma (*riddle*) that can be resolved only by inspiration, not by human reasoning (cp. Ps. 73: 16f.). *on the harp:* Elisha used music to obtain prophetic insight (2 Kings 3: 15), but nowhere else in the Old Testament is instruction accompanied by a musical instrument. However, this is a psalm and was doubtless composed for singing.

5. *why:* a rhetorical question expressing confidence. The psalmist's 'why' may also be a call for help (Ps. 10: 1) or a cry of dereliction (Ps. 22: 1), but is seldom, if ever, a request for elucidation.

6. Man's *trust* and his *boast* should be in God alone (Ps. 52: 7; cp. 2 Cor. 10: 17), for he 'cannot serve God and Money' (Matt. 6: 24).

7. *ransom:* in Israelite law it was sometimes possible to escape execution by paying a ransom (Exod. 21: 30), but no amount of money can purchase *release* from death when it has been decreed by God.

8. The cost of a legal ransom would probably be set according to the gravity of the crime and the offender's means, but it would be futile to contemplate offering God a ransom.

9. *the pit of death:* a synonym for Sheol (verses 14f.).

10–20. The end of all godless men is the same, futility and death, 'But God will ransom my life.'

10. *remember this:* the imperative suits the wisdom style of address, but the Hebrew, 'he will see', rather than 'he will remember' (N.E.B. footnote), offers perfectly good sense. *wise men:* the godly; *stupid men:* the wicked (see on Ps. 14: 1f.). The two types are frequently contrasted in the wisdom literature. *brutish men:* the self-confident braggarts who are contemptuous of reproof (Prov. 12: 1). The N.E.B.'s transposition of the last line to verse 11 introduces no new interpretation, nor does it greatly improve the poetic structure.

11. It has sometimes been thought that the statements in verses 10–12 contradict the hope expressed in verse 15. But the theme is that death is the great leveller. All men, good or bad, must leave their possessions behind, as must also the psalmist. He does not seek escape from the common fate of all men, but he can look in faith beyond death to entry into the fulness of God's presence (see on verse 15). But for the godless there is no such hope; for them *The grave* is the end, *their eternal home,* and the prospect of existence in Sheol never held much cheer for the ancient Israelite (cp. Ps. 88: 10–12). The narrow *grave*, soon to be *their dwelling* for ever, offers a stark contrast to the vast *estates* which they enjoy at present.

12. Cp. verse 20. *like oxen:* based on conjectural emendation. The Hebrew reads 'For men cannot abide in pomp'. Though poverty may cause early death, wealth cannot keep alive for ever.

13. *all who seek to please them:* this translation also depends on emendation. The meaning of the Hebrew is obscure, but most commentators find some reference to deluded followers of the wicked. The poor, dazzled by wealth and the apparent stability of those who possess it, begin to curry favour with them instead of turning to God (Ps. 73: 2–11).

14. The text of this verse is corrupt, especially in the second half, and, like most translations, the N.E.B. makes considerable use of emendation, but the general sense is clear. The godless are *like sheep* being driven to slaughter. The personification of *Death* (cp. Jer. 9: 21) and its characterization as a

shepherd present a striking contrast with the picture of God in Ps. 23. *Sheol*, Death's underworld realm, is the place of wasting disease, corruption and decay, all that is the opposite of the life that comes from God (see on Ps. 6: 5).

15. God can do what no amount of wealth could ever achieve (verse 7), he can *ransom* life. This insight goes a long way in preparing men to receive the one who gave 'his life as a ransom for many' (Mark 10: 45). The psalmist does not expect to escape the natural process of dying (verse 10), but he does believe that he will not have to spend the rest of eternity in underworld gloom. The psalmists constantly attest to the blessing and joy of knowing God's nearness (e.g. Ps. 4: 6–8) and also the horror of knowing his absence (e.g. Ps. 22: 1). They knew by experience that 'unfailing love enfolds him who trusts in the LORD' (Ps. 32: 10), but they also believed that Sheol meant the end of all communion with God (Ps. 88: 5). The inevitable conclusion is that God *will take* the faithful *from the power of Sheol* into the eternal enjoyment of his presence which has been so real in this life. The verb *take* is the same as that used of the translation (death?) of Enoch in Gen. 5: 24 and of Elijah in 2 Kings 2: 3, 9, but neither of these passages sheds much light on the nature of the psalmist's expectation.

16. *Do not envy:* cp. Ps. 37: 1, 7. But the Hebrew reads 'do not fear', a more fitting exhortation to conclude a psalm in which the main theme is introduced with the words 'why should I be afraid' (verse 5). This counsel is still addressed to 'all mankind' (verses 1–2).

17. This underlines the thoughts expressed in verse 11 (cp. Eccles. 5: 15).

18. *he counts himself happy:* literally 'he blesses himself', that is, instead of God, but no amount of self-praise or *praise* from other *men* can make any difference to his end.

19. *to join the company of his forefathers:* not in happy reunion, but in the gloom and darkness of Sheol (cp. Ps. 88: 12).

20. The N.E.B. text follows manuscripts which have the same wording as verse 12, but others provide the variant

reading 'men in their pomp cannot understand', and it may be observed that variants are sometimes introduced to refrains in Hebrew poetry as in Ps. 107 (cp. on Ps. 59: 6, 15). The conclusion of this psalm may therefore be a solemn warning that wealth can so blind a man that he becomes unable to distinguish between true and false riches. ✡

OUR GOD WILL NOT KEEP SILENCE

50

1 God, the LORD God, has spoken
and summoned the world from the rising to the setting sun.
2 God shines out from Zion, perfect in beauty.
3 Our God is coming and will not keep silence:
consuming fire runs before him
and wreathes him closely round.[a]
4 He summons heaven on high and earth
to the judgement of his people:
5 'Gather to me my loyal servants,
all who by sacrifice have made a covenant with me.'
6 The heavens proclaim his justice,
for God himself is the judge.

7 Listen, my people, and I will speak;
I will bear witness against you, O Israel:
I am God, your God,
8 shall I not[b] find fault with your sacrifices,
though[c] your offerings are before me always?
9 I need take no young bull from your house,
no he-goat from your folds;

[*a*] and wreathes him closely round: *or* and rages round him.
[*b*] *Or* I will not. [*c*] *Or* for.

for all the beasts of the forest are mine   10
  and the cattle in thousands on my hills.
I know every bird on those hills,   11
the teeming life of the fields is my care.
If I were hungry, I would not tell you,   12
for the world and all that is in it are mine.
  Shall I eat the flesh of your bulls*a*   13
  or drink the blood of he-goats?
Offer to God the sacrifice of thanksgiving   14
and pay your vows to the Most High.
  If you call upon me in time of trouble,   15
  I will come to your rescue, and you shall honour me.

God's word to the wicked man is this: 16
  What right have you to recite my laws
  and make so free with the words of my covenant,
  you who hate correction   17
  and turn your back when I am speaking?
If you meet a thief, you choose him as your friend;   18
  you make common cause with adulterers;
you charge your mouth with wickedness   19
and harness your tongue to slander.
You are for ever talking against your brother,   20
stabbing your own mother's son in the back.
All this you have done, and shall I keep silence?   21
You thought that I was another like yourself,
but point by point I will rebuke you to your face.
Think well on this, you who forget God,   22
or I will tear you in pieces and no one shall save you.
  He who offers a sacrifice of thanksgiving   23

[a] *Lit*. bisons.

235

does me due honour,
and to him who follows my way[a]
I will show the salvation of God.

⁂ In this psalm the worshipper finds himself participating in a drama. God appears in fire summoning the world to judgement, the judgement of the covenant people of whom the worshipper himself is a member (verses 1–6). God first addresses those who imagine their religious duty is fulfilled by observing certain formal rituals (verses 7–15) and then those who hypocritically recite his laws but have no intention of living up to them (verses 16–21). Finally he warns his people that he demands due honour and observance of his law (verses 22f.). The message is one frequently sounded by the prophets (cp. Mic. 6: 6–8) reminding the faithful that their religion is not just a matter of ritual or of philosophical morality, but of encounter with a God who lives, loves and judges. It is sometimes supposed that this psalm could have originated in a ritual of covenant renewal in which God's appearance on Sinai was dramatically re-enacted, his bond ceremonially reaffirmed and his people admonished by a cultic official. The date of authorship is uncertain.

1–6. God summons the world to the judgement of his people.

1. *God, the LORD God:* the psalm opens on an appropriately majestic note. Three separate titles are used in the Hebrew, probably as synonyms emphasizing the superlative splendour and power of God. *the world from . . .:* all the inhabitants of the earth, called to be witnesses at the judgement along with heaven and earth (verse 4).

2. *God shines:* light is a frequent symbol of God's presence, here signifying his 'majesty and splendour', as in Ps. 104: 1f. *perfect in beauty:* here describing Zion rather than God himself (cp. Ps. 48: 2).

[a] him who follows my way: *prob. rdg.; Heb.* him who puts a way.

3. God's *coming* on Zion is like his appearance on Sinai, amid *fire* and raging tempest (N.E.B. footnote; cp. Exod. 19: 16). The imagery may simply be traditional, but it is appropriate in a psalm that speaks of judgement on the basis of the Sinaitic law (verses 16–21). On the transference of God's seat from Sinai to Zion, see Ps. 68. *will not keep silence:* see verse 21.

4. *heaven . . . and earth:* summoned along with 'the world' (verse 1) as witnesses at Israel's trial (cp. Deut. 4: 26; Isa. 1: 2). Being older than man they can bear fuller testimony to his deeds, even from the beginning (Deut. 4: 32).

5. *loyal servants:* that is, those whom God has called to be loyal (*ḥasīd*) to his *covenant* demands and to whom he extends his promise of blessing (cp. on Ps. 30: 4). Great is their privilege, but also their responsibility; judgement must there-fore begin 'with God's own household' (1 Pet. 4: 17; cp. Amos 3: 2). *by sacrifice:* a reference to the original ceremony ratifying the covenant at Sinai (Exod. 24: 5–8), but also to its ritual reaffirmation in subsequent generations (cp. Jer. 34: 18).

6. To *judge* is the prerogative of God alone. The function of *The heavens* is to witness to his justice.

7–15. God's word to the religious.

7. It is not to pass sentence that the 'judge' has summoned his *people*, but to *bear witness against* them of their corruption, thus exhorting them to repentance. *I am God, your God:* an Elohistic adaptation (see pp. 4f.) of the introduction to the decalogue (Exod. 20: 2; Deut. 5: 6), reminding the people of God's authority, as the one who gave the covenant, to judge them.

8. The N.E.B. footnotes offer the generally accepted trans-lation of this verse and imply that God has no complaint about the regular frequency and assiduous care with which the rituals are performed. It is not to condemn all sacrificial worship that he speaks, but to correct the motives of the worshippers (see on Pss. 40: 6; 51: 16f.). *sacrifices . . . offerings:* here used as synonyms, but see more fully on Ps. 40: 6.

9–14. The caricature speaks for itself. It is not *your* animals that God needs, but the dedication of *your* hearts (cp. 1 Sam. 15: 22).

13. The naïve belief that the function of sacrifice was to provide God with food and drink was common in ancient religions and was doubtless also held by some Israelites.

14. *the sacrifice of thanksgiving . . . your vows:* the context would appear to suggest that the spiritual offering of thanksgiving in song (Ps. 69: 30) and psalm of praise (Ps. 61: 8) are meant, rather than the material 'thank-offering' (Lev. 7: 12) and 'votive offering' (Lev. 7: 16), though these too could express a heart-felt response of gratitude and obedience. *the Most High:* a title that suitably suggests God's unique majesty (see on Ps. 7: 17).

15. Here is a neat summary of a true relationship with God. *in time of trouble* man has no need to please or bribe God with sacrifices, only to *call upon* him in trust. Thus will he see God *come to* his *rescue* and then he will *honour* or praise (literally 'glorify') him with grateful devotion. God does not seek a worship that is calculated, but one that is a response to the knowledge of his saving grace.

16-21. God's word to the hypocrite.

16-17. *the wicked man:* a very strong judgement on one who belongs to the family of God's 'loyal servants' (verse 5), but then it is addressed to the man whose religious busyness has created the impression that he loves God's *laws*, while in reality he has little true care either for them or for the one who gave them (cp. Matt. 15: 6-9).

18. Contrast Ps. 1: 1f.; the man whose delight is in the law of the LORD does not 'walk the road that sinners tread'. The offences listed in verses 18-20 imply neglect of the simplest, yet primary moral duties prescribed in the second half of the decalogue (Exod. 20: 12-17).

20. *brother:* not simply a fellow Israelite. The parallelism suggests the closest possible family bond. When such intimate ties of kinship cease to have importance, the moral structure of social relationships has ceased to exist and religion becomes

utterly meaningless. The picture may be exaggerated and extreme, but it describes the limit to which man without God can descend and so stands as a warning to the faithful and a judgement upon them in so far as they tend towards this limit.

21. *shall I keep silence?*: cp. verse 3. God's silence is easily mistaken for indifference (cp. Pss. 10: 11; 73: 11) and therefore must be broken if his honour is to be upheld. But his silence is never purposeless, for it gives man the opportunity to examine himself *point by point* so that when the *rebuke* comes he recognizes it, learns from it and is edified. *You thought that I was another like yourself*: a common perversion of the biblical doctrine that man is created in God's 'image and likeness' (Gen. 1: 26), but God declares his infinite superiority in recurrent formulae, such as 'I am God, your God' (verse 7; cp. Hos. 11: 9).

22–3. God's final word of admonition and exhortation.

22. *you who forget God*: both the ritualist who neglects the spiritual, and the hypocrite who neglects the moral, the two most fundamental aspects of religion (cp. John 4: 24). *tear you in pieces*: like a lion; for the metaphor, see Hos. 5: 14.

23. This verse sums up the teaching of God in the psalm, the first half corresponding to verses 7–15 and the second to verses 16–21. As in verse 14, *sacrifice of thanksgiving* seems to refer to the spiritual offering of pure praise or *honour* (literally 'glory'; cp. verse 15). *my way*: literally 'a way', but probably correctly interpreted here as the way of obedience to the law of God (cp. Ps. 1: 6). True religion is this, that God shows man his *salvation*, while he responds with gratitude and obedience (see verse 15). ✳

A NOTE ON FURTHER READING

For background and comparative material see J. B. Pritchard, *Ancient Near Eastern Texts* (3rd ed., Princeton University Press, 1969).

For introductory books on the psalms see C. F. Barth, *Introduction to the Psalms* (Blackwell, 1966); H. Ringgren, *The Faith of the Psalmists* (S.C.M. Press, 1963); C. Westermann, *The Praise of God in the Psalms* (John Knox Press, Richmond, Virginia, 1965).

For a more comprehensive and detailed commentary see A. A. Anderson, *Psalms*, New Century Bible (Oliphants, 1972). For a more conservative approach see D. Kidner, *Psalms*, Tyndale Old Testament Commentaries (Inter-Varsity Press, 1973–5). For an older, but extremely valuable, commentary see A. F. Kirkpatrick, *The Book of Psalms*, The Cambridge Bible for Schools and Colleges (Cambridge University Press, 1891–1901).

INDEX

INDEX

form criticism 7f.

glory 24, 38, 41f., 68, 86, 110, 119, 130, 135f., 154

God:
    as creator 1, 41, 46, 78, 86f., 109, 130f., 150, 165, 219
    as gardener 17, 207
    as judge 1, 17, 22, 35, 37f., 44, 46f., 49, 55, 70, 77, 166, 204, 236f.
    as shepherd 31, 88, 105f., 128, 233
    as warrior 39, 72, 82, 161, 181, 210
    kingdom of 1, 20, 38, 84
    kingship of 1, 7f., 20, 48, 52f., 55, 78, 109–11, 130, 132, 149, 213, 219, 222f., 225f.
    majesty of, see God, kingship of
    presence of 24, 27f., 30f., 33, 47f., 59, 64–6, 68, 91, 94, 109f., 123, 135f., 143, 169f., 198, 201f., 220, 225, 233
    sovereignty of, see God, kingship of
    throne of 46f., 55, 215, 223
    victory of 24, 30, 46–8, 91, 93–5, 109, 112, 208, 213f., 220f., 222f., 226
    voice of 131
    wrath, of 22, 33, 39, 55, 77, 95, 124, 135, 182

gods (pagan) 66f., 86, 130, 140, 168, 223

Gunkel, H. 7

Hermon, Mt 131
Herod 20
holiness 99, 130
Holy of Holies 31, 55, 78
holy mountain 21, 24
hope 89, 98, 113, 125, 143, 151, 187
host of heaven (sun, moon and stars) 42, 87, 130, 150
humble (poor) 48, 62, 104, 114, 163, 173, 195, 232

Isaiah 77, 89
Israel (the people of God) 1, 7, 20, 46, 62, 91, 93, 103, 207f., 213, 220;

242

INDEX